Searcher
of
Majesty

Searcher
of
Majesty

by

Solange Hertz

' Bona Tempora Volvant '

Arcadia
MMXV

Printed in the United States of America

ISBN 978-0-9883537-8-7

Searcher of Majesty

Visit our website at www.tumblarhouse.com

*Nihil obstat:*Edward A. Cerny, S.S., S.T.D.
Censor Librorum

Imprimatur: Lawrence J. Shehan, D.D.
Archbishop of Baltimore
October 2, 1962

The *nihil obstat* and *imprimatur* are official declarations that a book or pamphlet is free of doctrinal and moral error. No implication is contained therein that those who have granted the *nihil obstat* and *imprimatur* agree with the opinions expressed.

In the Name of the Father
and of the Son
and of the Holy Spirit

PREFACE

THIS book is about God and Woman. I've dedicated it to our glorious father Saint Joseph, the just man who lived intensely, fruitfully, and perfectly with both.

Rather than to multiply prefaces, I'm borrowing one written some six hundred years ago by the author of *The Cloud of Unknowing*. It's still good, and says everything better than I would dare:

> I do not mind at all if the loud-mouthed, or flatterers, or the mock-modest, or fault-finders, gossips, tittle-tattlers, talebearers, or any sort of grumbler, never see this book. I have never meant to write for them. So they can keep out of it. And so can all those learned men (and unlearned too) who are merely curious. Even if they are good men, judged from the "active" standpoint, all this will mean nothing to them. But it will mean something to those who, though "active" according to their outward mode of life, are, by the inner working of the Spirit of God—his judgments are unsearchable—disposed towards contemplation. Not continually, maybe, as in the case of true contemplatives, but now and then willing to share in the deep things of contemplation. If such people see this book, by the grace of God they should be much inspired by it.

Actually, I wrote this book mostly to cheer us women up!

SOLANGE HERTZ

At Home
Feast of St. Joseph
March 19, 1962.

TABLE OF CONTENTS

Searcher of Majesty

CHAPTER 1

WHENEVER I smell something burning, I'm inclined to jump to the conclusion that some woman is thinking. A friend of mine who happens to be a research bacteriologist would agree with me. By her own admission she was once making some valuable first-hand observations on vegetable oxidation, when she was interrupted most inopportunely by her mother, who began sputtering and coughing most unscientifically, but finally managed to get out, "Where is all that smoke coming from?"

Billows of it, my friend soon saw, were being generated by several blackened carrots in the bottom of a saucepan on the stove; for it turned out that these were the vegetable matter under scrutiny, and they were suddenly oxidizing at a phenomenal rate. My friend had been leaning over them till now, oblivious to fumes, and so rapt in the wonders of natural mystery that these same carrots had ceased utterly to figure in her mind as part of the family dinner—the reason for their being on the stove in the first place.

"Oh, gosh, Mother!" she said when she came to—or something like that.

This, of course, is about all a girl can say to explain away the schizophrenia that so often splits us when a weak human nature forsakes a lower reality to grope admiringly for a higher. Something has to give, and usually does.

I remember some years ago dashing between trains into a confessional in a big city church and unburdening myself of what I considered a venial sin of intellectual pride. As I recall, I muttered something like, "Bless me, Father, for I let the stew burn while I was trying to figure out the circumincessions of the Blessed Trinity.

It was the end of a working day, and Father, no doubt about it, had had it. "Now you imitate the Blessed Mother!" he shot at me, adding for good measure, "She knew how to keep her mind where it *belonged*!"

This excellent advice was delivered in unmistakable accents of positively Mosaic indignation. Kitchen theologian, forsooth! Now even Sinai was smoking! It was no use pretending I didn't understand. Evidently my sin had been far more heinous than I ever suspected. Clearly I was a traitor to my vocation as wife and mother, if not to my very womanhood.

Well, it wasn't the first time a penitent had,

> ... looked for sympathy, but there was none;
> for comforters, and ... found none.
> Rather they put gall in my food,
> and in my thirst they gave me vinegar to drink. (*Psalm 68*)

There are lots of forms of Christ-like suffering. Accepting a stiff penance, I pulled my quivering psyche together as best I could and crept from the confessional, thoroughly chastened, nay, oxidized.

"He who hears you, hears Me," the Christ promised his priests.

It remained only for me to take my unknown confessor's advice, if I ever expected to rise from the spiritual quagmire into which I had so deeply, if unwittingly fallen. Having just promised that "with the help of Thy grace I resolve to sin no more, and to avoid all near occasions of sin," I perforce concluded I had better stop thinking about the Blessed Trinity. It was simply too fascinating for a housewife with stew on the stove.

As directed, I began instead dutifully meditating on the life of the Blessed Mother, so I could imitate her at this impasse. Naturally, this entailed figuring out precisely where her mind belonged so I could put mine there too.

"Hail, full of grace," Daughter of the Father!

"The Lord is with thee," Bride of the Logos!

"Blessed art thou among women," Temple and Instrument of the Holy Ghost!

This Lily of the Trinity, who quizzed an angel, then "ran in haste" until she finally *stood* in agony at the foot of the Cross, what did she think about while the stew thickened? Even she, I was sure, could think about stew just so long. A stew is finite; thinking isn't.

Well, to make a short story shorter, it was about two hours and fifteen minutes all told before I was busily cogitating circumincessions of the Blessed Trinity again. Obviously, that was where our Lady's mind belonged, with the rest of her; and so did mine. Didn't God make us for Himself?

Whenever I hear maudlin stories about unsympathetic confessors who supposedly drive their penitents out of the Church by gross lack of sympathy and understanding, I can't help laughing, though of course I shouldn't. It's obvious, however, that those sinners just didn't listen to what Father really said. They forget that Confession is a sacrament whose grace doesn't depend on human foibles, and that all things work for good for those who even try to love God. That apparently tired, crusty, anonymous priest was the agent of what I now know was one of the greatest graces of my life. Wasn't he the Christ? Didn't Christ come to lead us to the Father? Well, that's where he pointed me. No penitent could ask for more.

Almost a decade later, I'm still thinking about the Blessed Trinity; and not possessing the Blessed Virgin's privileges of integrated nature, I still burn an occasional stew, try as I will not to. When I do, however, I've learned to confess a sin against justice, that is, not giving the stew the attention rightfully due it. That's nothing so satanic as intellectual pride, but more in the category of petty thievery, which is terribly humiliating to thinkers of great thoughts. As for actually falling into pride, it's hard to see how speculating on the Blessed Trinity could ever lead to it; the effects are so humbling. As far as I know, the only people who might succumb are those who presume to understand the Trinity and explain It to others. They become formal heretics, poor things, and even so, that takes an awful lot of brains.

A married couple we know once announced gravely at a cocktail party that they had resigned their membership in the Protestant church they attended in order to become Unitarians. In the course of the evening I had occasion to ask the wife what had prompted this move. (I knew her to have descended from a long line of Presbyterian divines!) Her answer was—and I quote: "Ed and I finally came to the conclusion that we just couldn't swallow the Trinity!"

I could have told her we swallow the Blessed Trinity without any trouble at all every time we receive Holy Communion, but I knew, of course, what she meant. What could I say? I had to come clean and admit I couldn't either.

Looking back over our conversation, I see now that my friend may be actually closer to the truth than she ever was before, though to all appearances traveling in the opposite direction. She admits, bless her heart, that her mind can't comprehend the Blessed Trinity. Lots of people never get that far. Her only mistake is assuming it follows that the Blessed Trinity doesn't exist. This, please God, is merely an error in logic which can be remedied whenever she so desires.

It takes a long time for some people to perceive that, whereas natural education inevitably adds to the store of what it knows, supernatural education seems only to add to what it doesn't know. Certainly the more you think about God, the smaller and more ignorant you see yourself to be. After this kind of mental exercise any housewife can say with Dr. Carl Jung, "I'm not a bit taken in by intellectuals—I'm one myself, you know!"

It doesn't take a psychiatrist to see that every human being is an intellectual by his very nature as a rational animal. He can't help trying to swallow the Blessed Trinity, because he was made by the Blessed Trinity to keep trying. This is his eternal destiny.

Believe it or not, even women think. Eve did. Don't we smell something burning? This time, I'm afraid it's hell. Eve was the first lady intellectual simply because she was the first lady. She wanted to know the mystery of good and evil and "be like God," so it's easy to see why my unknown confessor had qualms. Eve thought the whole matter over, talked it out with the devil, and judging the fruit not only pretty and tasty, but "desirable for the knowledge it would give," she ate it.

Her sin didn't lie in her thirst for knowledge. This was God-given and legitimate, an integral part of her nature. Her sin consisted in satisfying her craving in her own way, contrary to God's injunction. You know the rest, but we can't stop here, because we would be left with a terribly distorted view of the female intellect and its role in the world.

We might turn instead to the Queen of Saba. She's a real bluestocking and a delightful character, who was so enamored of wisdom she traveled many miles "having heard of the fame of Solomon ... to try him with hard questions. And entering into Jerusalem with a great train ... (she) spoke to him all that she had in her heart," just as a woman would.

She was terribly taken with Solomon, who had an answer for everything. To express her admiration she gave "a hundred and twenty talents of gold, and of spices a very great store, and precious stones." Scripture adds, "There was brought no more such abundance as these which the Queen of Saba gave to King Solomon" (*III Kings 10:1,2,10*). We are also told that "King Solomon gave the Queen of Saba all that she desired, and asked of him: besides what he offered her of himself of his royal bounty" (*III Kings 10:12-13*).

Our Lord, the new Solomon, approved the wisdom-seeking queen as wholeheartedly as did His ancestor. Holding her up as an example against the pedantry of the Pharisees, He promised that "the Queen of the South will rise up in judgment with this generation and will condemn it; for she came from the ends of the earth to hear the wisdom of Solomon, and behold, a greater than Solomon is here!" (*Matt. 12:42*). He admired virtuous female curiosity, and said so.

Next to the Christ, the blessed housewife Mary is the greatest intellectual the world has ever known, her capacity for knowledge only faintly foreshadowed by Eve's and the Queen of Saba's. Because she was "full of grace," her mind's eye was utterly simple and perfectly enlightened, though like us she lived on earth through faith. We can be certain she kept her mind exactly where it belonged—in God—ever seeking humbly to penetrate the abyss of His wisdom.

"As it is not good for a man to eat much honey, so he that is a searcher of majesty, shall be overwhelmed by glory," warns Proverbs, such rich Food is God for the human mind.

Who is so overwhelmed with glory as this Woman, clothed with the Sun, who searched Majesty all her earthly life and searches It even now in Heaven? No wife and mother can imitate her without imitating her intellectual life, a life with God, which is not merely a meeting of hearts in love, but a meeting of minds in light. Saint Augustine doesn't hesitate to say, "Mary conceived first with her mind and then with her body" (*Sermo, 215, 4*).

At the Angelic Salutation in Nazareth, she "kept pondering what manner of greeting this might be," and after the Annunciation inquires, "How shall this happen, since I do not know man?" And like the Queen of Saba, she is told "all she desired and asked of him," for the angel answers to her satisfaction, closing with the words, "For nothing shall be impossible with God."

"For everyone who asks, receives," promises her Son, putting His seal on this sort of inquiry. Ask, and you shall receive; search majesty and faint with the honey of it.

Had the Christ never come, we could dispense with thinking about the Blessed Trinity. Natural humanity is perfectly satisfied with the God who is One, all-powerful, all-knowing, all-good, eternal, and whose existence can in fact be proved by five arguments from reason. Millions and millions of housewives have known no other and may have led good natural lives in His sight notwithstanding. Our Blessed Lady as a girl knew God this way, for she considered herself His handmaid at the time, as she candidly admitted to the Angel.

"Behold the handmaid of the Lord!" she said.

"But I," says the Christ to us, "have called you friends!" as St. John reported later. "No longer do I call you servants (or handmaids), because the servant does not know what his master does. But I have called you friends," He insists, "because all things that I have heard from my Father I have made known to you!"

This Man made known to us that God is Three as well as One. He had to tell us, because at Mary's fiat He caught us up forever into His triune life. At the risk of burning the stew a thousand times, we'll have to think about this cataclysmic elevation. I, for one, can't get over it. This is the Mystery of mysteries, utterly beyond all demonstrations from reason, but necessary to supernaturalized human intelligence if it is to achieve its new destiny. That's why God told us.

Now, what's tellable about the Blessed Trinity is soon said. In his famous Creed, St. Athanasius puts it very grandly, very insistently, drawing us into the abyss by the majestic simplicity of his language:

> Now this is the Catholic faith: that we worship one God in Trinity and Trinity in unity; neither confusing the persons nor distinguishing the nature. The person of the Father is distinct; the person of the Son is distinct; the person of the Holy Spirit is distinct. Yet the Father and the Son and the Holy Spirit possess one Godhead, equal glory, and co-eternal majesty. As the Father is, so is the Son, so also is the Holy Spirit. The Father is uncreated, the Son is uncreated, the Holy Spirit is uncreated. The Father is infinite, the Son is infinite, the Holy Spirit is infinite. The Father is eternal, the Son is eternal, the Holy Spirit is eternal. Nevertheless, there are not three eternals, but One eternal; even as they are not three uncreateds, or three infinites, but One uncreated, and one Infinite. So likewise the Father is almighty, the Son is almighty, the Holy Spirit is almighty. And yet there are not three almighties, but one Almighty. So also the Father is God, the Son is God, the Holy Spirit is God. And yet, there are not three Gods, but only one God. So too the Father is Lord, the Son is Lord, the Holy Spirit is Lord. And still there are not three Lords, but only one Lord. For just as we are compelled by Christian truth to profess that each person is individually God and Lord, so also are we forbidden by the Catholic religion to hold that there are three Gods or Lords. The Father was made by no one, being neither created nor begotten. The Son is from the Father alone, though not created or made, but begotten. The Holy Spirit is from the Father and the Son, though neither made nor created nor begotten, but proceeding. Consequently there is one Father, not three Fathers; there is one Son, not three Sons; there is one Holy Spirit, not three Holy Spirits. Furthermore, in this Trinity there is no "before" or "after," no "greater" or "less": for all three Persons are co-eternal and coequal. In every respect, therefore, as has already been stated, unity must be worshipped in Trinity, and Trinity in unity. This is what everyone who wishes to be saved must hold regarding the Blessed Trinity. (From the *Breviary*, Lesson for Trinity Sunday.)

On the face of it, this definition proves that somebody has done a great deal of thinking about God, because all it contains is by no means self-evident in the Gospels, the source of its revelation. Early theologians were not even sure, for instance, whether the Holy Spirit was truly a distinct Person, or simply a very high form of grace. The Greek Church still doesn't concede that the Holy Spirit proceeds equally from the Father and the Son. To this day there's no "filioque" in their creed.

St. Teresa reports in her *Autobiography* that once while reciting St. Athanasius' Creed,

> I was given to understand the mystery of One God and Three Persons with so much clearness, that I was greatly astonished and consoled at the same time. This was of the greatest help to me, for it enabled me to know more of the greatness and marvels of God; and when I think of the most Holy Trinity, or hear It spoken of, I seem to understand the mystery, and a great joy it is (xxxix, 36).

Well, it's no use pretending. All the stews I've scorched to date don't add up to anything like that. If you want to see the Blessed Trinity as I do, you'll have to lower your sights considerably. St. Augustine defines education as learning from others, but as I see it, this doesn't always mean other people. Material nature is "other" too, and everything outside us unfolds God's glory to the human intellect. Unknowable outside revelation, the Blessed Trinity is reproduced nowhere in natural creation, yet its "vestiges" are refracted everywhere, tantalizing us constantly, once we're in the know.

The best place to start pondering the Blessed Trinity is any place, doing whatever you're doing.

"Look, child," I found myself telling one of our struggling schoolboys here, "parsing sentences isn't as hard as you make out. Just look for the Blessed Trinity. It's in everything."

"In *sentences*?"

"Certainly. Find the Subject, the Verb and the Object—doer, doing, done. You'll find everything else in the sentence just hangs on them."

"Everything?"

"Every sentence works the same. *Mrs. O'Leary's cow kicked over the kerosene lamp, starting the Chicago fire.* Cow, kicked, lamp. See?"

"Oh," he said, and believe it or not, his English grades improved. But why shouldn't they? God created grammar.

St. Jerome once wrote to his friend Pammachius that in the case of Holy Scripture even the syntax contains a mystery. Still awed by the divine mystery in the least inspired sentence in the newspaper, I find the saint's comment a masterpiece of understatement. He must have been talking down to Pammachius, I've decided.

Even as a benighted unbeliever I used to be amazed at the way home decorating problems could be resolved by judiciously grouping recalcitrant objects in threes. One object with two others in close relation to the first proved especially good, as, say, a table flanked by two chairs; or a vase, an ashtray and a statuette on a coffee table. Add a second ashtray and the effect was ruined. Four of anything rarely seemed to work, and when it did, the effect was generally fat, full, and now no more. Five was fine, because three could easily be discerned in relation to the other two. Same with seven, and so on. Three proved invariably interesting, a natural nucleus for any further subsidiary combinations. It could be added to indefinitely, in what I know now is a pale vestigial reflection of Triune fecundity.

Please don't take my word for this. Try it yourself, if you haven't already. I found it positively irritating never to be able to depart from my formula without settling for second best, but finally I gave up, concluding it must be naturally satisfying to see the arrangements of the parts of the human body reproduced in the house the body occupied. You know, torso flanked by two arms, one nose with two eyes, one head with two ears, and so on. Poor atheists, they must be satisfied with small truths! Not that I had stumbled over anything new. The mysterious fitness of "threes" has bewitched mankind since thinking began. It's as inescapable to the notice of the garbage collector as it is to that of the scientist or the philosopher.

The garbage man knows firsthand that fruits and vegetables all have three parts: peel, pulp, and seed. The youngest scientist can see that a tree has root, trunk, and branch, and that all living things go through a cycle of birth, growth, and decay—in a visible creation which is animal, vegetable, and mineral. Matter itself can be gas, liquid, or solid, and solids must have length, breadth, and thickness. Anybody knows there's a past, present, and future, and that you can move up, down, or across through air, water, or earth, not to mention swallowing blarney hook, line, and sinker.

Certainly a housewife can't overlook the fact that rooms are composed of ceiling, walls, and floor. She must know, too, that any stool must have at least three legs if it's to stand without help. Doing spiritual reading in the mail order catalogue, she can contemplate any amount of merchandise in sizes small, medium, and large-in grades good, better, and best. Like Goldilocks stumbling into the abode of the three bears, she soon recognizes that housekeeping without reference to the Blessed Trinity is utterly impossible. Any porridge is either cold, tepid, or hot; chairs little, middle-sized, or big; and mattresses tend to be soft, hard, or "just right."

And I guess I know who Goldilocks is, all right. Don't let her fool you. She's really Aristotle in a blond wig, preaching his golden mean to the small fry, exploring the house of the Three Bears by sipping their porridge, sitting in their chairs, and sleeping in their beds. Natural ethics is just as trinitarian as everything else and finds even the lowliest virtue always exactly midway between two extremes.

This didn't escape St. Augustine, who found vestiges of the Trinity in classical philosophy, which he notes is natural, rational, and moral:

> Not that I would conclude that these philosophers, in this threefold division, had any thought of a trinity in God, although Plato is said to have been the first to discover and promulgate this distribution, and he saw that God alone could be the author of nature, the bestower of intelligence, and the kindler of love by which life becomes good and blessed ... There are three things which every artificer must possess if he is to effect anything—nature, education, practice. Nature is to be judged by capacity, education by knowledge, practice by its fruit (*City of God,* Bk. xl, 25).

St. Augustine no doubt also saw that man by his very nature craves unity, truth, and goodness, whom God sustains by creation, conservation, and concurrence, as scholastic philosophy tells us. I understand that in his teens St. Aloysius Gonzaga once accepted an invitation at Alcala to argue in public debate that the Blessed Trinity can be known through human intelligence alone. I would have loved to have been there!

In the spiritual world, the rule of three can be discerned ever more truly, the closer we approach the Godhead. Among angels, St. Thomas tells us, there are three hierarchies. Among men, God's chosen people were first distinguished carnally as Cohen, Levite, and Israel. Now become the Church, they subsist as priesthood, religious, and laity. Indeed God's entire plan for us unfolds in a threefold manner by way of Creation, Redemption, and Sanctification, reflected liturgically in the seasons of Christmas, Easter, and Pentecost.

Our Lord died on a wooden symbol of the Trinity, his name fastened to the top in three languages: Hebrew, Greek, and Latin. If we follow these apparently contrived little details any distance at all in the human life of Jesus, however, we soon see that every action of His was in fact a trinitarian operation in flesh, in some cases so revealed to the senses of the bystanders. One such was His baptism, when the Father was heard to speak, and the Holy Spirit was manifested by the visible sign of a dove.

O Emmanuel, God-with-Us! At His Death, Resurrection and Ascension—again a threefold action—all "vestiges" follow humanity's elevation into the Trinity Itself. In this triune Life, the Christian now lives and breathes, whether he likes it or not. His virtues are become inestimable—as also his sins.

This being the case, we may sometimes wonder why God waited so long to reveal the mystery of the Trinity to us. Few Christian wives and mothers could fail to see that the human family, composed of father, mother, and child, forms a particularly powerful vestige of the Trinity. Indeed the human family is so strongly reminiscent of the Trinity, it leads us to see at once one very good reason why God in His infinite wisdom didn't disclose His treble identity to the early Hebrews, as we feel He might have.

The Jews lived their early history surrounded by polytheistic pagans whose myths, like everything created, reflected the Trinity vestigially. Their plural deities were in fact for the most part god "families." The Sumerians, for instance, had a father-god called *An* and a mother-goddess *Ki*, who united to give birth to *En-lil*, and this trinity was repeated in varied form throughout Babylonia, Assyria and Egypt. The same was true in Chanaan, where Baal played the part of *En-lil*, *Astarte* was the mother, and *El* the father. As we know, the Hebrew prophets spent most of their time and risked their lives, trying to keep the chosen people from adhering to these fakes. Had God seen fit at this time to reveal Himself as three Persons to such a nation, surrounded by so many spurious trinities, surely the truth would have degenerated into little more than just another myth among others. The reason why God doesn't reveal Himself fully to us is, therefore, always the same anywhere or anytime: we aren't ready for it!

Nevertheless, many family trios in the Old Testament may be in fact trinitarian figures. The Siblings, Moses, Aaron, and Miriam, perhaps fall into this category on close examination. Abraham, Sara, and Isaac certainly do, and foreshadow unmistakably the Holy Family of Nazareth—this last the most perfect representation of the Trinity ever produced in flesh, inasmuch as it is a truly supernatural representation, and one of its members was the Second Person himself.

With the hindsight we now have, we can see that God did actually fill the Old Testament with literally hundreds of luminous clues to the great mystery; but for the Jews it was veiled as was the face of Moses, and as St. Paul laments, it continues so to this day. We Christians, on the other hand, "with faces unveiled, reflecting as in a mirror the glory of the Lord" (*II Cor. 3:18*), can see that the Lord God in Eden who says of Adam, "The man has become one of *Us*," was speaking the plainest truth.

Abraham "by the terebinths of *Mamre* as he sat at the entrance of his tent in the heat of the day" was visited by three strangers whom he nevertheless addressed as "my Lord," and who foretold to him the birth of Isaac. Abraham, we know now, had rare insight. So, too, Isaias is granted a sublime vision of the One God who is nonetheless pronounced thrice Holy by the heavenly court. Passing by these more obvious examples, we might turn to the Book of Josue, where there occurs the following well-known story:

> Then Josue, son of Nun, secretly sent out two spies from Sattim, saying, "Go, reconnoiter the land and Jericho." When the two reached Jericho, they went into the house of a harlot named Rahab, where they lodged. But a report was brought to the king of Jericho that some Israelites had come there that night to spy out the land. So the king of Jericho sent Rahab the order, "Put out the visitors who have entered your house, for they have come to spy out the entire land." The woman had taken the two men and hidden them, so she said, "True, the men you speak of came to me, but I did not know where they came from. At dark, when it was time for the gate to be shut, they left and I do not know where they went. You will have to pursue them immediately to overtake them." Now she had led them to the roof, and hidden them among her stalks of flax spread out there. But the pursuers set out along the way to the fords of the Jordan, and once they had left, the gate was shut.
>
> Before the spies fell asleep, Rahab came to them on the roof and said: "I know that the Lord has given you the land, that a dread of you has come upon us, and that all the inhabitants of the land are overcome with fear of you. For we have heard how the Lord dried up the waters of the Red Sea before you when you came out of Egypt, and how you dealt with Sehon and Og, the two kings of the Amorrites beyond the Jordan, whom you doomed to destruction. At these reports, we are disheartened; everyone is discouraged because of you, since the Lord, your God, is God in heaven above and on earth below. Now then, swear to me by the Lord that since I am showing kindness to you, you in turn will show kindness to my family; and give me an unmistakable token that you are to spare my father and mother, brothers and sisters, and all their kin, and save us from death." "We pledge our lives for yours," the men answered her. "If you do not betray this errand of ours, we will be faithful in showing kindness to you when the Lord gives us the land."
>
> Then she let them down through the window with a rope; for she lived in a house built into the city wall. "Go up into the hill country," she suggested to them, "that your pursuers may not find you. Hide there for three days, until they return; then you may proceed on your way." The

men answered her, "This is how we will fulfill the oath you made us take: When we come into the land, tie this scarlet cord in the window through which you are letting us down; and gather your father and mother, your brothers and all your family into your house. Should any of them pass outside the doors of your house, he will be responsible for his own death, and we shall be guiltless. But we shall be responsible if anyone in the house with you is harmed. If, however, you betray this errand of ours, we shall be quit of the oath you have made us take." Let it be as you say," she replied, and bade them farewell. When they were gone, she tied the scarlet cord in the window.

They went up into the hills, where they stayed three days until their pursuers, who had sought them all along the road without finding them, returned. Then the two came back down from the hills, crossed the Jordan to Josue, son of Nun, and reported all that had befallen them. They assured Josue, "The Lord has delivered all this land into our power; indeed, all the inhabitants of the land are overcome with fear of us" (*Josue 2:1-24*).

Those whose faces are unveiled soon may suspect that we have here not only a good story, but a miniature allegory of the triune God's plan for the salvation of mankind. Here a figure of God the Father, Josue "sends" the Son and the Holy Spirit as two "spies" to reconnoiter the fallen world. They are harbored by the sinful elect in the person of Rahab, who, nevertheless, believes and hides them on her "roof." (The roof in Scripture is often a figure of the higher intellect, where faith abides.)

Before disappearing out the window to elude their pursuers for "three days," the men give Rahab a pledge in the form of a red cord to be tied at her window. Recalling the blood of the sacrificial lamb put on the doorposts of Egypt, this can certainly be taken as a figure of the redeeming sacrifice of Christ. Eventually returning to Josue (God the Father), the two announce that conquest is certain, that "all the inhabitants are overcome with fear of us." At the destruction of Jericho, Rahab the elect is spared together with all her kin precisely because she "hath hidden the messengers."

Thus interpreted, this is the story of the Church and of every redeemed soul who willingly harbors the Son and the Holy Spirit whom the Father sends within human souls to establish His Kingdom. Trying to fathom this story to the bottom in all its details would be like trying to swallow the Blessed Trinity, but even this much betrays the rich trinitarian content latent in Scripture.

While we're on the subject, St. Teresa says elsewhere in her *Autobiography*:

I was once recollected in that companionship which I have ever in my soul, and it seemed to me that God was present there in such a way that I remembered how St. Peter said: "Thou art the Christ, the Son of the living God"; for the living God was in my soul. This is not like other visions, for it overpowers faith; so that it is impossible to doubt of the indwelling of the Trinity in our souls, by presence, power, and essence. To know this truth is of the very highest gain; and, as I stood amazed to see His Majesty in a thing so vile as my soul, I heard: "It is not vile, My child, for it is made in My image" (*Relation* ix, 17).

And with that, we fall headlong into the vortex of the mystery which lies within us, for in the interior world of the human soul, the vestiges of the Blessed Trinity which teem in the natural world intensify and come to a point like rays of light concentrated by a high-powered lens:

> God created man in His image.
> In the image of God He created him.
> Male and female He created them (*Gen. 1:27*).

Who in his right mind could ever have suspected such a thing? That only God could have revealed us this, our most intimate secret, proves we don't know the first thing about ourselves. How are we like God? Inasmuch as generations of acute theologians have so far been unable to provide us with any kind of clear definition on this important question, please don't expect an explanation from me off-hand.

Properly awed by the magnitude of the problem, I can only accept that women are made to God's image as well as men. It's evident they must search Majesty for their own answers within themselves, as St. Teresa did. It's true she was granted special visions of what took place in her soul, but we are possessed of the reality they portrayed no less than she, each to her own degree. It remains that no woman made to God's image can know herself without knowing God—nor can she know God without knowing something of herself. If this reciprocity didn't exist, the interior life would be just the hollow, self-centered mockery the world judges it to be.

St. Teresa, taught by our Lord, rhymed the poem:

> Soul, thou must seek thyself in me,
> And thou must seek for me in thee.

As it is, those who try know it's a dangerous, vital, exhilarating business. "Search not into things above thy ability," warns Sirach. Many would argue it's safer and humbler to follow his advice and let well enough alone, "For it is not necessary for thee to see with thy eyes those things that are hid" *(3:23)*. Unfortunately, Sirach qualifies this easy way out. He adds, "But the things that God hath commanded thee, think on them always!" *(3:22)*.

That's the trouble. We have to search Majesty. God tells natural man as He did Father Abraham, to "walk in my presence and be perfect." This calls forth the full limit of natural human capacity, living in God's "presence," though not in His intimacy. To Moses God explains why man made in His image must be a perfect man: "For I, the Lord your God, am holy!" *(Lev. 19:1)*. This is enough, but the Christ, who made gods of us, tells us to be perfect, not as man can be perfect, but *"as your heavenly Father is perfect!"* Who but God could set such standards, or establish such a relationship? We are commanded to measure ourselves against divinity!

This is awful. Who can imitate what isn't known? Obviously this is impossible. Lest we use this excuse against Him, God the Son, Second Person of the Blessed Trinity, became man so that triune Divinity might be made plain to us.

> God, who at sundry times and in divers manners spoke in times past to the fathers by the prophets, last of all in these days has spoken to us by his Son, whom he appointed heir of all things, by whom also he made the world; who, being the brightness of his glory and the image of his substance, and upholding of all things by the word of his power, has effected man's purgation from sin and taken his seat at the right hand of the Majesty on High (*Heb. 1:1-3*).

Theologians in the tradition of Duns Scotus are of the opinion that, if Adam and Eve had never sinned and never needed a redeemer, God would, nevertheless, have become Man, if only to supply them a visible model of fully developed human perfection. Such a model would be indispensable if man were to achieve a supernatural end within the intimate life of God. We might also argue, didn't God make man in His image precisely because God intended to become man? St. Francis de Sales, Suarez, St. Albert the Great, and many mystics were of the opinion that from the beginning, the Incarnation was the true motive for creating the universe. Otherwise, they contend, why would Christ be Head of the angels, who could in no wise profit by redemption?

Without the divine Model, who could know on the human level how to be as *poor* as God, who empties Himself eternally as an outpouring of Persons? The person who became man "did not consider being equal to God a thing to be clung to but emptied himself, taking the nature of a slave and being made like unto men," so that He might pour Himself out on earth to the last drop of His blood, divested even of His material clothing, in order to teach us the poverty of God.

We must know God, to be as *chaste* as God is chaste, who is thrice-holy, yet ever One, outside of Whom nothing is, and who as Man asked, "Which of you can convict me of sin?" (*John 8:46*).

Only God can teach us to be as *obedient* as God is obedient. The servant of all His creation, He rains on just and unjust alike, sustaining all things by His power and Love. As Man He washed the feet of other men, doing always the will of the Father and becoming "obedient unto death, even to the death of the cross," coming, "not to be served, but to serve."

"Be you, therefore, imitators of God," said St. Paul, who understood all this so well. "And walk in love, as Christ also loved us and delivered himself up for us an offering and a sacrifice to God to ascend in fragrant odor" (*Eph. 5:1,2*).

"For I have given you an example," He told them in farewell, "that as I have done to you, so you also should do" (*John 13:15*), and He left to prepare for each of us a place in the bosom of the Trinity. We must know God to understand why poverty, chastity, and obedience perfect faith, hope, and charity, and why these theological virtues are three which lead us to the Trinity by enlightening our minds, cleansing our memories, and strengthening our wills. By them we overcome the flesh, the world, and the devil, for even evil—which is *nothing*—must be so in a trinitarian way to oppose a trinitarian God.

Even under the Old Dispensation, God commanded us to love Him "with thy whole heart, thy whole soul and thy whole mind," as the price of being His own special possession. There's a noble congruity in loving a trinitarian God three ways, with heart, soul, and mind. I wonder, are we, like God, trinitarians? If we're made in His image, we must be, both naturally and supernaturally.

Like God, we are mostly hidden, especially from ourselves, but like Him we also produce certain "vestiges." For instance, when a housewife possessing mind, memory, and free will thinks of herself thinking, and takes pleasure in the thought, she re-enacts within herself to some extent the very circumincessions I burnt the stew over. "God himself is a spirit," reminds theology, "and the manner of divine generation is entirely spiritual. It is an act of the divine intellect. God the Father understands. There is nothing for Him to know or understand, except Himself. We can distinguish, therefore, the Thinker and the Thought-Of."

> God the Father, if you like, sees Himself reflected in the mirror of His mind. It is the perfect image of Himself that He sees, One "Who is the radiance of His Father's splendor, and the full expression of His being" (*Heb. 1:3*). That image is His Son. We, too, having a mind that is spiritual, can think of ourselves. We have the beginnings of the trinitarian operations, but they are merely inchoate; they do not carry to completion: the contemplated image of self never becomes a distinct person that is other than self.

Walter Hilton, also a mystic like St. Teresa, puts it another way:

> The soul of man, is a life with three powers—memory, understanding, and will—made in the image and likeness of the Blessed Trinity, whole, perfect, and righteous. The *memory* has the likeness of the Father inasmuch as it was given power to retain His image, neither forgetting it nor being distracted by creatures. The *understanding* was made clear and bright without error or darkness, as perfect as it might be in a body not glorified and so it has the likeness of the Son, who is eternal Wisdom. The *will* was made pure, springing up to God without love of the flesh or of creatures, by the sovereign goodness of the Holy Ghost, and so it has the likeness of the Holy Ghost, who is divine Love.
> So man's soul, which may be called a created trinity, was perfected in the memory, sight, and love of the uncreated Blessed Trinity, which is God ... But when Adam sinned, choosing to squander his love on himself and creatures and to take pleasure in them, he lost all his nobility and dignity, and you also in him, and he fell from the blessed Trinity into a horrible, dark, wretched trinity; that is, into forgetfulness and ignorance of God, and into a monstrous love of himself. (*Scale of Perfection,* Bk. II, Ch. 43.)

Hilton sums up the whole of the spiritual life in a desire "to recover a semblance of that dignity; that our soul may be restored by grace, as it were, to a shadow of that image of the Trinity, which it originally possessed, and which it will have in its fullness in heaven" (*Scala,* Bk. I, 42).

"The Trinity so loves to find Its own image and likeness in Its creation!" exclaimed Sister Elizabeth of the Trinity, the modern apostle of the Divine Indwelling.

St. Augustine pronounced no endeavor so arduous or so rewarding as meditation on the Blessed Trinity, which will engage our minds, memories, and will for eternity.

"O eternal Trinity, you are a deep sea," cried also St. Catherine of Siena, "into which the deeper I enter, the more I find; the more I find, the more I seek!"

Because the Blessed Trinity is an indemonstrable, fully supernatural mystery, it gives itself to us only supernaturally, and *really*. It's no hobby for spiritual dilettantes. "The kingdom of heaven is like leaven, which a woman took and buried in three measures of flour, until all of it was leavened" (*Matt. 13:33*), said the Second Person, who is all textbooks in one Word. When Christ the leaven, which Holy Mother the Church "took and buried" in our "three measures of flour"—our own trinitarian image—begins His work there, we can expect to rise to unprecedented heights. Because we are corporeal, we inevitably come to reflect and participate in—each to her own degree—the perfect divine life lived in flesh by God on earth. "Therefore, whether you eat or drink, or do anything else, do all for the glory of God!" says St. Paul (*I Cor. 10:31*).

Dishwashing? Well, "whatever you do in word or work, do all in the name of the Lord Jesus," says the Apostle, and as I remember, the Lord Jesus was very particular about both the inside and the outside of the cup being clean, so washing dishes can't be unimportant. Besides, there is a special reward in eternity for dishpan hands. Our Lord promised St. Gertrude that "in the Resurrection, when the body will be raised incorruptible, each of its members will receive a special recompense for the labors and actions which it has performed in My name and for My love."

"O Lord, show me some way whereby I may bear this life!" groaned St. Teresa, like many another woman who yearned to chuck it all and take off for heaven.

And our Lord replied, "Think, My child, when life is over, thou canst not serve Me as thou art serving Me now, and eat for me, and sleep for me. Whatsoever thou doest, let it be done for Me as if thou wert no longer living, but I; for that is what St. Paul said."

Dishwashing in Christ and the Blessed Trinity isn't all done in the head, like simple arithmetic. In fact, St. Thomas wouldn't allow that even simple arithmetic can be done entirely in the head. Following Aristotle, he says, "It is as ridiculous to say, the soul alone understands, as to say, alone it builds or weaves."

Elaborating for us in modern idiom, Fr. Sertillanges says:

Thought is born in us after long processes of preparation in which the whole bodily machine is at work. The chemistry of the cell is the basis of everything; the most obscure sensations prepare our experience; this experience is the product of the work of the senses, which slowly elaborate their acquisitions and fix them through memory. It is amid physiological phenomena, in continuity with them and in dependence on them, that the intellectual operation takes place. No one thinks, even if he is only utilizing an acquired idea, without calling up a whole complex of images, emotions, sensations, which are the culture medium of the idea ... The change by which we pass from ignorance to knowledge must be attributed, according to St. Thomas, directly to the body and only accidentally to the intellectual part of us. (*Intellectual Life,* p. 34).

It's easy to see from that how St. Paul could talk about the Word of God penetrating even into "joints and marrow." It's also easy to see that nobody but a housewife can think as a housewife thinks. Not even a theologian can think about God for her. God's Majesty is to be searched specially by each one of us, because He made each one of us specially to search Him. As we search His Majesty, He searches our hearts, and whoever ponders in her heart finds Him, as did the blessed housewife Mary, Seat of Wisdom, Mother of Good Counsel.

Believe it or not, women are especially good at this pondering business, producing knowledge in love within our souls, as God the Father produces the Son in the Holy Spirit. Men criticize women for thinking with their hearts, but that's the way women are made to think. Because they're built this way, female thinking sometimes sinks to earth but on the other hand, it rarely takes off for the wild blue yonder of impractical theory as male thinking sometimes does. When a woman really thinks, there are practical repercussions: we have two Eves, the old and the new, to prove it. In fact, about all a woman has to worry about is keeping her thinking straight, so reliably does she "do" thought as she goes along. The knowledge and love joined in God, shall man put asunder?

Fiat, said Mary for all of us, thinking it over. I think I smell something burning.

"I have come to cast fire upon the earth, and what will I but that it be kindled?" (*Luke 12:49*).

I guess the kitchen stove is as good a place for fire to start as any. Here *goes.*

The Exploration of Inner Space

CHAPTER 2

IF THERE'S one pastime I hated when I was a little girl, it was playing with dolls. Having nonetheless persevered as a wife and mother for nearly a quarter-century despite this handicap, I feel I've earned the right to come out and say so, even in print. It's bound to be known on Judgment Day anyway. Not that I didn't want to play with dolls, mind you. I just couldn't get the hang of it.

I do remember gathering a bunch of them around a table once, when I was about seven years old, setting toy teacups and things out to play "party" like everybody said little girls were supposed to, and even putting cookie crumbs or what not in the plates, all in proper tradition. Then I sat back and wondered what to do next. I looked at the dolls, and the dolls stared back glassy-eyed at me. The stupid creatures just sat.

If you wanted them to eat anything, you had to sneak the crumbs out of the plates unbeknownst to yourself and pretend they had eaten them—pretty much as those Babylonian priests did with the idol *Bel*, to fool the king. Then you had to make all the conversation, answering yourself in a squeaky falsetto, and what to talk about I never found out. I couldn't think of anything worth saying even at real tea parties, and still can't.

This doll-playing, I figured, was for invalid girls who couldn't get outdoors and build tree huts, or who didn't happen to have a whole family of nine cats, complete to grandmother and great-uncle, as I had. The closest I ever came to enthusiastic doll-playing was dressing up the cats and putting them around the table, with bits of raw hamburger in the plates and milk in the teacups. Boy! What a party! Cats, now, can be counted on to behave like real children. Squash them into chairs and they jump right out. Give them something they like to eat, and they lap it up; give them something they don't like to eat, and they try to sneak away and under. Whatever they did, they always left a dandy mess, for real. At this distance I have to admit that these nine cats provided me with far firmer preparation for motherhood than any number of those marcelled effigies I so often found under the Christmas tree.

Still, once the eats were gone, my heart wasn't in tea parties any more than the cats'. By the time they had slithered out of their gynemorphic ruffles, I was ready to call it quits. Maybe you think I suffered from a defective imagination, but not so. What I hated about doll-playing wasn't so much the inanity of the dolls, as that insufferable make-believe that went along with it. That got on my nerves. How other little girls stood it, I never learned.

Now, with nine live cats, you can do something real. You can, for instance, be an explorer. This was my favorite game, bar none, mostly because it wasn't a game. I was really exploring, the cats coming along tails in air if they pleased. If they didn't, I'd most likely go alone, for exploring doesn't depend on congenial company. Staff in hand, carrying lunch in a napkin, I'd make my way into the nearby grapefruit grove, where you never could tell what would turn up.

There was absolutely no pretense involved. It took all the imagination a girl had to figure out where to look for what next in that limited acreage. You either found something or you didn't. On good days, there might be a perfectly whole snake skeleton lying in plain sight, or then again, maybe only a rusty key to some unimaginable sardine can. Useful knowledge frequently turned up, as for example, the results of eating a grapefruit that was too green. Inevitably there were times when I would come across another stray cat, who would be surreptitiously added to my collection, his presence usually detected too late for the home authority to take any effective counter-measures.

A skinny, freckle-faced boy called Max sometimes went along on these expeditions. He put me on to a peculiar sort of little round nut which grew at the root end of a coarse grass thereabouts. We never discovered its name, but it turned out to be edible. Explorers learn to eat whatever they find to sustain life en route, and luckily our parents never found out how seriously we took exploring. Max, I'm sorry to say, eventually fizzled out as an explorer, as did most of my other friends. He was tired, he said, of always going through "the same ole grapefruit grove." He was a boy, and moved on to wider fields.

Unfortunately, anything beyond the grapefruit grove was off limits for me, so I determined to make the best of it and explore what I could until I grew up and could get to the Himalayas. When I was older, I thought I'd be a spy; then becoming stodgier, an archaeologist—just so it was delving into the unknown. It's hard to believe, but it never occurred to me that just because I was a girl, I would grow up and be a housewife, cooking and setting tables for the rest of my life. What the doll dishes were all about never dawned on me until I already had a very bad case of dishpan hands. By then, of course, the die was cast.

I hadn't meant to go on so about myself, but I'm afraid there's no help for it. As Dam Hubert van Zeller points out, anyone who presumes to write honest books on "spiritual" subjects has only his own experience to fall back on, and ultimately, like the poulterer endeavoring to satisfy his customers at all costs, he ends by placing himself on the slab for sale along with the other birds. This being the case, I may as well go on and tell you I've washed several tons of dishes to date, and set enough tables to reach the Himalayas and back again.

To round out the picture, however, I must admit that no childhood occupation so prepared me for my lot as playing explorer. No matter how high the dishes pile, there's always "the same ole grapefruit grove" lying there waiting to be explored. So help me, I'm still at it, and still amazed at what turns up.

Whoever thinks exploring is an exclusively masculine calling is, I suppose, thinking purely in terms of the Himalayas, or the moon, or such places. There's no denying that women generally are second-rate at this type of endeavor, though even here we must be very careful about categorizing. Almighty God sent us a saint, called Joan of Arc, to remind us that a woman's profession is whatever profession He calls her to. It may not be the one she wants, or the one the world wants her to have, nor even, sometimes, the one for which she is most suited biologically. St. Joan wore not just men's pants, but men's armor. Somehow or other, she made an excellent general, finding woman's place astride a horse in army camps and battlefields.

Exploring can be the most feminine of pursuits, especially if we understand that all explorers don't brave natural elements, suffering hunger and thirst, following sketchy maps, going out to discovery and conquest. Some brave all these dangers, but spiritually, and travel in the opposite direction, going in to uncharted wilderness. In fact, to accept fully a vocation, as a woman is to lend oneself to a plunge into an ever deepening mystery.

Woman's vocation is a mystery. Woman is a mystery. She is mysterious not only to men, but especially to herself. Rather than face the mystery within themselves, many women prefer to live out their lives as second-rate, small-size men. It's unnatural, but it's easier.

"A career on the outside for every housewife!" cry women college presidents.

Well, we have to admit there are days when it's hell in the same ole grapefruit grove, especially when you don't know what to look for, or when a dark blue sock has somehow got into the wash with the best white damask dinner napkins. Unfortunately, it's in the grapefruit grove that woman's real potential is developed. We escape problems on the inside by running outside, but we never solve them that way. "We suffer terrible trials because we do not understand ourselves!" said St. Teresa.

What makes a housewife a drudge is an inside problem. Until she solves it, whatever skills and talents she lavishes on the outside world will do no lasting good to anyone, least of all herself. If the world is to be saved from the horrors of our time, one half of its population must in fact rediscover itself as the "interior sex," and find the courage to explore for this same benighted world the riches hidden in the grove. This is the real work of woman. There's no make-believe about it, simply because it can't be seen. In comparison with it, a woman's exterior occupations are the ones which turn out to be make-believe. For this kind of exploration her Creator has specially fitted her, making her more sedentary, more passive, more introspective than man by nature, and this applies, I discovered, even to tree-climbing tomboys.

"The kingdom of heaven is within you," says the Christ, telling us plainly that God is to be found where His image is.

There are no maps for use in these forays, only sketchy tales told by occasional travelers who have ventured into this unknown territory. They all say differently, yet their stories all agree in the essentials. For one thing they maintain that the world inside is immense, full of surprises and vastly various, everything outside it somehow reflected in its depths.

"The heart is unsearchable, who can know it?"asked Jeremias (*Jer. 17:9*).

Indeed the complicated immensity of the human inner world is such a truism, it's rather taken for granted. It's rarely speculated on by anyone but specialists, much as only astronomers give really sustained thought to nebulae in the outer cosmos. As for actually entering the inner cosmos, few amateurs venture unless driven. This, I suppose, is why so much secular literature on the subject deals with purely pathological aspects. We're inclined to take cognizance of the interior universe only when something has gone terribly wrong with it, say, some star has blown up, or there's been a total eclipse. Basing our knowledge of interior space on the plentiful evidence collected by psychiatrists and psychoanalysts from mutilated souls lying on their office couches—perhaps by way of the opium dreams of the unfortunate Thomas De Quincey or the alcoholic fancies of Edgar

Allan Poe—we are properly terrified of ever entering into ourselves at all.

Here's a snatch of what De Quincey reported in May, 1818, returning from one of what he called his "oriental" dreams,

> ...which always filled me with such amazement at the monstrous scenery, that horror seemed absorbed, for a while, in sheer astonishment. Sooner or later came a reflux of feeling that swallowed up the astonishment, and left me, not so much in terror, as in hatred or abomination of what I saw. Over every form and threat, and punishment, and dim sightless incarceration, brooded a sense of eternity and infinity that drove me into an oppression as of madness.
>
> Into these dreams only, it was, with one or two slight exceptions, that any circumstances of physical honor entered. All before had been moral or spiritual terrors. But here the main agents were ugly birds, or snakes, or crocodiles, especially the last. The cursed crocodile became to me the object of more horror than almost all the rest. I was compelled to live with him; and (as was always the case, almost, in my dreams) for centuries. I escaped sometimes, and found myself in Chinese houses with cane tables, etc. All the feet of the tables, sofas, etc., soon became instinct with life: the abominable head of the crocodile, and his leering eyes, looked out at me, multiplied into a thousand repetitions; and I stood loathing and fascinated.

Similar notes could be culled in most any mental hospital, but De Quincey was a drug addict of high literary talent, and makes much better reading. With gems like this and "The Pit and the Pendulum" circulating in educated milieux it's small wonder the words *morbid* and *introspection* have practically merged into one in modern vocabularies. Healthy people, we are led to believe, get out more, and very healthy people stay out.

Luckily for the human race, the same ole grapefruit grove doesn't present this aspect to all explorers! Walt Whitman had a wonderful time disporting himself in his, and being an indefatigable poet as well as an unusually extroverted introvert, he tried to put some of his private cosmos into words. In the remarkable long poem he called forthrightly the *Song of Myself*, he takes us on a guided tour of natural creation as he sees it in himself, beginning:

> I celebrate myself, and sing myself,
> And what I assume you shall assume,
> For every atom belonging to me as good as belongs to you.

God be praised in poets! They understand without being told that the many are always found in one! This is deep natural knowledge, and no one with the courage to be himself fails to acquire it. That's why, I suppose, pantheism is the standing temptation of poets. Few escape it entirely. As he says:

> Mine is no callous shell,
> I have instant conductors all over me whether I pause or stop,
> They seize every object and lead it harmlessly through me.

Bringing in his wake machinists, the grass, lunatics, whale flukes, pimples, and anything else he happens to encounter, Whitman can say:

> The old husband sleeps by his wife, and the young husband
> sleeps by his wife;
> And these tend inward to me, and I tend outward to them,
> And such as it is to be of these more or less I am,
> And of these one and all I weave the song of myself.

And he cries in self-defense:

> Dazzling and tremendous, how quick the sunrise would kill me, If I could not now and always send sunrise out of me!

Philosophers see this too. Schopenhauer as a matter of fact stated his own conclusions on this score in one sentence. "The world," he said, "is my idea." Subjectivity can hardly go further! More deadly than pantheism, here is the worst temptation besetting the interior explorer: self-centeredness. When he discovers on looking inside himself what a marvelous, fascinating cosmos he is, he's liable to fall in love with himself, as Lucifer did, and relate all reality to his own center. "For no man can make a god like to himself" (*Wis. 15:16*) warns Scripture. As Whitman admits:

> I resist anything better than my own diversity.

But the minute an explorer becomes content with what he finds, he has ceased to be an explorer. Like Cain, he has left the presence of the Lord and "founded a city," settling into squat four-square finitude. This kind of staying put may look like interiority; it isn't. It's interiority standing still—a world of difference.

Do I contradict myself? asks Whitman disarmingly, with characteristic child-like directness.

> Very well then I contradict myself.
> (I am large, I contain multitudes.)

Incapable of tallying all the baffling data his own soul supplies him, he confesses to his readers that,

> I concentrate toward them that are nigh, I wait on the door-slab.

Nobody who writes about the interior life can do more than that really. Whitman, whose name *wiht*-man in Anglo-Saxon means *creature-man*, is aptly given to these trenchant natural insights!

The door-slab is about as far as a poet can go by common means. He can describe just about anything in his interior universe, provided he stays on this side of the slab, in that fascinating limbo where body and soul join, which we call *psychological*. It's a busy realm of imagery, where the milling evidence collected from the outside world by the senses is sifted into symbol, stored and classified in the memory, and presented meanwhile to the intellect to be acted on or not by the will. Even so, this is already very, very mysterious, very trinitarian.

Here psychiatrists and philosophers penetrate little farther than poets. It can be a very dangerous spot to linger on. St. John of the Cross, who isn't called "the first modern psychologist" for nothing, warns:

> It is to these senses of imagination and fancy that the devil habitually betakes himself with his wiles—now natural, now supernatural; for they are the door and entrance to the soul, and here, as we have said, the understanding comes to take up or set down its goods, as it were in a harbor or in a store-house where it keeps its provisions. And for this reason it is hither that both God and the devil always come with their jewels of supernatural forms and images, to offer them to the understanding; although God does not make use of this means alone to instruct the soul, but dwells within it in substance, and is able to do this by Himself and by other methods (*Ascent of Mt. Carmel*, Bk. II, Ch. 16, 4).

St. Augustine, scanning his own store-houses in utter amazement, applies to God for an explanation:

> Great is the power of memory, a thing, O my God, to be in awe of, a profound and immeasurable multiplicity; and this thing is my mind, this thing am I. What then am I, O my God?
> What nature am I? A life powerfully various and manifold and immeasurable. In the innumerable fields and dens and caverns of my

memory, innumerably full of innumerable kinds of things, present either by their images as are all bodies, or in themselves as are our mental capacities, or by certain notions or awarenesses, like the affections of the mind—for even when the mind is not experiencing these, the memory retains them, although whatever is in the memory is in the mind too—in and through all these does my mind range, and I move swiftly from one to another and I penetrate them as deeply as I can, but find no end. So great is the force of memory, so great the force of life while man lives under sentence of death here.

What am I to do now, O my true Life, my God? I shall mount beyond this my power of memory, I shall mount beyond it, to come to You, O lovely Light. What have you to say to me? In my ascent by the mind to You who abide above me, I shall mount up beyond that power of mine called memory, longing to attain to touch You at the point where that contact is possible and to cleave to You at the point where it is possible to cleave. For the beasts and the birds have memory, or else they could never find their dens or their nests or all the other things their way of life needs; indeed without memory they would be unable to have a way of life. So I must pass beyond memory to come to Him who separated me from the four-footed beasts and made me wiser than the birds of the air. I shall pass beyond memory to find You, O truly good and certain Loveliness, and where shall I find You? If I find You beyond my memory, then shall I be without memory of You. And how shall I find You if I am without memory of You? (*Confessions*, Bk. X).

St. Augustine asks questions only mystics and small children dare put. They alone have the simplicity to rush across Walt Whitman's door-slab and enter a region where the senses are left behind and even poetry must falter. Like St. Peter walking on the water, they can sustain themselves only by faith. This is a crucial stage on the interior journey, for here the explorer either runs home, settles down on the slab, or plunges headlong into a land "waste and void," where "darkness covers the abyss, and the spirit of God stirs above the waters" (*Gen. 1:2*). If he goes forward, he comes upon a "new creation," an elevation of the one "in the beginning." Self-lovers never make this leap, because as St. Augustine guessed, here one must leave self behind.

"Amen I say unto you, unless you turn and become as little children, you will not enter into the kingdom of heaven" (*Matt. 18:3*).

"Everyone of you who does not renounce all that he possesses, cannot be my disciple," (*Luke 14:33*) stipulated the Man who said, "I am the Door," and who warned us that "many will seek to enter and will not be able" (*Luke 13:24*).

Walter Hilton, an English mystic who crossed the slab, tried to tell others what this experience is like:

It is as if a man has been a long time in the sun, and then comes suddenly into a dark house. He will be as if blind at first, and see nothing, but if he will wait a bit, he will soon be able to see about him; at first large objects, and then small, and then everything that is in the house. It is the same spiritually; he who renounces self-love and acquires knowledge of himself is in the dark to begin with. But if he preserves and continues with assiduous prayer, and often repeats his determination to love Jesus, he will come to see many things, great and small, of which he was at first unaware. The prophet seems to have promised this when he said: "Then shall thy light rise up in darkness, and thy darkness shall be as the noonday. And the Lord will give thee rest continually, and will fill thy soul with brightness" (*Is. 58:10-11*). (*Scale of Perfection*, Bk. II, Ch. 27)

Everything outside the door-slab of self serves only to give us an inkling of the wonders that lie inside, where God's image isn't merely "vestigial" as in matter, but real and efficacious, the very shape of the human structure raised by grace. The contemplation of sensible creation only prepares for the higher self-knowledge which goes hand in hand with the knowledge of God: "If thou know not thyself, O fairest among women," counsels the Bridegroom to the soul seeking Him, "go forth, and follow after the steps of the flocks, and feed thy kids beside the tents of the shepherds" (*Can. 1:7*).

Without God's grace, travel beyond this point is clearly impossible. St. Teresa, who lived in an age of chivalry," thought,

> ...that we should regard the soul as a castle, made entirely of diamond or very clear crystal, in which there are many rooms, just as in heaven there are many mansions. And well-considered, sisters, the soul of the just is nothing less than a paradise where, as our Lord himself says, he takes his pleasure. Then, what kind of a place will it be, do you think, in which a King so powerful, so wise, so pure, so rich in all good things, will take delight? I find nothing with which to compare the great beauty of a soul, and its vast capacity. And truly, our intelligence, however keen, can scarcely grasp it, any more than we can understand God, to whose image and likeness, as He himself says, He has created us ... It is no small pity and shame, that by our fault, we do not understand ourselves, nor realize who we are.
>
> Would it not show great ignorance, my daughters, if a man were questioned about himself, and he did not know who he was, nor could he say who was his father or his mother, nor to what country he belonged? Then if this would argue great stupidity, ours is greater beyond comparison, when we do not endeavor to find out who we are, except that we inhabit these bodies, and we understand but vaguely that we have souls, because we have heard that this is so, and the Faith declares it to us. But we seldom consider what we possess in this soul, or who is within it,

or how great is its value, and thus we pay little heed to preserve its beauty with all care. This we bestow entirely on the rude setting, or enclosure of the castle, that is to say, on our bodies. (*Interior Castle,* First Mansion, I.)

There speaks a real housewife, who knows what housekeeping is all about! St. Teresa would be quick to point out that a housewife's house is simply a material image of this interior castle. Inside is where the real housekeeping goes on—the dusting and decorating, the tea parties, the stew-burning and all the rest of it. Be they carried on in a two-room apartment, a split-level in suburbia, or in the Governor's Mansion, these activities are the palest parodies of what takes place in the housewife's soul. Every human soul God ever created is a housewife in this sense; and in this sense housewifery is the universal human vocation.

Think for a minute about keeping house—the cooking, the cleaning, the marketing, the mending, the constant tidying up and organizing which a housewife must engage in to maintain a poised *status quo* in her home. The never-ending struggle against dirt, decay, and disorder is a material shadow of the battle every Christian wages in his own interior against sin, ignorance, and death. So also the acquisition of virtues and the delicate spiritual adjustments of the inner life are simply "interior decoration" in the true sense of the words.

Think, too, of all a house contains—the emergency supplies on the shelves, the books, the little treasures, the homely but useful objects; the painting of great-uncle Edward, the water that courses in and out of the pipes, the sun that streams in the large—and small—windows; the places to eat, to sleep, to play, to cry; the clothing for four seasons; not to overlook the skeleton in the closet.

Every house has its "working parts" and its parlor, open to all, but what about the attic and the basement—the unused "upper room" of contemplation and the murky depths of the semi-conscious? Does the housewife's industry extend to these? Does she make full use of the house she keeps? Is she, indeed, a really good housekeeper, or does she stash anything she doesn't want to cope with behind closet doors or in jammed drawers? Does she spend all her time shopping, making her house not a home, but a warehouse? Does she houseclean neurotically, always intent on "order," but neglectful of harmony? Does her house afford food and shelter to anyone but herself? Does she patiently repair the still serviceable slipcover, glue the slipping chair rung? Or does she get rid of these annoying problems by throwing out the chairs, like the baby with the bathwater?

On earth the householder must be always ready to "bring forth from his storeroom things new and old," as the Mass for a Holy Woman makes clear. In a well-appointed house the new and the old both have their place. A house filled exclusively with factory-fresh utensils and furniture not only lacks character-it sins against the Fourth Commandment. "Honor thy father and thy mother" means also, honor the things of thy father and mother, respect the old and the traditional, give history its place. Living at peace in one's soul—house must entail putting up patiently with inconveniences and inherited defects, even old traumas and broken dreams, doing the best we can with what we have, throwing out junk, but refurbishing the reclaimable. This doesn't prevent us from yearning with all our heart for the great day when the Lord and Master will come home to stay and "make all things new!" (*Apoc.21:5*).

Ah, who shall find a good housekeeper? Far and from the uttermost coasts is the price of her!

Housework is so rich in mystical significance, even dusting a table can be an examination of conscience. Preparing dinner is a whole course in doctrine. How many of us drudges realize that when we set the table, feed the children, and clean up afterwards we are in fact reflecting in millions of homes the sacred actions of the High Priest himself at Mass? Do you have feeding problems in your family? Well, so does He! There's no home-related activity a housekeeper can engage in that's without spiritual overtones. Does she collect antiques? Well, coming across an old battered chest with "good lines" in an old barn and taking it home to refinish and set up in a place of honor gives her just a taste of what the divine Missionary must feel in His Sacred Heart when He is able to reclaim a disfigured soul and set it up in His House, the Church.

As for just sitting in a chair, well, that's a minor sabbath. My goodness, a chair! Have we ever really given a chair the thought—I should say the *respect* it deserves? Who is worthy to sit, actually *sit* in a chair? To give us an inkling of the transcendent exaltation of Christ's Sacred Humanity after His Ascension, the Creed can only babble after St. Paul, "He sitteth at the right hand of God the Father Almighty. From thence He shall come to judge the living and the dead." And this same Christ promised those who followed Him that they too would sit on twelve thrones, judging the tribes of Israel. A chair, at the very least, may well be at the end of the earthly search for majesty.

My house is full of chairs, tall, short, straight, squashy, rocking, hard and upholstered. All have one common characteristic, however; they were all made to be sat in. Any chair is made to support the human

body in a state of—not inertia, like a bed—but decorous rest. Sitting in
a chair properly makes one automatically feel secure, in abeyance, and
majestic. There are "chairs of philosophy" and "chairs of mathematics"
in universities, accorded to persons who know something and can rest
secure in their knowledge. The pope speaks officially, *ex cathedra*,
from a chair when he pronounces on dogma.

Even the Pilates exercise their God-given worldly authority "sitting
on the judgment seat." At the far end of the scale we have, alas, electric
chairs and toilets, because God's wisdom "reacheth from end to end
mightily" (*Wis. 8:1*)—even to hell.

At the upper end of the scale, Richard Rolle intimately associated
the corporal act of sitting with contemplation. In a surprising little aside
in his *Incendium Amoris*, he tells us:

> Whenever I wanted to enter into contemplation while standing,
> walking, or even reclining, I was aware that I failed greatly from these
> goals and considered myself, as it were, forsaken. Wherefore, driven by
> necessity to attain the greatest devotion possible and to persevere therein,
> I decided to sit down. I was not unaware of the reason for this: whenever a
> man stands or walks, his body becomes fatigued and thus his spirit is
> shackled and somewhat wearied in the face of this effort. The spirit does
> not find its greatest peace nor its perfection in this, because, according to
> the philosopher, the spirit only gains prudence while sitting in quietude.
> Whoever, therefore, prefers contemplations while standing and not sitting,
> should know that he is still a long way off from the heights of
> contemplation.[1]

In this life, women are better suited for prolonged sitting than men.
Physiology alone would proclaim it. It's important, for I think we are
meant to sit in chairs somewhat in the manner that God "sits" within us.
If anyone who had never seen human beings were to describe what he
thought they were like from the evidence given him by the chairs they

---

[1] *Ut si velim stando vel ambulando contemplari, vel procumbendo,
videbam me multum ab illis deficere, et quasi desolatum me existimare. Unde
hac necessitate compulsus ut in summa devotione quam habere possem et
perseverare, sedere elegi. Hujus rei causa non ignoro quia si homo multum
stet vel ambulet corpus eius fatigatur et sic impeditur anima et quodammodo
lacescit pro onere. Et non est in sua summa quiete, et per consequens nec in
perfectione, quia secundum philosophum, sedendo et quiescendo fit anima
prudens. Qui ergo adhuc magis stando quam sedendo in divinis delectatur,
sciat se a contemplationis culmine longe distare.* (Deanesley edition,
Longmans, Green & Co., p: 185.)

sit in, what would he say? He would be very much in the same position
we're in when we try to form an idea of God from the evidence given
by the shaky seats made to His image, which He occupies here on
earth. Like chairs, we bear a vital relation to Him whom we are meant
to contain, but what He is in himself we can never know without actual
contact with Him.

The only perfect human "chair" the world has ever produced for
Him, which gives truest evidence of Him, is our Lady, Seat of Wisdom.
There are beautiful Byzantine Madonnas, painted by unknown artists
back in the days when Christians painted theology and the inside of
their subjects, which teach so well the mystique of chairs. In one
picture I have in mind our Lady sits in a chair which is circular and
womb-like, withal carved and turreted like a city wall. She holds the
Child before her, presenting Him to the beholder from her marvelous
resting-place like the holy Jerusalem "which is built as a city that is in
unity with itself"(*Ps. 121*).

From this painting the Blessed Housewife speaks clearly:

> *In omnibus requiem quaesivi*: In all these I sought rest, and I shall
> abide in the inheritance of the Lord. Then the Creator of all things
> commanded and said to me; and He that made me rested in my tabernacle,
> and He said to me: Let thy dwelling be in Jacob, and thy inheritance in
> Israel, and take root in Mine Elect. ... And so I was established in Sian,
> and in the holy city likewise I rested; and my power was in Jerusalem.
> And I took root in an honorable people, and in the portion of my God, His
> inheritance, and my abode is in the full assembly of the Saints.

Mothers, cities, houses, chairs, souls—what mysterious vessels
they are! They are mysteries of emptiness, waiting to be filled. Woman,
whom St. Peter in fact calls "the weaker vessel," is herself surrounded
by vessels of all kinds, "one for honorable, another for ignoble use," as
St. Paul would put it. The only woman who can really explain such
things to us is the one we call Spiritual Vessel, Vessel of Honor,
Singular Vessel of Devotion. She is the Ark of the Covenant, a House
of Gold.

With her help, perhaps we can continue. Saint Teresa considers this
point:

> Let us consider, then, that this castle has, as I have said, many
> apartments, some above, others below, and at the sides; while at the
> center, in the midst of these, is the principal room, where much secret
> intercourse is held between God and the soul. It is necessary to pay great
> attention to this comparison; perhaps, by it, God willing, I shall be able to

give you some idea of the favors He is pleased to bestow on souls, and the different kinds of favors. (*Interior Castle*, First Mansion, I.)

Please, St. Teresa, go on!

Now, turning to our lovely and delightsome castle, we have to see how we may enter it. I seem to be saying something foolish, because if this castle is the soul, clearly there is no question of how to enter, since they are one and the same thing, and it would seem to be crazy to tell a person to go into a room who was already in it. But you must understand that there are many degrees of entering, and many people remain in the precincts of the castle, where the guards are, and they make no effort to pass inside, nor do they know what is in this precious place, nor who is therein, nor even what rooms it may have (*ibid.*).

Lots of people never get beyond the door-slab, is what I think St. Teresa is saying.

For so far as I can understand, *prayer and reflection are the gateway into this castle.* ... Souls who do not pray ... are so accustomed to mix with the reptiles and beasts that are round about the castle, that they have contracted their habits, and though by nature so richly endowed as to be capable of conversing with God, there is no curing them (*ibid.*).

(Do you suppose one of those reptiles might be poor De Quincey's crocodile? I wonder, did De Quincey ever read St. Teresa?)

Developing this analogy, the saint goes on to compose one of the most sublime treatises ever written on the life of prayer, inviting every housewife to make herself at home in her own house. She envisages spiritual progress as progress from the outside in, through seven "mansions," into the bridal chamber of the King in the deepest center of the soul.

Nobody's castle is exactly like anyone else's. The architecture of each is quite different, both as to style and room arrangement. I suppose some have long corridors with sudden turns; others have all the rooms opening one into another. Some have high walls; others are built open to the air, like tropical pavilions. There are Spanish haciendas, English Georgians, Indian bungalows, little grass shacks, and I guess even igloos and tree huts. Any man's home is his castle; the variety in earthly architecture is only a poor reflection of the diversity in the structure of souls.

Whether large or small, however, all spiritual houses are big enough to contain the universe, for they were all designed as private residences by the divine Architect Himself, to suit Himself, and no one else. It's essential that the housewife in such a place know her business, because she's not just the housekeeper there, or the wife there, but the Queen. Because the King is God, however, the house is more than a castle. It's a temple, dedicated and consecrated. This raises the vocation of the housewife to such a pitch, only Scripture, written by God Himself, is capable of describing it truly—no offense intended to St. Teresa, or Walt Whitman, or De Quincey.

"Do you not know that you are the temple of God and that the Spirit of God dwells in you?" inquires St. Paul, aghast at our ignorance. "If anyone destroys the temple of God, him will God destroy; for holy is the temple of God, and *this temple you are!*" (*I Cor. 3:16-17*). "Do you not know ... that you are not your own? ... Glorify God and bear Him in your body!" (*I Cor. 6:19-20*).

I think you'll agree the same ole grapefruit grove has taken on an entirely new aspect viewed from this height. Here De Quincey's crocodile is nowhere to be seen, and the Song of Myself has assumed the proportions of an eternal roundelay with the Most Holy Trinity. We suspect the world we're exploring now isn't entirely Schopenhauer's idea, or even St. Teresa's or St. Paul's.

The temple of which St. Paul speaks isn't of human architecture, "made by hands." It's a supernatural edifice, produced in love and silence, built by the Man of Peace, the true Solomon whose precursor entertained the Queen of Saba, and who *in silence* built the first Temple in Jerusalem. As Scripture tells us, "The house, when it was in building, was built of stones hewed and made ready: so that there was neither hammer nor axe nor any tool of iron heard in the house when it was in building" (*III Kings 6:7*). So does the supernatural build silently with the natural it finds at hand, previously "hewed and made ready" to house God.

No more beautiful description of the human soul exists than the one emerging from the imagery depicting Solomon's Temple in the Third Book of Kings. The porch, the winding stairs, the oblique windows, the doors of olive wood, the roof of cedar-all are presented in the language of supernaturalized poetry, whose meanings are discovered only by the most intrepid interior searchers.

The prophet Ezechiel developed and raised these "house" images to such mystical heights that this part of his work, St. Jerome tells us, was forbidden to Hebrew readers under thirty, so liable is it to profanation and so opaque is the language to the spiritually immature. Laying no claim to being under thirty, I must still confess my deficiencies in this area.

It isn't that I haven't read the text and looked up all the words. I have. It's just that I'm too sinful to get their full implications.

If you pray enough and God enlightens you, however, you do get them, and can read Ezechiel for yourself. I'll confine myself to pointing out that Ezechiel here opens to our view a threefold concentric vista of God's Temple. Taking us well beyond the door-slab, Ezechiel shows us not only the human soul in supernatural dimensions, but also the Temple which in Christ's mystical body on earth, both of these giving way in turn to the vision of the Temple of the New Jerusalem which will emerge in glory as the Church Triumphant at the end of time. Pondering on any one of these levels will yield more treasure than you would believe the ole grapefruit grove could ever contain.

"God ... set me upon a very high mountain," avows Ezechiel in his humility, beginning to recount the wonders he saw. Leaving De Quincey and Walt Whitman very, very far behind, he takes us through the porches, the courts exterior and interior, the kitchens and the storerooms of the Temple, into the very Holy of Holies. He describes the altars, the appurtenances and decorations of the sanctuary; introduces us to the personnel; and even takes us on a tour of the outer property. The redeemed housewife, wandering through her new home with Ezechiel's help, is dumbfounded at the extent and variety of this hitherto unsuspected domain which is hers.

"Can this be me?"

And well may she shiver when she hears Ezechiel say, "And the spirit lifted me up and brought me into the inner court: and behold the house was filled with the glory of the Lord!" for this house is nothing but herself.

With that I must confess I don't understand the modern penchant for calling a housewife a "homemaker." If this well-meant euphemism is supposed to add to my dignity as a human being, I can't see how! When you come right down to it, homemaker is more applicable to husbands, who, like God, make things and beget families. I think *housewife* is one of the most beautiful words in the English language, once we see what a house and a wife truly are: the dwelling and consort of Almighty God!

Housewifery is the most delicate and demanding of vocations. God says:

> They who have set their threshold by my threshold, and their posts by my posts: and there was a wall between me and them: and they profaned my holy name by the abominations which they committed: for which reason I consumed them in my wrath ... But thou, son of man, shew to the

house of Israel, the temple, and let them be ashamed of all that they have done. Show them the form of the house, and of the fashion thereof, and all its ordinances, and all its order, and all its laws, and thou shalt write it in their Sight: that they may keep the whole form thereof and its ordinances, and do them!

But where is God?

"Search *me!*" the poor housewife might say.

And Saint Paul would agree: "For holy is the temple of God and this temple you are."

"In His temple," King David informs her, "all say, 'Glory.'" That's the *Song of Myself* in a higher key.

Of Scales and Perfection

CHAPTER 3

P RACTICAL household hints for running the interior castle abound in Scripture, and it doesn't do to ask a lot of questions before trying a few. What housewife cares why crushed eggshells settle coffee grounds, provided they do before the guests arrive? She can take a course in physics when the crisis is past.

Settling spiritual sediment is a bit more difficult, but apparently not impossible, for Scripture gives many hints on how to do it. As the evidence presented in the last chapter may lead us to suspect, singing is one of them. If you can't pray, *sing*. Then, if you don't feel like singing, *pray*. The spiritual housewife St. James says, "is any one of you sad? Let him pray. Is anyone in good spirits? Let him sing a hymn!" (*5:13*). I gather it's best, if possible, to do both, because *bis orat qui cantat*. Whoever sings his prayer prays double, or so runs the monastic adage, compressing in four words centuries of hard experience.

Whether or not the singer has a good voice to start with and can stay on key doesn't seem to matter at all. St. James certainly throws caution to the winds. He says *"Anyone!"* When Scripture, which is God's truth, says *anyone* can sing, the words must mean more than they say. If really anyone can sing, then this mystery is worth looking into.

Understanding that with Latin Rite Catholics Gregorian plainsong is official in the Office, I ventured to make inquiries about it. I had come across an article written at upper liturgical levels which informed me soberly that the "Solesmes interpretation" was under fire, wherein I soon saw that for a song called plain there were an awful lot of complicated opinions on how to sing it. According to the reporter, Dom Ictus, maintained thus and so, but Dom Plagal and Dr. Flex clearly contended otherwise, whereas I hadn't even settled on my own version of the *Et cum spiritu tuo*.

This polemic, incidentally, appeared in a foreign periodical, for at the time of which I speak most Americans were pretty well satisfied with "Jesus' Heart All-Burning" in D Major, interpreted on the spot by whoever could sing the loudest. Determined, nevertheless, to discover what was really what in case Gregorian ever caught on in the American provinces where I live, I later had occasion to approach a young choirmistress in a liturgically advanced center in the United States, and I made the most of it. Everybody there seemed to be singing Gregorian as easy as pie, so I introduced myself and asked her please to explain to me what it was that Solesmes was doing that some other people didn't agree with.

She looked me over and in a moment said solemnly, "I really couldn't explain it to you. Even if I did, you wouldn't understand it."

Seldom have I suffered more salutary humiliation. What she said was egregiously true, but how could she have known it on such short acquaintance? She must have been a prophet. How else could she have known just by looking at me that I didn't have a clandestine doctorate in *Hypo-locrian Melodies of the Tenth Century*? Never before had I suspected that my musical ignorance showed, and could be clearly seen by casual observers; but thank goodness I found out.

Let's face it. To this day I have no comprehension of what Solesmes is up to. The trouble is, the minute a human being admits to just anybody that he's totally ignorant, he begins to suspect, like Socrates, that he's really highly educated. So let me tell you about the music of the Church, call it Gregorian, Ambrosian, plain, complicated, or whatever you like. It's not often you can hear about sacred music from someone who isn't an expert, but if you continue reading this, you will.

I can't know anything theoretical about liturgical song, having not so much as read one book on the subject. All I have ever done is sing it as best I could, because somebody has to if there is to be High Mass according to the rubrics around here for Christmas, Easter, and funerals. Needless to say, I've never sung with a Gregorian choir as such, for these "levites and singing men" perform a liturgical function for which women by nature are incapable. I do sing, however, as part of a group I have come fondly to think of as "Fools for Christ," because, like me, they just do the best they can, open-mouthed, for the love of God. If the rest of the congregation suffers, well so do we.

"To the end that the faithful may take a more active part in divine worship, Gregorian chant ought to be restored among the people, at least in all that concerns them," said Pius XI in *Divini Cultus*. "It is in truth altogether necessary that the faithful should not behave like strangers or mute spectators. Moved by the beauty of the liturgy, they ought to take part in the sacred ceremonies."

Well, some of us do.

In the past few years, our ranks have boasted by turns a beautician, a disc jockey, a golf pro, a bacteriologist, one professional singer, a couple of secretary-typists, a published novelist, several high school students, and any number of housewives like myself. Some have beautiful voices, some don't. Some can stay on key no matter what happens, some stay on most of the time, and some only occasionally. Some sing loud and well, some loud and wrong. Some sing so timidly the caliber of singing can't be ascertained at all. Some sing fine as long as there's a stronger voice to lean on, whereas others have apparently irresistible urges to soaring solo flights and are hard to hold to the modest limits of the ecclesiastical mode.

In other words, Fools for Christ are a fine, representative cross-section of the People of God, who must perforce be beauticians, disc jockeys, housewives, and all the other kinds of laymen there are. If only professional choristers are to join in the apocalyptic Voice-of-Many-Waters at the end of time, the vast majority of us are sunk! Unless Christ's grace is void, these are precisely the people destined to join the angelic choirs in eternity, so we needn't be surprised to find them in training already, Like the Bible, the music of the Church is for everybody, *now.*

There's something terribly mysterious about music, any music. Scientists have been able to catch little more than the vibrations it sets up in flight; and philosophers have speculated on its deeper secrets in vain. Dying at birth, the sound of music nevertheless has power to conjure up the most varied emotions, setting up concomitant vibrations in the human soul, arousing the most diffident and calming the most turbulent. When a wily adman sings, "Glatz's Crunches in your lunches/Keep you rolling with the punches!" many a bemused housewife finds herself dropping a package in her shopping cart, so persuasive is the power of song.

Music effects some rapprochement in that mysterious zone where body and soul are joined together and spirit is translated into act. That's plain. How it does, I don't know, but Ezechiel may have shed some light on the problem when he reported that in the mystical temple, "the chambers of the singing men in the inner court" were just outside the inner gate. Music is very close to the interior powers of the soul, and in fact Ezechiel says the inner court "was on the side of the gate that looked to the north: and their prospect was towards the south" (*40:44*), from whence the Queen of Saba came.

The south, often used in Scripture as a figure of carnal life, may well be used so here, for music—although the most spiritual of the arts—operates by and is directed to the senses. Produced by means of matter like all the arts, music, nevertheless, remains the most indefinable and mysterious to mankind, withal the most mathematical. Its mathematics provide a subtle analogy to the measurements of Ezechiel's Temple, so prodigal and surprising are the dimensions.

Scripture leads us to believe that good music exerts power over the devil. At the time of King Saul's mental collapse, when "the spirit of the Lord departed from Saul, and an evil spirit from the Lord troubled him" (*I Sam. 16:14*), music was sought as a remedy. Saul's servants ask permission to "seek out a man skillful in playing on the harp, that when the evil spirit from the Lord is upon thee, he may play with his hand, and thou mayest bear it more easily" (*16:16*). Singled out for his musicianship, the young David is brought, and "whensoever the evil spirit from the Lord was upon Saul, David took his harp, and played with his hand, and Saul was refreshed, and was better, for the evil spirit departed from him" (*16:23*).

Cataloguing all the uses of music in Scripture proves that then, as now, it graced banquets, weddings, funerals, military triumphs and children's games. Shepherds played it. Angels sang it. Even harlots played the harp and sang like the sirens to lure customers; whereas good women often followed the example of Miriam, who "took a tambourine in her hand, while all the women went out after her with tambourines, dancing" in their praise of God (*Exod. 15:20*).

Searching into the ever higher purposes of music, we find it sometimes the handmaid of prophecy. When the kings of Israel, Juda, and Edam ask Eliseus' counsel concerning their quarrel with Moab, the prophet has no offhand advice for them.

"But now bring me a minstrel!" he commands.

"And when the minstrel played," runs the story, "the hand of the Lord came upon him," whereupon Eliseus is soon able to acquaint his inquirers with the forthcoming rout of their enemy.

Eliseus' predecessor, Samuel, apparently kept a whole troop of such players about him, for after anointing Saul king, he orders the new monarch to go "to the hill of God. ... And when thou shalt be come down from the high place, with a psaltery and a timbrel, and a pipe, and a harp before them, and they shall be prophesying. And the spirit of the Lord shall come upon thee, and thou shalt prophesy with them, and shalt be changed into another man" (*I Sam. 10:5-6*). (Goodness, no wonder that young lady could tell at a glance I didn't have a Ph.D.! Music and prophecy go together, it seems.)

In this connection, I see a note to our family Bible reads:

In a number of passages in the Old Testament there is reference to groups of prophets. This aspect of Old Testament prophecy is to be distinguished from the office of the individual prophets. The individual prophets were especially chosen by God, and they spoke in the name of God, transmitting His revelations and instructions to the people. The functions of the groups of prophets was to foster a more fervent religious spirit among the people, and to live a life in accordance with that ideal. They chanted the praises of God to the accompaniment of musical instruments; and sometimes their fervor reached the stage of religious exaltation.

Now perhaps we might ask how this kind of music-making finds its way into the spiritual housewife's household hints. As a matter of fact, when the Israelites saw what happened to Saul, they asked pretty much the same question.

When he,

> ...came to the foresaid hill ... behold a company of prophets met him: and the spirit of the Lord came upon him and he prophesied in the midst of them. And all that had known him yesterday and the day before, seeing that he was with the prophets, and prophesied, said to each other: What is this that hath happened to the son of Cis? Is Saul also among the prophets?" (*I Sam. 10:10-11*).

The experience was repeated on a later occasion. Hunting down David, who had fallen from favor and had sought refuge among Samuel's prophets, Saul sends messengers to ferret out the fugitive. It's no use, however, for when the messengers "saw a company of the prophets prophesying ... the spirit of the Lord came also upon them, and they likewise began to prophesy" (*I Sam. 19:21*).

After three such tries, Saul goes for David himself, only to succumb in his turn to the musical hypnosis of the singing and playing prophets. Forgetting all about David and the purpose of his visit, the king—emotionally unstable at best—stripped himself of his garments, and prophesied with the rest before Samuel, and lay down naked all that day and night."

And Scripture closes again with, "This gave occasion to a proverb: What! Is Saul too among the prophets?" (*I Sam. 19:24*).

This, the Jews thought, was pretty funny.

And I'm afraid any spiritual housewife who begins to take music into her prayer, or prayer into her music, is going to get this proverbial reaction from people who don't happen to know what's been going on in the real world of music since Jubal strummed the first harp and tootled the first flute.

What! Is the housewife too among the prophets?

Well, if she sings the Word of God among the People of God, how can she help but be? Certainly the point of the foregoing story is plain: Prophecy is highly contagious.

"But now bring me a minstrel!"

Certainly David the Psalmist never got over his association with Samuel and his singing prophets. No mean musician in his own right, as king he instituted our first liturgical music as we know it, integrating it into the divine ritual at the Tabernacle before the Temple was built.

"He set singers before the altar," says Jesus ben Sirach in his memorial, "and by their voices he made sweet melody" (*Ecclus.47:11*).

Coming into Sion:

> All Israel brought the ark of the covenant of the Lord with joyful shouting, and sounding with the sound of the cornet, and with trumpets, and with cymbals, and psalteries, and harps. And when the ark of the covenant of the Lord was come to the city of David, Michel, the daughter of Saul, looking out at a window, saw king David dancing and playing, and she despised him in her heart (*I Par. 15: 28-29*).

Michol was a queen-housewife who just didn't understand music. She thought her husband was making an awful fool of himself. I'm afraid that's because she didn't understand prayer, either; for if we are to believe Scripture, there's a close and mysterious connection between the soul's music and its relations with God.

Music is pre-eminently an external manifestation of God's order and harmony, which produce God's peace. This is, again, a trinitarian reflection. The angelic multitudes, praising God at His birth on earth by announcing "Peace among men of good will," are usually represented as singing the Good News, for anything but ordered utterance at a time like this would be supremely incongruous. Disordered sound is only noise, whether from angels or the best Stradivarius.

Though revealing eternal verities, music is the most "temporal" of the arts. Produced in and through time itself, it most nakedly depends on it for existence. It puts into human ears a sharp echo of the first creation, when "in the beginning (of time) God created the heavens and the earth," leading us straight into the Blessed Trinity.

"I am ... the beginning," says the Christ (*Apoc. 22:13*). "In the beginning was the Word," witnesses St. John (*1:1*).

The heavens and earth created in the beginning will give place to the new only when time ceases. Then, John Dryden says, "Music shall untune the sky," for there is no disorder in the decrees of God.

"The earth was waste and void," says Scripture. "Darkness covered the abyss, and the spirit of God was stirring above the waters."

In sacred song, the "breath" which sings is this same Holy Spirit. Setting in motion the ordered vibrations of the human voice by which melody is created, He extends in time the primordial harmony. This is an unseen supernatural operation whose effects can nevertheless be heard and felt, for such music is a sacramental of the Church. Ordained to accomplish what it signifies according to the measure of faith, it orders and harmonizes the interior activity of the soul as potently as ever did the singing of Samuel's prophets. No wonder David's playing drove away Saul's evil spirit! No devil can stand God's order and harmony, even in sound.

On the other hand, if Glotz can bully a wary housewife into buying unwanted Crunches by purely natural psychological impact, what can't the liturgy of the Church drive her to! Whoever exposes himself fully to *Spiritus Domini replevit orbem terrarum* at Pentecost or *Dominus dixit ad me* at Christmas may well end up like Saul, spiritually "stripped of his garments and prophesying with the rest." Well sung, a Gregorian antiphon has all the psychological impact of the most coercive singing commercial, endowed with supernatural force. Obviously, singing prayer is one of those household hints that work, whether you understand the underlying principle or not.

Scripture tells us King Hiram of Tyre brought David's son "great plenty of thyine trees" (*III Kings 10:11*). These high-grade cypresses Solomon turned "into stairs in the house of the Lord, and in the king's house, and harps and psalteries for the singing men" (*II Par. 9:11*). If the pagan Hiram's navy brought the material for stairs and musical instruments in the Temple of the Lord and of the king's house, this must mean that material, sensual nature contributes something very valuable to the interior life. "Never were there seen such thyine trees in the land of Juda!" exclaims the chronicler.

Somehow stairs and musical instruments seem rather divergent, but are they? On stairs we ascend and descend, just as we do on musical scales, and "scale," I'm afraid, means "stair." At least Walter Hilton thought so, who wrote the *Scala Perfectionis*, a treatise on progress in perfection. With this clue in hand, it would seem the spiritual ascents of the Temple, as well as those in the human soul, are of the same stuff as its spiritual music. Both must be orderly progressions, ascents and descents as on Jacob's Stair whereon the angels moved up and down. If this is true, then music is indeed a powerful sacramental figure of the progress of the soul to God. It's clear that not just any music will do.

When Solomon dedicated the first Temple on Mt. Sion, and the Ark was brought into it from its former Tabernacle, "both the levites and the singing men ... clothed with fine linen, sounded with cymbals, and psalteries, and harps, standing on the east side of the altar, and with them a hundred and twenty priests, sounding with trumpets" (*II Par. 5:12*).

And something marvelous happened at the sound of the music, for,

> ...when they all sounded together, both with trumpets, and voice, and cymbals, and organs, and with divers kinds of musical instruments, and lifted up their voice on high: the sound was heard afar off, so that when they began to praise the Lord, and to say: Give glory to the Lord for he is good, for his mercy endureth forever: the house of God was filled with a cloud. Nor could the priests stand and minister by reason of the cloud. For the glory of the Lord had filled the house of God (*II Par. 5:13-14*).

Centuries later, when the Temple was being re-built after the Babylonian captivity, the Israelites couldn't wait for the work to be finished and dedicated. Like the angels at the Nativity, "when the masons laid the foundations of the temple of the Lord, the priests stood in their ornaments with trumpets: and the Levites the sons of Asaph with cymbals, to praise God by the hands of David king of Israel. And they sung together hymns ..."(*1 Esd. 3:10-11*).

We can hardly do less. Speaking to us human temples, St. Paul says, "Be filled with the Spirit, speaking to one another in psalms and hymns and spiritual songs, singing and making melody in your hearts to the Lord!" (*Eph. 5:18-19*), for what took place publicly in Solomon's Temple was merely a foretaste of what is destined to take place secretly in our own souls. It takes place daily in the Church at the singing of the liturgy and will do so eternally at the end of musical time.

Of the sublime interior melodies sung to God in this life in the depths of Christian hearts we know next to nothing. However, "in the days of David and Asaph from the beginning there were chief singers appointed, to praise with canticles and give thanks to God" (*Neh. 12:45*); and we may believe that in modern times, too, there are "chief singers" among us who can tell us a little something about the interior music inaudible to the natural ear.

We might, for instance, apply to Richard Rolle of Hampole, who in the last chapter enlightened us on the significance of sitting. By a special grace from God, Rolle seems to have been able to hear the heavenly harmonies within him. Writing much on the mystical life, he divided it into three stages roughly analogous to the classical purgative, illuminative, and unitive ways, but he characterized them as *calor*, *dulcor* and *canor*—heat, sweetness and *song*, this last typifying the highest possible perfection on earth.

Rolle's "song" is supra-material, a seraphic music founded wholly in charity, which takes place in the kingdom of heaven within and is a special extraordinary reward of the contemplative life. By it all the soul's activity is reduced to heavenly order and harmony, banishing every worldly care and grief. In the company of angels, the soul spends itself in "melodious meditation." After hearing this angel-song, Rolle tells us he could no longer bear to listen to the music of earth, not even that of the liturgy. (I shudder to think how Fools for Christ might have affected him!)

He says:

> Active souls rejoice in the exterior sounds of music, we pass over on the earthly tones of the organ to the sweet fire of contemplation of the Creator. They do not grasp our joys; we fail to fathom theirs, because we seek to be removed from all musical chantings, while we sing within ourselves the divine delights with resounding voices of joy. And now in general we have stopped singing and withdraw from that richness of invisible melodies so that while we have not fled in body from those noisy activities, we truly might learn that no one has ever been able to delight in the love of God unless he has left behind straightway the vain consolations of this world. Hence is evident the highest level of love of God: after such very great ardor and sweetness have been divinely bestowed, the most holy lover joins them to his song, and now he feels himself as it were, wrapped in a cloud, surrounded on all sides by an ineffable harmony and melodious song of praise with the tingling touch of a seven stringed harp. And this is indeed more suited to solitude and not to a group, for one dare not refuse with safety his mind thus (*Incedium amoris.*)

Indeed this mellifluous song seems at times to have taken him over bodily, for Rolle's Latin style is extraordinarily musical in itself. The alliterative sonority becomes so liquid in spots, the reader often risks letting the sense go to take his pleasure with the sound alone. Defying translation, passages like the following abound in his work:

... modicum masticantes molliciem mundialis rnagnificentie, in muneribus male multiplicatis moriuntur (Melos, X).

Or again, ... *pacienter ad patriam properent perhennem, utpote qui pergunt per pacem placentem, portas penetrantes perfectionis parate, et pascuntur in pratis puritate plenis (Melos, XIII).*

In speaking of Hell, he uses sibilants with telling hisses: *Stulti ac stolidi stabunt in stagnum et sulfur sentient sufflans singultum (XVI),* or, *"Siquidem quia in sceleribus sudabant et sanguinem siciebant, curn severitate a celigenis separati non salvabuntur, sed subito soluti in cinerern sustinebunt singulturn sine subsidio in sulfure sempiterno"(XX).*

Well, this isn't meant to be a term paper on medieval Latin, but was language ever so limber? Horace and Cicero may wince, but Swinburne and the prayerful can only acknowledge a master. The hidden harmonies Rolle heard are plain only to Him who is—not a searcher of majesty—but the searcher of hearts. All we know is that those whose pitch and rhythm ate in perfect accord with His are saints or holy angels. Down here we can occasionally hear ourselves "speaking to one another in psalms and hymns and spiritual songs," and faint echoes of the music of the spheres can be detected now and then by any housewife, but mostly we deal with music in parable, in the night of faith.

The musical parable which goes by the name of Gregorian chant is, I understand, the child of ancient Hebrew psalmody wedded to the classical modes of Greece. As such it speaks naturally for both heart and intellect. Regardless of all the technical niceties involved, however, technical skill and voice quality are not the most important elements in singing Gregorian. *Sacred song is not primarily a musical exercise, but a spiritual exercise.* The most real difficulties of execution stem, I do believe, from failure to grasp this fundamental fact.

Gregorian's techniques depend on spirit, and not the other way round, for what is born of flesh is flesh, in music as in every other human endeavor. Ascending and descending the stairs of the interior temple, its words, pitch, and rhythm are to liturgical prayer what the body is to the soul, and the balance between chant and prayer is no less delicate and exasperating to maintain. This means Gregorian is unalterably rooted in the Cross, and only fools for Christ can be crazy enough to sing it as it should be sung. This accounts for the fact that many excellent professional singers with highly developed diaphragms and years of experience behind them literally can't sing it. Though they invariably get the notes right, they remain like the Pharisee tied to the letter of the Law, or like the Herodians enslaved to purely natural gusto. This also accounts for the fact that young children often sing it so well and spontaneously if given the chance.

In fact, Gregorian is the song of a little child. If it's difficult to sing, that's because it's so implacably simple. Its notes don't leap and jump long intervals, but flow one into another at close quarters, very much as a small child croons to himself in the crib, before he is able to carry the complicated and artificial thing we have come to call a tune. There are no tunes as such in Gregorian, but only beautiful untrammeled melodies made for the pure in heart. Like the good housewife content in her own house, they rarely exceed an octave, but they compass the universe. So no wonder the urge to sing Gregorian often grows with the life of prayer! Love, and sing as you will!

Plainsong is so plain. It gives our little human fakeries no quarter. There's no place to hide. For one thing, there's no part singing in chant. Made for singers who are One, its melodies are sung in uncompromising unison, a feat any experienced singer can tell you isn't easy. Individual variations and peculiarities which might pass unnoticed in the hurly-burly of part singing are immediately discernible in Gregorian, which is also quite detached from accompaniment, thank you. Not depending on tricky instrumental interludes to make its point, Gregorian is at its best full-throated and *a cappella*, for it was created for God's own instrument: the human voice.

The only other instrument officially allowed in celebrating the liturgy is the organ. Closely imitating human song, it also "breathes" its music, and indeed can reflect God by parodying a whole multitude of human voices at once. So far lacking sufficient singers, only by the roar of an organ can we reproduce something of the mighty torrent St. John heard before the throne of God. We must remember that to "organize" means above all to make music, and when the Richard Rolles organize, they sing. Legend has it that when St. Cecelia sang and played the organ, an angel came down from heaven to listen, and I shouldn't wonder he was curious.

Whatever the volume, however, Gregorian breathes best in an atmosphere of austere poverty. It lives on a very modest scale, whose notes are neither sharps nor flats[2] and whose length is of even duration. There's no restlessness in them, no jerky syncopation, no running about from key to key and back again. There is, alas, no beat, but only rhythm. Its antiphons lap back and forth like waves on the seashore and, like these, appear in all assorted sizes.

Worldly souls given to a steady diet of popular records may as well try to cram the sea into march time as Gregorian. What comes out can never be the music of the Church, but only the music of a worldly soul

---

[2] Except b flat, to avoid diminished fifths and augmented fourths.

trying to bring the Church down to his level. "For not by measure does God give the Spirit!" *(John 3:34)*. Anyone who can't for a time forget the music of the world will never get the hang of this primordial and apocalyptic chant which prefigures the fulfillment of St. John's vision on Patmos, "a voice of a great crowd, and as the voice of many waters, and as the voice of mighty thunders, saying ... 'Let us be glad and rejoice, and give glory to Him!'" *(Apoc. 19:6-7)*.

And that brings us to the second distinguishing characteristic of Gregorian. It's not just the song of a small child; it's the song of the crowd, the many, the "thousands of thousands" (Apoc. 5:11) of small children who make up the kingdom of heaven. That proves conclusively it can't be the exclusive property of specialists and specially trained soloists.

St. James said, "Anyone."

Except for those occasionally specified by the rubrics, solos are strictly forbidden in the Church of God. Although each of us must sing his own indispensable Song of Myself in the gigantic production, it is borne upwards on the surging song of his fellows into the full richness of the *Opus Dei*. In the Song of Songs, all humanity sings the part of the Bride. This eliminates any possibility of audience-performer relationships on our part, "in order to be honored by men" *(Matt. 6:2)*.

Solo-singing is dangerous for the spiritual life, laying performers open to vanity and despair, and audiences to sensual passivity, if not outright misery. Scripture tells us angels sing, but would you believe it, I can't find one angelic solo recorded? Apparently the heavenly choirs are all group singers, and on earth we do well to imitate them.

"A concert of music in a banquet of wine is as a carbuncle set in gold," says the wise Sirach, prophesying music at Holy Mass. "Hinder not music!" *(Ecclus. 32:7,5)* he pleads.

A female relative who has dedicated her life to seeing that young children be not hindered from singing sacred music as only they can do it, once informed me that it was my misfortune to have studied coloratura singing even briefly in my youth. Though opera lost nothing when I desisted, I see her point ever more clearly. *Je suis Titania reine des fées* is indeed not the best preparation for the hushed expectancy of *Et valde mane* in later life. Both speak of dawn, but there the similarity ends. Titania may make an excellent fairy queen, but she's no soul of prayer. She's a terrible showoff, and this sort of thing, being rooted in pride, is death to the praise of God.

You can trust me here, because I learned it the hard way.

I'm still trying to shed Titania. The exasperating thing about her is that you can't just turn your back on her during services, by having nothing more to do with her trills and frills. You have to get her out of your system, like the old Eve she is, through the death of self, and that goes on every waking hour both in and out of church. What I'm trying to say is that, even before starting to sing Gregorian, Titania has to learn a little humility.

You know this isn't easy. First of all she has to be taught that for the moment, what she is singing may be more important than she is. Then she has to learn that how she sounds isn't the most important part of her singing. Worst of all, poor Titania has to sublimate that urge to solo, that Song of Myself heard above others. When this happens, she may begin to suspect that, unlike opera, the libretto is here more important than the music, that the music exists for the Word of God, and not vice-versa. Naturally, this will entail finding out what the words mean! Titania may have to do outside reading in Scripture, poor girl.

If she does, Titania has made a beginning on singing Gregorian, speaking to a just God in song, and not vocalizing before an admiring congregation. The music is meant to clarify the text, the words themselves setting the metre. Often called "heightened speech," it lingers here and there, points out this and that, and underscores what is most significant. This kind of singing is learned more from prayer and meditation on what one sings than from notation. Though this last must never be disparaged, we must remember the human voice is the only musical instrument endowed with speech. Both naturally and supernaturally, it sings the Word. This is a trinitarian function, not to be gotten around just anyhow.

To appreciate the spiritual qualities of chant, one has only to lay the beautiful Ambrosian *Gloria* from Mass XVIII alongside, say, the popular *Gloria* by Antonio Vivaldi. The latter, written when baroque music was at its headiest height, is gorgeous by purely musical standards. Its brilliant resolutions, sharp contrasts, and apparently inexhaustible melody may well leave its hearers stunned. In fact this kind of music is stunning. Titania would find it made to order.

The words of the sacred text are made the sport of the human voice. In the last movement, by the time the singers have bandied about the *Cum Sancto Spiritu* some thirty times in four parts, for about seventy measures of a closely packed allegro fugue, they might just as well be singing "Glotz's Crunches" for all the sense and reverence left. This sort of thing drove St. Pius X to bless us with his *motu proprio* on sacred music, for which we should all be grateful.

Needless to say, baroque music dotes on long, complicated instrumental interludes between bursts of song, perhaps to allow singers to get their wind, or to allow the musicians to show off too, or perhaps simply to delight the congregation. Whatever the rationale, giving oneself up to such flamboyant gymnastics may border on sacrilege for sensitive souls who don't normally bandy about the all-holy Name, or come to church for sensual enjoyment.

It needn't surprise us overmuch to learn that Vivaldi himself, known to his contemporaries as "the red priest," was defrocked a year after his ordination. Gossip had it that his offense was interrupting his Mass to dash into the sacristy and jot down some musical phrase that had just occurred to him! Whether or not this is true, it might well be, for Vivaldi's music itself betrays its composer's inverted spiritual values, where music is concerned. He is said to have become very pious in later life, however, so I trust that he will understand why I make such an example of him.

"In praying, do not multiply words, as the Gentiles do!" (*Matt. 6:7*).

But let's not fret. All of this is pretty academic, because the "many" will never in a hundred years master Vivaldi's *Gloria*. That kind of music isn't the song of the poor and hidden. Technically difficult, it is still very great art and, as such, honors God; but spiritually, it gives us very little. Its appeal will remain legitimately with the concert-goer, or with those whose response to religion is primarily emotional. Furthermore, it takes about an hour to sing.

The Ambrosian Gloria in contrast takes about three minutes to sing and is a revelation of revelation, in which the sense of awe of the composer in the face of what he presumes to say is such that he can hardly stir beyond three notes. Not until the phrase, "We give Thee thanks" does he venture to sing out lyrically in a serene burst of gratitude to take in more than two notes or more on a syllable, only to return immediately to his musical cloister. The word *Christe* he subsequently adorns with the same embellishment, but subtly enriched in its beginnings. Repetition of these modest devices at the "sins of the world" and at the last *Jesu Christe* is the limit accorded to nature in this sublime and starkly simple prayer of the creature before his God, trying to praise Him in spirit and in truth through the medium of song.

When the singer reaches the *Cum Sancto Spiritu*, this is no empty phrase, for he has simply come to rest in the Holy Spirit in Whom he sings. The words need be sung only once, without measure. And this isn't purely academic, for the Ambrosian *Gloria* is technically very simple. Moving and profound as it is, anybody can sing it, by the thousands of thousands, if they want to. Like the parables of Jesus, it is very, very great art, whose genius escapes analysis entirely. Only the greatest musicians can play universal themes on five notes for everybody.

Titania has to learn it's not natural enthusiasm that puts over the New Song of the elect, but the force of the Christ life within her. This spells the death of schmaltz, three-quarter time, and some fifty-seven varieties of musical sentimentality. Chant conveys rich emotion, but is never "emotional" like opera. It isn't meant to be listened to as music, but heard in the soul. It is an aid to prayer, a means of making contact with God, to be used as Eliseus and David and Solomon used music. We are never encouraged to make a sensual response to chant, but a spiritual offering.

Hymns in beer-and-pretzel or little-German-band tempo have no place in church. Good in themselves, they unhappily make us think of beer, pretzels, and parades instead of God. This is fine for souls at the summits of sanctity, for whom all things are pure; but for us Titanias I'm afraid they just spell beer, pretzels, and parades. By the same token, vibratos, arpeggios, glissandos and crashing cadenzas have to go the way of Titania's *troupe folle des lutins* who follow her flying chariot singing of earthly lusts and pleasures. As in the opera, these are doomed to disappear with the night, *au rayons de Phoebe qui luit*, meaning here the rays of the Sun of Justice Himself.

It doesn't follow that plainsong is the only sacred music worth singing. That's not true, as we know. I use it here only as a salient example of the very best we have. Outside canonical norms, who could overlook some of the American negro spirituals? When it comes to conveying religious awe, expectancy and humility, the school of St. Ambrose may well look to its laurels!

The apocalyptic, "My Lawd, what a mawnin! My Lawd, what a mawnin,/When the stars begin to fall!" is full of human yearning for God and heaven, so far and yet so near. And it's so simple. In *Rocka-My-Soul*, the singer who reports, "My soul went down in the valley to pray,/My soul got happy and stayed all day," might have been St. John of the Cross, so well does he understand what a day is and how great heights are scaled only by descending into the depths. The untutored spirituality found in *Steal Away* or *Nobody Knows the Trouble I See* proves the Holy Spirit is the "Father of the Poor," no matter where men suffer.

Lacking the Ambrosian, "Bring me a minstrel!" I say there's nothing academic about this, because singing can be a potent tool in spiritual formation, all the while it praises God. The congregational choir is nothing if not a mystical body in miniature. A fool for Christ doing his best as part of Christ's body, singing and "praying twice over," will immediately become painfully aware of his own inadequacies both as a singer and as a person.

Spiritual doctrine abounds in group singing, as it does in true group activity of any kind. Just trying to keep the pitch when the voice at one's elbow keeps tugging downwards is like the agony of resisting the persistent temptation of a bad companion. As in real life, it's often the one singer on key or in tempo who sounds bad, and it isn't the fellow who's loudest who's right. The mysteries of vicarious suffering and atonement are evident, too, for if one singer makes a mistake the whole product suffers. When Titania can contrive, furthermore, to cover the mistake of another, quietly taking it unto herself as her own, all the while maintaining the pitch for everybody, we know she's making solid progress, both musically and spiritually. She's a bigger fool for Christ than ever, I'd say.

Like King David, the divine Singer must have singers, for "by their voices, He makes sweet melody" (*Ecclus. 47:11*). Would we have Him who sang David's psalms on earth be dumb in us?

"Shut not the mouths of them that sing to thee!" prayed Esther's uncle Mardochai in a national emergency (*Est. 13:17*).

Richard Rolle again is worthy of quotation on this point:

> Indeed the lovers of the world can know the words or formulas of our preaching, but not, however, the songs of our chanting; because they read the words but cannot grasp the sweetness of the notes and harmony of these odes. O good Jesus bind my heart in the thought of thy name, for now I am not strong enough to sing of it. Thus have mercy on me by bringing to completion what you have begun. The truly passionate lover of Thee is swept up into a joyous state of melodious meditation that it is impossible for such sweetness to come from the evil spirit, such fervor to arise from any creature, such a hymn from human talent; and if I persevere in these, I shall be saved. (*Incendium Amaris.*)

Titania says, "Amen." She's a good girl at heart.

The Home Calculator

CHAPTER 4

"SHOW them the form of the house!" Ezechiel was commanded. "Let them measure the building."

No problem in arithmetic to compare with this one has ever been presented to plain humanity. When first brought by God into the vast spiritual temple, Ezechiel reports he saw:

> ...a man, whose appearance was like the appearance of brass, with a line of flax in his hand, and a measuring reed in his hand, and he stood in the gate. And this man said to me: "Son of man, see with thy eyes, and hear with thy ears, and set thy heart upon all that I shall show thee: for thou art brought hither that they may be shown to thee: declare all that thou seest to the house of Israel."

This heavenly surveyor appears elsewhere in Scripture. He returns "with the measuring line in his hand" in the prophecy of Zacharias, when the old Temple in Jerusalem is due to be rebuilt after the Babylonian captivity; and in the Apocalypse, where St. John describes the New Jerusalem, he emerges again, this time "with a measure, a golden reed, to measure the city and the gates thereof and the wall" (*Apoc. 21:15*) in a final display of his craft. Whoever he is, I don't think it would be wise to overlook him in any tour of God's dwellings.

Ezechiel continues:

> And behold there was a wall on the outside of the house round about, and in the man's hand a measuring reed of six cubits and a handbreadth: and he measured the breadth of the building one reed, and the height one reed. And he came to the gate that looked toward the east, and he went up the steps thereof: and he measured the breadth of the threshold of the gate one reed, that is, one threshold was one reed broad. And every little chamber was one reed long, and one reed broad: and between the little chambers were five cubits. And the threshold of the gate by the porch of the gate within, was one reed. And he measured the porch of the gate eight

cubits, and the front thereof two cubits: and the porch of the gate was inward.

And the little chambers of the gate that looked eastward were three on this side, and three on that side: all three were of one measure, and the fronts of one measure, on both parts. And he measured the breadth of the threshold of the gate ten cubits: and the length of the gate thirteen cubits. (*Ezech. 40:3ff.*)

Somehow we can't help feeling Ezechiel, while the measuring continued, may have been as mystified as we are who read this today. Being mystified, I'm sorry to say, isn't quite the same as being mystical, but one thing is certain: a mathematical aptitude is very little help here. If anything, it's a hindrance, for the first thing a mathematician will note in these verses is that the numbers don't add up right, and he might be tempted to doubt the validity of Scripture as a consequence. As we proceed in the text, it becomes painfully clear that the outside measurements of the building are hopelessly smaller than some of the smaller rooms on the inside, and all the measurements are by no means given. Proportions seem odd, too, in this spiritual looking-glass house, where windows may be the same size as doors, or even whole walls. Even allowing for the difficulties of translation, nothing quite adds up. After a few lines of this, only an extraordinarily literal-minded mathematician or one without any sense of humor would attempt to figure it out literally.

I'm happily unencumbered by much math aptitude. When *A* rows upstream at two miles an hour and *B* downstream at three-and-a-half miles an hour, they just meet whenever they meet, with little help or interference from me. When I entered grade school and was told that two plus two made four, I thought the teacher was pulling my leg. From where I sat, two plus two didn't make anything.

"You can't fool me," I informed her, though I was careful to couch it more respectfully. Obviously, any grade-schooler could see there were four there all along. "Two-plus-two" and "four" are exactly the same thing. "Unless two plus two make at least five, what's been made?" I said.

"Two plus two equal four," patiently explained the teacher. "That means two and two are the same as four."

Well, that's what I was complaining about. So why bother? I foolishly intimated as much.

Here, my teacher must have decided, was a girl-child with a serious mental block. We reached something of a stalemate, which I'm ashamed to say I resolved finally in a most cowardly way, by agreeing to be a good girl and play the arbitrary little game this teacher called "arithmetic," in which nothing ever happened, but in which the same amount of anything you started with was expressed in as many different ways as possible. Divided, multiplied, subtracted or whatever, you never could end up with anything more than you really had in the beginning, as far as I could see.

There was no end to the foolishness. When we started to multiply, I heard to my amazement that One multiplied by Zero equaled, not One, but *nothing at all.* That nothing multiplied once could equal nothing I readily conceded, but why One should suddenly "not be" because it was never multiplied, I simply couldn't fathom. I didn't say so, however. Since then I've had the satisfaction of learning that the most intrepid metaphysician hasn't yet uncovered sufficient proof that anything at all, once it exists, can be utterly annihilated (though of course it may suffer change). In grade school I would have been so happy to tell him that whole numbers, even big ones, could be made to disappear forever just by waving a Zero over them.

I was amazed at how arithmetic could box you in. Already resigned to having no place to go numerically, I now faced the prospect of seeing the whole science fall away from under me should some unscrupulous master-mind perversely multiply the whole thing by nothing. Nevertheless, I continued dutifully learning the rules of this silly game, and by never asking questions or letting my mind dwell unduly on its nagging absurdities, I managed to stay on the honor roll. (Speaking of absurdity, it's typical of mathematics that an irrational number is called a "surd," not an "absurd" which does seem more like it.) Anyway my ready adaptability seemed to please my teachers, whom I rather liked and couldn't bear to disappoint. Then, too, I hated to admit I was stupid. I concluded I had happily overcome my "block."

I hadn't. To this day I can't see what happens in arithmetic, and I was never even momentarily tempted to take any advanced course in the subject that wasn't absolutely required for graduation. Nobody, I figured, could be really happy just counting things for the rest of his life when, no matter how many ways he counted, he not only never made any more, but might lose the whole shebang.

Relating this childhood disillusionment some thirty years later to a luckless mathematician who drew me for a dinner partner, I was delighted to hear him say, "Oh, I know! It's terrible the way children are introduced to mathematics, being led to believe that numbers represent a reality they can never convey!" I was also cheered to learn from him that something is being done about it. It seems that educators are now going to give children in grade school some inkling of what's really what, and teach them right off about the principles of higher mathematics. This, he assured me, would fire their enthusiasm right at the start.

Nobody, alas, ever told me in grade school that there might be something to look forward to once I mastered the multiplication table. They never told me Two could have "powers" and be raised indefinitely, precisely *because* it was finite, to 2^2, 2^3, 2^4 and so on. Nor was I told about how algebra could use two-plus-two to ferret out some number you didn't even know, but which until you did, you called "X." They certainly didn't tell me about the calculus, where two-plus-two might not equal four at all once you got going. In calculus, I now understand, the value of two can change right along as it follows an object spiraling through mathematical space.

Now, I don't mean to say I would have gone on and taken calculus. I'm not seriously contending that the world kept a great creative mathematician on the wrong side of the slide rule when it discouraged me. One glance into the tangled bowels of my checkbook would soon dispel these illusions. I'm just saying that arithmetic would have been a deal more meaningful to me, and my teacher more respected, had I known that two-plus-two had possibilities.

It would have helped, too, if somebody had told me that really great mathematicians were far more likely to be found staring vacantly out the window or tripping absent-mindedly over curbstones than meticulously scribbling endless variations of two-plus-two in tight formation across a tidy notepad. If only some math teacher had admitted to me that Einstein wasn't especially good at arithmetic, but a whizz at sitting in an old sweatshirt with his shoes off, just *wondering*!

Don't think I'm sneering at two-plus-two, I wouldn't dare. Scripture would prove me a heretic in short order, teaching emphatically as it does that everything in creation rests upon apparently arbitrary building-blocks which are basic to the whole. Ezechiel's vision conveys this explicitly, for we are told that the man who measured the temple used for his purpose throughout "a measuring reed of six cubits and a handbreadth."

The Egyptian cubit used by the ancient world in Ezechiel's day was roughly eighteen inches long, I understand, being the distance from one's elbow to the tip of the third finger. The handbreadth or *palm* was about three inches. We know that the standard reed in general use was six cubits, but there was known to be also the "*royal* cubit," which measured an additional palm in length. This royal cubit, Scripture tells us, was the unit used in Ezechiel's reed, whose length consequently measured seven standard cubits in all, instead of the customary six.

Now, the number seven throughout sacred writings is a symbol of perfection. To the early Christians it meant specifically the union of the human with the divine, seen as the sum of four plus three, wherein the world equaled four and the Blessed Trinity equaled Three. Apply *that* to problems of room arrangement, and see what happens! If I, as an unbeliever, had only known!

On the face of it, you might be tempted to argue that nothing happens in this equation any more than anywhere else in arithmetic, but you'd be dead wrong. I couldn't begin to interpret all the mysterious number symbolism in the interior temple, where there are so many X's, but at least I know it's symbolism, true symbolism, and that this is one time I'm faced with numbers which represent *actual reality*. If only I knew the reality!

When we consider that God reveals Himself in the minds of theologians as *One* substance, *Two* processions, *Three* Persons, *Four* real relations, *Five* notions, and so on to the infinity of numbers *ad extra*, we may suspect that numbering isn't always just counting. Reading the Book of Numbers alone with this in mind should lead us to a number of conclusions. In the passage from Ezechiel just quoted, where "the little chambers of the gate that looked eastward were three on this side, and three on that side," we readily detect God's presence. Until better offers, I personally like to think these words refer to the Triune Indwelling in Mary, the "east gate" of the Mystical Temple, which Christ entered when He "went up the steps thereof." The Three Persons find perfect rest in both her soul and her body, "on this side ... and on that side," in heaven and on earth. Mary, the House of Gold, is also the Gate of Heaven, and through her we enter the Temple of the mystical body of Christ and all that lies within. With her help, perhaps we can understand something of what Ezechiel is trying to tell us.

He tells us squarely enough that the man's measures were taken by "the truest cubit, which is a cubit and a handbreadth." There is, therefore, something special about this mysterious royal cubit by which alone the measurements of God's spiritual home can be truly taken. Simple enough in itself, its findings make little or no sense until we understand that with the seven-cubit reed in hand, we have left simple arithmetic behind. We are now engaged in a higher calculus, an elevated algebra where two-plus-two might make anything, having been raised to infinity. As natural calculus is designed to deal with variables in relation to fixed quantities, so is Ezechiel's royal cubit meant to deal with us in relation to the Immutable Godhead.

Only saints really grasp this spiritual mathematics, and by God's mercy, some of them have had the goodness to try to explain its essentials to us. Just as in grade school I had two-plus-two in common with Einstein, so, too, in the mystical life I have the same *reed* in common with the saints. In the mystical life, the basic measure for taking the dimensions of God's House is *prayer*. It's not just the ordinary prayer of the creature towards his Creator; it possesses an extra three inches. It's a supernatural prayer, wherein the Blessed Trinity, Itself, takes part in the soul. With this divine reed in hand, Ezechiel's "man" is measuring the entire Temple, not excepting the inmost Holy of Holies. Simple arithmetic never had such possibilities!

There is a spiritual calculus, generally called contemplation, by which, believe it or not, any number of numbers can become *one*; but most of us are no more conscious of its existence than grade school children are of higher mathematics. If we hear at all of it, we're mostly warned against it, despite the fact that it's the normal end of the life of grace begun in baptism and is the prayer we all shall enjoy in heaven.

Browsing, not long ago, through a library copy of Father Garrigou-Lagrange's solid work on *Christian Perfection and Contemplation*, I noted, without too much surprise, that some forty-five pages had been systematically cut out. A glance through the Table of Contents revealed that the missing sections dealt with "The Degrees of the Mystical Life from the Fourth to the Seventh Mansions—The Essential Character of Contemplation, How It Proceeds from the Gift of Wisdom and the Gift of Faith—Growing Elevation of the Special Inspiration of the Holy Ghost in Beginners, Proficients, and the Perfect." And finally, "The Gifts of the Holy Ghost, Relation to Infused Contemplation and the Mystical Life." (There are individuals, I'm afraid, who might try to put the Holy Ghost on the Index.)

Apparently whoever tore these pages out was afraid some housewife like myself might get hold of them, not get the drift of the higher calculus, and go straight to hell in a mist of self-delusion. This in spite of the fact that Fr. Lagrange's work bears a highly respectable *Imprimatur*. It also takes up specifically the question of whether contemplative doctrine is for everybody and of a nature in itself to lead some souls to presumption and others to discouragement. Fr. Lagrange concludes that the generality of Christians need not be kept in ignorance of higher prayer just because there are fools among them. Were we to follow seriously that line of reasoning, we should have to outlaw knives because some people will inevitably cut arteries, and return to Prohibition because others insist on getting drunk.

This attitude towards higher prayer has often been a source of puzzlement to saints, and I believe St. Teresa may be speaking for all of them in the following. Expecting only the best from her readers, she says:

> It will be a great advantage, when the Lord shall grant you such favors, to know that they are possible, and those to whom He does not grant them, may praise Him for His great loving-kindness. And just as it does us no harm to think on heavenly things, which the blessed enjoy, but on the contrary, we rejoice, and endeavor to attain to their happiness, so neither will it injure us to see that it is possible for a God so great to communicate, even in this exile, with evil-smelling worms, and to love a bounty so kind, and a mercy that is measureless.
>
> I am certain that whoever is scandalized to hear that it is possible for God to grant this favor here below, will be found greatly wanting in humility and neighborly love (!). For indeed, how can we fail to rejoice that God grants favors to our brotherman, since it does not hinder Him from doing the same for us, and that His Majesty manifests His greatness, be it in whom it may?"
>
> It is not because those are more holy to whom He grants certain favors than are those to whom He refuses them, but that His greatness may be recognized, as we see in St. Paul and the Magdalene, and that we may praise Him in His creatures. It may be said that such things seem to be impossible, and it is well not to scandalize the weak, but it is a lesser evil that they should not believe in them, than that those to whom God grants them should fail to profit by them ... but those who do not believe this are not likely to experience them, because *He is very pleased when we place no limits upon His works*. Therefore, sisters, let not those whom the Lord does not lead in this way, ever discredit it!

The author of the Cloud says much the same thing. He laments:

> If you ask me how you are to begin, I must pray Almighty God, of His grace and courtesy, to tell you Himself. Indeed, it is good for you to realize I cannot teach you. It is not to be wondered at. For this is the work of God alone, deliberately wrought in whatever soul He chooses, irrespective of the merits of that particular soul.
>
> For without God's help, neither saint nor angel can even think of wanting it. And I fancy that Our Lord is willing to do this work as readily and as frequently—indeed, perhaps even more so—in those that have been lifelong sinners, as in those who have, comparatively, never grieved Him very much. And He will do this, that we may recognize Him to be all-merciful and almighty, and that He does what He likes, and when He likes. Yet He does not give this grace nor begin this work in a soul that is unwilling to receive it...

Don't think I would presume to explain to you what contemplation is, even if I knew, when all its beneficiaries agree its outstanding characteristic is that it can't be described. It can be experienced, though in itself it can't be felt, and it makes use of no words, no meditations, no formal pious practices. In referring to it, the mystics are reduced to such paradoxical designation as a "ray of darkness," "a cloud of unknowing," or simply, "the way of *nada*"—nothing.

Nescivi. "I knew not," admits the Bride of the Canticle, who certainly knows more than all the doctors of mystical theology put together. It follows that a contemplative who can give a detailed analysis of his prayer thereby proves he is no contemplative.

"Desist! And confess that I am God," counsels the Holy Spirit through the Psalmist (*Psalm 45:11*).

St. Thomas was content to define contemplation as a "simple gaze on truth," and modern theology does little better, dubbing it "an infused loving knowledge of God." The tomes written about it by mystical theologians deal perforce only with human activity in relation to it, the self-denial required not to obstruct its development, or the ordinary and extraordinary effects it may produce in us.

There are many excellent masters of the subject, among them the classic St. John of the Cross, giant of the mystical theologians. In American idiom, the plain-spoken work by the Capuchin Father Gabriel Diefenbach, *Common Mystic Prayer*, is a gem and a heart-warming introduction to the whole glorious subject. To such teachers I humbly refer you. Like the feller in the cowboy movie perpetually standing at the crossroads, I can only tell you, "They went thataway!" I was thirty-two years old myself before I found out that much, but someday I hope to join the chase.

A soul who habitually prays "thataway" bears the same relation to a soul using discursive prayer that Einstein bears to the grade school computer. The numbers are the same, but the answers are different. Little children who progress that far aren't likely to pass much time scribbling figures, adding up their indulgences and good works on a note pad. Like great mathematicians, they're more likely to take off their shoes as Moses did on the holy ground before the burning bush, content to "hide their faces" before *Him Who Is* (*Exod. 3:5-6*).

"Contemplative prayer is *simple*!" exclaim all the mystics. Simple as energy. Nobody agrees on what it is.

"$E=mc^2$" says Einstein, telling us simply what he thinks energy is.

As we've already noted, simple isn't easy, in prayer, in singing, or in higher mathematics. Einstein didn't arrive at his simple equation easily, and it isn't easily comprehended, either. No mystic ever said he found his prayer easy, especially at first. Why should he? He's at grips with the Divine Simplicity, which contains Einstein's equation, Einstein, energy, two-plus-two, and everything else; and whoever finds that easy, is no contemplative!

To a literary man having difficulty with praying simply, the Benedictine master, Dom Chapman, wrote, "It is as easy as jumping into a fire, which you had not seen, and has the same effect. It burns your clothes first, then your flesh, and then your bones. It is a fearful thing to fall into the hands of the Living God."

But what could be simpler?

Another thing all the mystics agree on is that contemplation is a free gift from God, as St. Teresa and the *Cloud's* author just said. Trying to acquire it by force, or imagining you have it when you don't, gets you exactly what you deserve. I believe no story in Scripture illustrates this better than the famous tale of Susanna and the elders which occurs at the end of the Book of Daniel, in a two chapter section declared apocryphal by both Protestants and present-day Jews.

Susanna, a figure of contemplation described as "exceedingly delicate and beautiful to behold," is the virtuous wife of a rich Hebrew called Joakim, whose home is the social hub of the community. Scripture says Susanna was in the habit of "walking in her husband's orchard ... when the people departed away at noon," for contemplation walks with God in silence and solitude as man walked with God in the garden of Eden. Overcome by the dazzling heat, the senses (the people) have no part in the intimate seclusion of Joakim's orchard (which might easily have been a grapefruit grove).

Anyway, one day, sending out her maids (probably the imagination and affections), Susanna proceeds to "wash herself" according to her custom, for contemplation purifies as it enlightens. She is spied upon by two wicked and utterly respectable old men who had been "appointed judges that year." Each, unknown to the other, becoming "inflamed with lust towards her," they agree to join forces to make her yield to them. She refuses in spite of all threats, whereupon they take their revenge by publicly charging her with having committed adultery with some fictitious young man. Acting in their official capacity, they intend to destroy Susanna by having her condemned to death by due process of law.

This happens all the time. Anyone who catches sight of beautiful and delicate contemplation falls in love with her; but carnal souls who know only elementary spiritual arithmetic try to force her to their level, wishing to possess her on their terms. Not knowing the required calculus, they try to measure her by the ordinary reed, not the royal cubit. Of course she refuses herself to them, because she is chaste; and in their spite they try to destroy her, falsely representing her as evil.

"It's a waste of time!" they say. "You'll go nuts!"

In St. Teresa's day, contemplatives were sometimes told their prayer was the work of the devil, who was leading them to hell. Today they are told it's probably the result of a disturbed psyche and will lead only to the psychiatrist's couch.

Was it one of those old men who tore the pages out of Fr. Lagrange's book? I don't know. I do know, however, that a priest to whom I turned with the evidence in hand said, "Now you be careful reading that!"

Again, "Who hears you, hears Me!" We must be very careful indeed, for contemplation has her own special heretics: the quietists. They are the dove-sellers in the interior Temple. Practically their every error can be laid to seeking to apply the rules of human logic to the workings of divine wisdom. Quietists—from Molinos, Roja, and Mme. Guyon on down to our own parishes—would reduce contemplation to a system, supplanting God's action by negative human effort, as if all one had to do to become a contemplative was to keep as inactive as possible, both interiorly and exteriorly. God, quietism assures us, will then rush automatically into the vacuum, whereas actual results are inertia, contempt of active works, and ultimately, loss of the sense of sin.

The healthiest and cheapest antidote I've ever heard for this disease is Dom Chapman's famous, "Pray as you can, and don't pray as you can't!" Prayer, after all, is for everybody.

The prophet Daniel, who quickly suspected what Susanna was up against, arose to defend her as our Lord defended Mary against her sister Martha. He cleared her reputation by a very simple stratagem, asking each elder separately what kind of tree Susanna and her alleged paramour had been sitting under when they were apprehended.

"A mastic tree!" says the one.

"A holm tree!" says the other.

To appreciate the depth of the teaching here, we must allow that these respectable judges can also represent the higher powers of the soul, perhaps the reason and the memory, who also try to spy on contemplation, seeking to draw her down to their limited ken during prayer. When queried, each gives its own interpretation of what goes on, and speaking falsely, they can't even agree in their falsehood.

The same thing happened at the trial of Divine Wisdom Himself when "the chief priests and all the Sanhedrin were seeking witnesses against Jesus, that they might put Him to death, but they found none.

For while many bore false witness, their evidence did not agree" (*Mark 14:55-56*).

Only the Daniels, who are of the truth themselves, can recognize the innocence of the Son of God or of Susanna at sight. So too, the mystics teach us, when this same Divine Wisdom is at work in the higher forms of contemplative prayer, the whole personnel of the interior temple becomes incapable of any helpful activity. This was figured at the dedication of Solomon's Temple, for, as we saw, "When they began to praise the Lord ... the house of God was filled with a cloud. Nor could the priests stand and minister by reason of the cloud. For the glory of the Lord had filled the house of God" (*II Par. 5:13-14*).

"My house is a house of prayer!"

Though I readily admit this is beyond me, I'm prepared to believe every word of it. It's something to try to become worthy of, and to look forward to someday either here or in heaven. Anyway, as Dom Chapman also says, "The less you pray, the worse it goes!"

As for the dangers to be run in reading about such heavenly wonders in the souls of others, well, no one will deny there are terrible risks in being baptised at all and presuming to lead a supernatural life within the Blessed Trinity. It's a shame never to try calculus for fear of flunking out.

"I was often thinking," says St. Teresa, "how St. Peter lost nothing by throwing himself into the sea, though he was afterwards afraid." And she cautions, "Satan, I believe, does great harm, for he hinders those who begin to pray from going onwards, by suggesting to them false notions of humility. He makes them think it is pride to have large desires, to wish to imitate the saints, and to long for martyrdom" (*Vida, Ch. XIII, 4,5*).

Let us pray for this grace. Like St. Peter desiring to walk on the water, let's ask the Lord, "Bid me come to thee over the water," and hope that in our case, too, He will answer, "Come I" as He did to Peter.

Inevitably, the deepening lay spirituality of our century has been accompanied by a rediscovery of contemplative prayer. Indeed, how can there be deep lay spirituality without it? Simple prayer is the only hope of the saint in the street for whom the fixed orisons of monastic tradition are artificial at best, and often impossible. The only time the layman can count on praying is all the time.

As Father Merton has so astutely pointed out, perfect vocal prayer is rather the special gift of the desert solitary, not of those whose hands and lips must be busy with the work of the world. Curiously enough, it seems our Lord didn't teach formal prayer at all, until He was constrained to do so by His disciples, and then after His public ministry was well under way. On reading the Gospels, we sense He gave them the Lord's Prayer almost reluctantly, as if He felt they weren't quite ready for it. Truly, how many of us are possessed of the necessary spirit for informing the words as we repeat them? It's easier, certainly, to be content merely with the words, which can make the prayer vocal, but can't make the vocal prayer.

Simple informal prayer, on the other hand, was the salvation of the early Christians trapped in pagan surroundings, whenever they could find no time or place to themselves. Still the layman's secret weapon, this "prayer without ceasing" can alone be counted on to bring the Blessed Trinity potently and constantly into the marketplace, where converts are contacted in the flesh. Let's ask God to grant us all this grace. Why not "have large desires and imitate the saints"? Martyrdom of one kind or another will follow in due course.

Of course, if you're green in the spiritual life, it's easy enough at first to imagine you're getting somewhere fast. I remember looking a very holy monk straight in the eye some years ago and lamenting I had been stuck in the Fifth Mansion for some time without being able to progress any further. How he kept a straight face, I'll never know, but he did. This kind of self-control is probably just one of the dividends of holy living. Instead of crumpling up with laughter, he congratulated me soberly on having reached so far as that, and lamented in return that his was a much sadder case.

"After forty years in religion," he sighed, "I'm still trying to get into the First."

After that I soon climbed down into the moat. "Move over," I said to De Quincey's crocodile, who did.

But don't think I'm not still trying. Any real perseverance in prayer worthy of the name will show you up for the fool you are in short order. That you can depend on. As long as God promises His grace to the humble, the only problem is how to be humble, said the Little Flower. The humble soul has nothing to fear at any stage of the spiritual life; the proud one is always in danger.

Domine, non sum dignus ut intres sub tectum meum, "Oh, Lord, I'm not worthy to entertain you under my roof," apologizes the inadequate housewife.

"The house is a mess!" apologizes Martha, smoothing her apron and wondering where she left her lipstick. Nothing reveals her deficiencies to a housewife like having someone very important appear at the front door. It's worth a hundred examinations of conscience.

"But come on in anyway!" begs Mary, intent on the Guest.

She knows instinctively He's looking more for good company than complicated soufflés, and she does her best.

Everybody knows there are times when things are more at sixes than sevens. Any housewife reading parts of St. John of the Cross on a very bad Monday might conceivably imagine herself in the last stages of purgation near the summits of perfection, but I don't think she could keep up the illusion long if she had any sense of humor. For instance, try this passage describing some of the sufferings encountered in the Dark Night of the Soul:

> Wherefore the spirit experiences pain and sighing so deep that they cause it (her soul) vehement spiritual groans and cries, to which at times it gives vocal expression; when it has the necessary strength and power it dissolves into tears, although this relief comes but seldom. David describes this very aptly in a Psalm, as one who has had experience of it, where he says, "I was exceedingly afflicted and humbled; I roared with groaning of my heart." This roaring implies great pain; for at times, with the sudden and acute remembrance of these miseries wherein the soul sees itself, pain and affliction rise up and surround it, and I know not how the affections of the soul could be described save in the similitude of holy Job, when he was in the same trials, and uttered these words: "Even as the overflowing of the waters, even so is my roaring." For just as at times the waters make such inundations that they overwhelm and fill everything, so at times this roaring and this affliction of the soul grow to such an extent that they overwhelm it and penetrate it completely, filling it with spiritual pain and anguish in all its deep affections and energies, to an extent surpassing all possibilities of exaggeration. (*Book II, Ch. IX.*)

Housewives do go through dark nights, and when it's the one St. John describes, I'll bet there's no imagining it. On the other hand, speaking for myself, I find nothing can look quite so dark as what I've come to call the "Dark Night of the Hall Closet." There are any number of these closets in the housewife's interior castle, and it's terribly easy to walk into one by mistake. It's stygian inside with the door closed, in fact much darker than any night could be; and worst of all, closets lead absolutely no place. It's essential to get the door open as soon as possible and face up to looking foolish before you smother.

Reading mystical literature without plain common sense easily traps you into dead-end closets, but then, as St. Teresa so often pointed out, if you don't have common sense, there's little hope for you anyway. The one thing she dreaded in her convents was what she called "a melancholy nun," and one requirement she insisted on in all postulants was "a good understanding." Mistaking the grace we have for the grace we haven't can be the result of plain stupidity.

That *doctor discretus* Walter Hilton put it this way:

> A hound that only runs after the hare because he sees other hounds run, rests and turns home again when he is tired. But if he runs because he sees the hare, he will not stop, although he is tired, until he has caught it. It is the same in the spiritual life. Whoever has a grace, however small, and deliberately gives up acting on it, and strives after one that has not yet been given to him, because he sees or hears that other men have it, may indeed run a while, until he is tired, but then he will turn home again, and he will be lucky if he does not get home lame as a result of his fancies (*Scale of Perfection, Bk. I, Ch. 41*).

From where I sit, a girl who concludes she's having visions when it's her glasses that need changing is going to have a bad time of it just reciting the Our Father and the Hail Mary. I'd hate to think that on her account pages must be torn out of wonderful books on prayer which other girls with good sense and the beginnings of great grace might be reading with profit to the whole world. The world needs such women.

Anyway, the doctors of the Church agree that genuine prayer is soon known by its effects, even by the soul herself, and simple prayer breeds simplicity of life. Though she can't report anything definite going on in her interior house, the housewife can't help noticing that her housekeeping has become less haphazard, more meaningful, and in fact, the house seems at times almost to keep itself. Many little chores that once tied her down are suddenly seen to be utterly superfluous. There's a new orderliness, a new sense of proportion.

"He set in order charity in me" (*Cant. 2:4*), says the Bride of the Canticle. When love gets a sense of direction, everything falls into place.

Exterior activity, too, becomes progressively more unified. Tastes become simpler. The flashy items in the clothes closet dwindle automatically to what is really necessary. There's less busy-ness and more accomplishment. Fewer words are used, but more is said. More time is spent and less is wasted. So, too, thinking is more and more about God, and less about self. Prayer itself is no longer divorced from exterior activity, but becomes nothing so much as an inarticulate and constant craving for God.

"Cling so closely to the feet of Christ, that even if He wanted to send you to hell, He'd have to go there with you!" advises Blessed Claude de la Colombière.

This kind of presumptuous humility is the fundamental *ascesis* of the simple soul. Whoever prays this way is no longer interested in hoarding virtues. She avoids sin primarily because she sees it's a hopeless obstacle to the union she craves. When she discovers a bit too much dessert can stand between her and God, mortal sin just takes care of itself! "Let the dead bury the dead!"

Any addle-pate can see it's not being saintly that gets us God. It's entertaining God that makes us saintly. Holy Mass, sacraments, commandments, counsels, liturgy, penance and everything else are simply means of bringing Him into the Holy of Holies of the human soul, so He may live and act there.

"I am the Lord who search the heart," He told Jeremias (*17:10*). "You blind fools! for which is greater, the gold, or the temple which sanctifies the gold?" He asked the Pharisees (*Matt. 23:17*).

"Visit this dwelling, we beseech thee, O Lord," prays the Church every night at Compline.

Schopenhauer was only scratching the surface. The housewife with the seven-cubit rule discovers her house isn't her idea at all, but God's, and therefore the center of the universe. In her house the Father begets the Son eternally, both pouring forth the Holy Spirit on all flesh.

Domine, non sum dignus ... sed tantum die verbo et sanabitur anima mea. Just a word from You, and the housecleaning will be finished in a jiffy. *Sanctifica tabernaculam tuam!*

This Word is spoken by the Father in the depths of the house, in which order is gradually set by the Holy Spirit who proceeds from them. With the incompetent but willing housewife's permission, the Holy Spirit soon takes over the entire management of the premises.

"The Spirit also helps our weakness," says St. Paul. "For we do not know what we should pray for as we ought, but the Spirit himself pleads for us with unutterable groanings. And he who searches the hearts knows what the Spirit desires, that he pleads for the saints according to God" (*Rom. 8:26*).

"The Holy Spirit, whom the Father will send in my name, he will teach you all things," promised the Word himself. (*John 14:26*).

Spiraling ever more deeply into these Trinitarian operations, the housewife sees that every time she receives Holy Communion there is sacramentally re-enacted in her soul and body something like the ascension of the Sacred Humanity into the bosom of the Trinity. Again God's glory enters Solomon's temple, and again and again the Holy Spirit is sent. St. Teresa tells us:

Once after Communion, I saw how His Father within our soul accepts the most Holy Body of Christ. I have understood and seen how the Divine Persons are there, and how pleasing this offering of His Son is, because He has His joy and delight in Him, so to speak, here on earth; for it is not the Humanity alone that is within us in our souls, but the Divinity as well, and thus it is so pleasing and acceptable unto Him, and gives us graces so great (*Rel. ix, 20*).

St. Teresa's vision was given by God for all of us. Every sacrament the soul receives intensifies the divine life within her. Soon not only is her own house filled, but it has overflowed the entire neighborhood, as it did at Pentecost!

Without leaving her doorstep, she has access through God into the central being of all His creatures. The universe is found in her house no longer ephemerally reflected in the sensory images it leaves in the memory, which Walt Whitman found so fascinating; nor does it exist only in the thoughts she thinks about it in the understanding, where Schopenhauer found it. Now the universe can be found there essentially, as it is contained in the Triune God Who dwells in her, and whose very life is hers by participation. Because this is true, I had to start this book, just to be sure you knew it too. There's no summit meeting anywhere in the world at which the housewife can't be present; no secret conclave escapes her influence. None of her children need go to school without her; nor is there any benighted soul from here to the Himalayas she can't help spiritually and materially, simply by applying at any moment to the Lord of her household for the one thing necessary.

This is prayer.

When the prophet tells us to "deal thy bread to the hungry, and bring the needy and harborless into thy home," he was speaking a beautiful and very accurate figure of this prayer for others which is strangely enough the very stuff of the most intimate and private conversation with God under one's own roof. "Then shall thy light break forth as the morning," he promises (*Isa. 58:7-8*).

"In the manner by which the Father is related to the Son by communication, and the Son to the Holy Ghost, so are interior souls related to one another and to mankind. Nature does not enter into this mode of communication: that which is born of the spirit is spirit," says Father de Langeac. If the housewives of the world—and spiritually that means all the souls in the world—came to grips with this kind of calculus, atheist communism would fall to bits tomorrow, the Gospel would be preached in every nation in short order, and Christ would soon reign visibly among us in glory.

Please, stay home and *do the housework*! Measure the building!

"And with what measure you measure, it shall be measured to you," said the Christ, putting the royal cubit in our hands.

"That, being rooted and grounded in love, you may be able to comprehend with all the saints what is the breadth and length and height and depth and to know Christ's love which surpasses all knowledge" (*Eph. 3:17-19*), speaks that rapid calculator St. Paul, who even on earth rose to the third heaven.

> For thus saith the Lord of hosts. Yet one little while and I will move the heaven and the earth, and the sea and the dry land. And I will move all nations: *and the desired of nations shall come*: and I will fill this house with glory: saith the Lord of hosts. ... Great shall be the glory of this last house more than of the first!(*Agg. 2:7-8*).

That'll be a Sunday. My Lawd, what a mawnin!

As the Lord said to Moses, "On the seventh day everyone is to stay home and no one is to go out" (*Exod. 16:29*), for "the Trinity," explains Sister Elizabeth, "is our dwelling-place, our home, our Father's house which we should never leave."

Even now.

Is There a Doctor in the House?

CHAPTER 5

"ONCE upon a time there was a young girl named Mary. She was so pure and good, and she loved God so much, she didn't have to know anything. She did housework all her life and never exercised her mind, because God wanted her innocence preserved. What God wants most of all from women is blind obedience and servile work. Mary was so abysmally uneducated she couldn't sin, and she was so simple and pious, God made her the Mother of His only-begotten Son."

This kind of blasphemous fiction rarely gets printed as baldly as you see it here, because obviously it wouldn't stand a chance; but that doesn't mean it isn't being distributed. Like a sweet-smelling deodorant, it creeps into baby-blue scenes of life at Nazareth, May Day music, children's prayers composed by grownups, or just general conversation. It perfumes everything without alarming anyone, masking more offensive odors that might arouse suspicions. Its author, the father of lies, whose greatest talents necessarily lie in the field of fragrant fiction, sees to its diffusion.

Ignorance, he would have us believe, is the very stuff of innocence. Though they go hand in hand, says he, ignorance in itself can be a very good thing, the touchstone of true simplicity. "'Tis folly to be wise," when presumably it's so sanctifying to be plain stupid, and so on. There's hardly a woman alive he hasn't forced to subscribe to this falsehood in some degree at one time or another; and the Mother of God herself he has dared to use in evidence.

This heresy takes various forms, running all the way from the one just cited to the often heard, "What's the use of all that education for Dolly Mae when she's about to get married anyway?" Lack of ignorance, it would seem, just makes a housewife restless and hard to live with.

"Any girl with an IQ over 90 is going to endure martyrdom in marriage unless she has plenty of outside interests." In other words, intelligence bottled up in a house may lead to dementia.

"Finest mother I ever knew never could get past the third grade. Kids all turned out to be college presidents." (Who's arguing?)

Eventually the Chinese will be brought in. "Give a woman knowledge, and you give her a knife." And high time, too.

"It's certainly not what she knows that makes a woman great. Look at the Blessed Mother!"

That would seem to settle it, but only if you don't look at the Blessed Mother. You must also keep from reading the Gospels, a dispassionate, prayerful reading of which will quickly dispel any illusions that might be entertained of our Lady as "Ignoramus Most Holy," a quiet little peasant girl who never raised her eyes above her sewing, never indulged in mental speculation of any kind, and for whom the crudest counting on her fingers more than sufficed.

Satan has never been a match for the Blessed Virgin, and here as elsewhere she refutes him utterly. We have already suggested that she was an intellectual, and that she used her mind fully to enlighten her will, "keeping things in mind and pondering them in her heart."

"Philosophy ... is born in wonder," says our home book of *Introductory Metaphysics*. "Wonder is the child of knowledge and ignorance. It arises when we know something, but do not know the explanation for it. We then naturally ask ourselves how it can be as it is."

"How shall this happen, since I do not know man?" asked Mary of Nazareth, for she of all people was a philosopher, a true "wisdom-lover." Though we can never match her, we're all called to imitate her to the limit of our capacity.

This is very hard. "But if any of you is wanting in wisdom," suggests St. James "let him ask it of God who gives abundantly to all men, and does not reproach; and it will be given to him. But let him ask with faith, without hesitation!" (*1:5-6*). Believe it or not, simple faith leads normally to perfect knowledge, if no obstacle is put in its way.

The Annunciation isn't the only indication in the Gospels of our Lady's active intelligence. There are many others peeping out at us from between the frugal but fruitful lines of the well-known stories about her. For instance, there's the *Magnificat*.

And Mary said:

> My soul magnifies the Lord,
> and my spirit rejoices in God my savior,
> Because he has regarded the lowliness of his handmaid,
> for behold, henceforth all generations shall call me
> blessed,

Because he who is mighty has done great things for me,
and holy is his name;
And his mercy is from generation to generation
toward those who fear him.

He has shown might with his arm;
he has scattered the proud in the conceit of their heart.
He has put down the mighty from their thrones
and has exalted the lowly.
The hungry he has filled with good things
and the rich he has sent empty away.
He has given help to Israel his servant,
mindful of his mercy,
As he promised our fathers,
toward Abraham and his descendants forever
(*Luke 1:46-55*).

In presenting our Lady to us as an outstanding example of an uneducated holy woman, the devil must somehow get around the *Magnificat*, which in point of evident learning and beauty of language compares most favorably with the finest compositions in the Bible. Trying various methods, he has suggested she never said it in the first place, that these words were actually Elizabeth's the educated priest Zachary's wife; and he can produce hallowed manuscripts to support his contention. The Pontifical Commission scotched this gambit in 1912 by officially pronouncing the *Magnificat* Mary's, as evidenced by the "harmonious testimony of nearly all the codices both of the original Greek text and of the versions."

It has also been suggested that the *Magnificat* was a brilliant piece of editorial work on the part of St. Luke and others, and is at best a hodge-podge parody of various passages of Scripture cleverly put together and attributed to our Lady. Though never calling in question the *Magnificat's* divine inspiration or its appropriation to our Lady, I understand modern Catholic scholarship tends to give the devil his due more than formerly. Accorded a critical hearing, all reasonable hypotheses concerning the word-for-word authorship of our Lady's poem are being gravely sifted.

Until the experts find a better explanation, however, I must confess I find the simplest explanation the most satisfying, and the most rational. For my money, Mary composed the Magnificat pretty much, if not entirely, as it stands. Acting under divine inspiration, St. Luke got it from her firsthand, relaying to us what *Mary said*. Why apologize? Why anyone should find this strange, searching for far-fetched reasons to the contrary, I'm too prejudiced to see. I want Mary to have written the *Magnificat*! I, too, am a housewife who wrote poetry in her youth, and bad as it was, I can still quote lots of it. So why not Mary, of all people?

Anyway, who says she composed the *Magnificat* on the spot? The sacred text certainly doesn't. All it says is, *Mary* said it. She might have composed it anytime before or after, setting the innermost sentiments of her soul into formal rhythm as any poet writes occasional verse. This was an occasion, not only for her, but for us! She was almost bound by tradition to commemorate it, much as Miriam composed a refrain to celebrate the destruction of Pharaoh's chariots in the Red Sea, or as Debora wrote a poem about Jahel's victory over Sisara. Though we may have just about lost this art today, being too rushed to savor great events as these women did let's not therefore conclude women never did this sort of thing.

No one will deny that the *Magnificat* does parallel many passages in the Old Testament. Its opening lines are strongly reminiscent of the Canticle of Anna, which begins, "My heart exults in the Lord, my horn is exalted in my God" (*I Sam. 2:1*). As far as I'm concerned, this proves our Lady knew Anna's Canticle well, and loved it. By the same token it can be proved she was used to praying the Psalms and knew them by heart, for there are several verses in her poem similar to ones occurring in the Psalms and Isaias as well.

To mention only one instance among many possible ones, the Blessed Virgin's closing words, "He has given help to Israel his servant, mindful of his mercy, as he promised our fathers," may have derived from Isaias' prophecy which reads,

> But thou, Israel, art my servant, Jacob whom I have chosen, the seed of Abraham my friend: In whom I have taken thee from the ends of the earth. ... Thou art my servant. I have chosen thee and have not cast thee away (*41:8-9*).

The Psalmist put it, "He has remembered his kindness and his faithfulness toward the house of Israel. All the ends of the earth have seen the salvation by our God" (*Ps. 97:3*).

Without parading pedantry unduly, the point here may be that, like all the prophets, the Queen of Prophets laid no claim to originality. On the contrary, she found in her heart the entire summation of these very prophecies. She knew Scripture so well, and was so steeped in its teaching, she breathed it as her own breath, either deliberately paraphrasing or hardly aware she was so doing, so imbued was she with its spirit and meaning. The *Magnificat* is not the speech of an ignorant woman, though of a divinely simple woman. Could she who produced Christ not have produced Scripture which is Christ, the Word of God?

After Mary's Child was born, we are told His first visitors to the cave were simple shepherds who at the direction of an angel "went with haste, and ... found Mary and Joseph, and the babe lying in a manger, and that when they had seen, they understood." Simplicity, we have seen, is easily enlightened even in stables. This isn't the whole story, however, for Scripture tells us also that Mary was visited not only by the unlettered but by the learned—the Wise Men, who arrived much later, after a long journey begun when they had "seen his star in the east."

"And entering the house (ah, the house), they found the Child with Mary his mother and falling down, they worshipped him." Our Lady could have been neither prejudiced against, nor awed by the educated. In fact we know she accepted gifts from them when they "opened their treasures" before her and her Child. The Holy Spirit here deploys a most beautiful allegory, an action picture of human learning shown "falling down and worshipping." Then, "opening its treasures," before God and His human Mother, it proffers what is trinitarian homage—gifts of gold, frankincense, and myrrh—to a Triune God on earth who is King, God and Man. Nowhere is there, I suspect, a more succinct statement of the true end of education: to give glory to God. This is the *Gloria in Excelsis* of the erudite.

That our Lady herself knew a thing or two about opening the treasures of the intellect for God is made clear in yet another familiar story about her. It's the Fifth Joyous Mystery in her Rosary, and it tells how she and her husband found their lost boy in the Temple:

"And it came to pass," relates St. Luke, "that they found him in the temple, sitting in the midst of the teachers, listening to them and asking them questions. And all who were listening to him were amazed at his understanding and his answers. And when they saw him they were astounded" (*Luke 2:46-8*).

Here is mystery unutterable. Here we peer for an instant into the problem which has fascinated theologians for centuries. How can God be a man? How can a man possessing full divinity and enjoying the Beatific Vision suffer? Equally incredible, how can He who knows all things "advance in wisdom and age and grace before God and men," learning experientially from day to day like any other boy, as St. Luke's Gospel affirms our Lord did? We know He did, but *how*? Here is knowledge and ignorance well-calculated to produce plenty of wonder.

Mary and Joseph were astonished, says Scripture. At what? Not at
His learning, I do believe, but at finding Him where they did. "When
they saw Him, they were astonished," it says, not when they heard Him,
or at what He was saying. It's evident they had been wearily searching
for Him everywhere, and surely one of the first and most obvious
places they must have returned to look was the Temple, the very hub of
Jerusalem. Reading carefully, we mark that Scripture doesn't say He
had been there for three days while they looked for Him; Scripture
merely says that's where He was when He was located.

Apparently He wasn't there at first, nor at any other likely spot.
Any good parent knows pretty well the haunts his child is likely to
frequent, as well as what friends or relatives or public places he might
be drawn to drop in on. Every good parent knows where his child's
interests lie, and what his characteristic reactions are in crises. Mary
and Joseph undoubtedly looked in all the obvious places and asked the
obvious questions of all the obvious people, because that's the point of
the story. The wonder was, he seemed to have disappeared into thin air.
Barring kidnapping or other foul play, normally tractable, but missing
children are located in a matter of hours, not days.

Where was He for three days?

"In the bosom of the Blessed Trinity!" opines St. Aelred, who like
all saints has a genius for getting to the heart of mystery.

I'm inclined to go along with the holy Aelred. "The boy Jesus
remained in Jerusalem, and his parents did not know it," runs the text.
This was, I think, His first "ascension," a joyful prefiguration of the
glorious one to come. As His Nativity from a Virgin's womb prepared
His Resurrection from a sealed tomb, so His disappearance in
Jerusalem, "the habitation of peace," prepared the greater
disappearance from our sight into the clouds of heaven when His work
on earth was accomplished.

"Did you not know that I must be about my Father's business?"
leads so easily into His parting promise to the Apostles, "And I send
forth upon you the promise of my Father." And St. Luke says He
added, "But wait here in the city, until you are clothed with power from
on high," for no disciple is above his master.

Be that as it may, it remains that Mary and Joseph were astonished
at finding Him with the doctors in the Temple, and sadly astonished
that He would have deliberately put them through such mental agony.

"Son, why hast thou done so to us?" asks His mother with good
reason, not only of Him, but of all of us.

She didn't ask Him where He got all His "understanding and his
answers," because that, I think, she knew very well. Indeed, Scripture

in no wise says His parents were amazed at these, though a hasty reading might leave that impression. It's at this point of the story, as a matter of fact, that is blasted forever the devilish concept of our Lady as an uneducated, ignorant-but-lovely woman.

This happens when we ask a very simple question.

Just where did the twelve-year-old God-Man get those answers?

This mystery teaches implicitly that our Lord learned as man in the ordinary way. Because He was true man, His human learning reached Him by human channels, not from private visions and revelations without effort on His part. Granted His unclouded intellect and perfect sense faculties, He still had to receive knowledge from some other human being, just like the rest of us. Without fear of contradiction, I suggest one of these human beings was His Blessed Mother. Another was St. Joseph.

From what I've been able to gather on the subject, there was no compulsory public education as we know it in our Lord's day. Elementary schools were probably attached to the synagogues, but the teachers of young children under twelve would be primarily the parents. Although education among the Jews consisted almost exclusively in religious instruction coupled with practical instruction in a useful trade, Israel as a whole was far from being an illiterate nation. A child was taught to read in order that he might read Scripture; taught what science there was that He might appreciate God's universe; taught to sing that he might praise God "in the vast assembly," and taught a craft in order to do God's will by supporting himself and his family, practice charity, and support the Temple.

In other words, education was clearly understood to be just what it should be—a means to God. Secular learning as such was subordinated to this higher purpose, outside which it had no *raison d'être*. The peculiar situation which pertains among Christians today, whose secular education has advanced far beyond and independently of religious knowledge, would have been incomprehensible to the devout Jew of our Lord's time. This, he would argue, was not education, but vanity, and of course he'd be right. Of what use, indeed, is knowledge that doesn't know enough to "fall down and worship" its very Source? The main task of the secular Christian today may well be to lead natural knowledge to its supernatural destiny.

In this task women play a very important part, because to them belongs the fundamental orientation of the human being before school can influence him one way or another. Although coeducation in schools was unknown in Israel, coeducation itself is as old as mankind, for it has always existed in the home. Both girls and boys came in for all the home training that was available, and in wealthy families, tutors were sometimes employed for more advanced teaching. Of the beautiful Susanna Scripture says, "For her parents, being just, had instructed their daughter according to the law of Moses" (*Dan. 13:3*), so we know female education was hardly considered a waste of time.

That our Lady was already admirably conversant with the Scriptures has already been noted, and though we know the Holy Family was poor, tradition seems to suggest that she herself was born of well-to-do parents. Apocryphal writings would have it she was reared and educated in the Temple from an early age. Taking these tales with several salutary grains of salt, no one would argue that her natural education in point of accumulation of information could compare with a college graduate's today, but certainly she was well educated according to the norms of her time.

More important, her education was properly theocentric. Even humanly speaking, this places her well beyond the orbit of the average bluestocking today, whose head may be crammed with facts, but who has to look around for what to do with them. She's fortunate if her so-called education doesn't drive her to a highly successful professional career completely outside God's will for her!

We know that both Mary and her husband were of the royal line of David. This made them true Hebrew aristocrats for whom learning would have much meaning, and perhaps they fell into that well-known class of people we all know who are gently bred and cultivated, but don't happen to have a great deal of money. They were educated people in the true sense of the word, which means "to draw out of a person something latent or potential." In other words, they were thoroughly "brought out," for no teacher can supply what doesn't lie in embryo in the pupil already. Mary and Joseph were educated primarily because they were godly and perforce used mind as well as heart fully in His service.

That Joseph was a carpenter in no way argues that he was coarse or non-intellectual, even in the special sense of that maligned word. The Jews never allowed themselves to look down on manual labor as some educated morons do, and in fact the rabbis customarily supported themselves by plying a trade on the side. St. Paul, brought up in this tradition, saw no conflict whatever between preaching and tent-making—any more than a housewife should see conflict between cooking and teaching, or parsing Sanskrit and shelling peas. These intellectual and manual tasks have deep mystical interrelationships, and the truly educated see them!

Can anyone seriously contend that St. Paul, the "chosen vessel" destined to build up the perfect Tabernacle among the Gentiles was a *tent-maker* by accident? Tent-making and tabernacle-building are one and the same thing, both mystically and semantically speaking, and the one occupation was as much God's will for him as the other. So too, the just man Joseph. Destined to provide for the God-Child on earth by his labor, and ultimately to act as Quartermaster for the whole Mystical Body, dispensing "things made" to that end—was he a carpenter, an artisan, and maker of "things" by accident? Surely not. St. Joseph's role in the Church had to be "hidden." If the early Church had been allowed to see him in his true light, he might have been mistaken for Divine Providence itself, so transcendent is his function!

Our Lord at the age of twelve was certainly in great part the educational product of His holy parents, especially in consequence of their poverty. We know our Lord was literate, for we are told He customarily rose to read the Scriptures in the synagogue at Nazareth; but He never went on to the advanced formal study of the theological schools in Jerusalem, for we read that the Jews wondered at His erudition. "How does this man come by learning, since He has not studied?" (*John 7:15*).

Miraculous? Only in that Christ himself is a miracle. How large a part His Mother contributed to His human education can't be ascertained, but it's safe to believe it was considerable. Teaching is like cooking in more ways than one. The best chefs and professors may be men, still, it's the women who do most of the cooking and teaching.

The Book of Proverbs, the oldest educational handbook among the Jews, says in the very first chapter: "My son, hear the instruction of thy father, and forsake not the law of thy mother."

In many passages throughout its pages reverence for the instruction of parents is stressed, along with abundant advice on how to bring up children and what to teach them. Listen:

"He that spareth the rod hateth his son: but he that loveth him correcteth him betimes" (*13:24*).

"Chastise thy son, despair not: but to the killing of him set not thy soul!" (*19:18*).

"The rod and reproof give wisdom: but the child that is left to his own will bringeth his mother to shame ... Instruct thy son, and he shall refresh thee, and shall give delight to thy soul" *(29:15,17)*.

Here, I believe, is the long-sought answer to juvenile delinquency. There's no doubt that our Lord himself was taught from His infancy according to the precepts of this divine book on child guidance and wasn't left to His own devices.

After His escapade in the Temple, when He answers His Mother's reproach with the lofty, "Did you not know I must be about my Father's business?" Mary and Joseph tell Him firmly it's time to go home.

"And he went down with them and came to Nazareth, and was subject to them," says Scripture for our instruction.

St. Paul tells us that St. Timothy, whose father was Greek, was taught Scripture by his mother Eunice and his grandmother Lois, so an educated Hebrew woman was not an unheard-of rarity in the early Church. Being able to teach her children something was simply part of being a good mother, and when, as in Timothy's case, the father couldn't supply the necessary instruction, the mother considered herself wholly responsible. (Timothy became a bishop.) It's conceivable that this may have been true for a time in our Lord's case, for we know St. Joseph probably died sometime between the episode at the Temple and the marriage at Cana, where Mary appears alone. If he passed away while our Lord was still young, the responsibility must have fallen very heavily on His Mother.

In any society, I'm afraid it follows that if a girl is going to be a mother, she can't be too educated. It's possible that a career woman can be poorly educated, or knowledgeable only in one line, and still get by, contributing competently enough in the controlled and largely artificial conditions of an office, a hospital, or a classroom. For a housewife, however, there are no protective, arbitrary limits to her sphere of action. Like Holy Wisdom, she must be all things to those in her care, because her craft is the whole human being, not just the nine-to-five executive part of him, or the sick patient part of him, or even the Latin student part of him. She can't be content with the trade school education directed solely to earning a living which has sadly become the norm in many of our best universities. For her, more is required, in fact nothing less than all the liberal arts in their full scope. No housewife is equal to such demands, but it's what she needs!

Elizabeth Leseur, who managed to live a life of intense union with God in the pagan atmosphere she shared with an unbelieving husband, left the following entry behind her in her private journal. Dated September 20,1899, it reads:

> I set myself to study philosophy, and it interests me greatly. It throws light on many things and puts the mind in order. I can't understand why it is not made the crown of feminine education. What a woman so often lacks is true judgment, the habit of reasoning, the steady, individual working of the mind. Philosophy could give her all that, and strip from her

so many prejudices and narrow ideas which she transmits religiously to her sons, to the great detriment of our country (*A Wife's Story*, Burns Oates, 1933).

"I proposed in my mind to seek and search out wisely concerning all things that are done under the sun," says Ecclesiastes, because as he explains, "this painful occupation hath God given to the children of men, to be exercised therein" (*1:13*).

How could a mere housewife, of all people, think she's any different?

Above all, "Let her be learned in heavenly doctrine!" prays the Church for every bride who gets her nuptial blessing.

Mme. Leseur knew Latin, English and Russian, besides French. She read constantly in the Scriptures and the Latin classics, and if we are to credit her journal, she bemoaned daily the lack of contemplative spirit in ordinary human lives, where it properly belongs. She saw that natural knowledge, to be used properly, must be coordinated and unified by philosophy.

Cardinal Newman would agree. He says:

> ... all knowledge forms one whole, because its subject matter is one; for the universe in its length and breadth is so intimately knit together that we cannot separate off portion from portion, and operation from operation, except by a mental abstraction; and then again, as to its Creator, though He of course in His own Being is infinitely separate from it, yet He has so implicated Himself in it, and taken it into His very bosom by His presence in it, His providence over it, His impressions upon it, and His influences through it, that we cannot truly or fully contemplate it without contemplating Him ... The comprehension of the bearings of one science on another, this belongs, I conceive, to a sort of science distinct from all of them, and in some sense a science of sciences, which is my own conception of what is meant by philosophy, in the true sense of the word, and of a philosophical habit of mind (*The Scope and Nature of University Education*, Discourse II).

Considering philosophy's encompassing femininity in relation to knowledge, it's not impertinent that the patron of Christian philosophers (and theologians!) should be a woman: St. Catherine of Alexandria. The story goes that she so exasperated the Emperor Maxentius, not only by resisting his amorous advances, but by trouncing his fifty best philosophers in open debate, that he eventually insisted on beheading her personally. This, alas, often happens to ladies who inadvertently beat men at their own games, and we aren't surprised to learn that St. Catherine's was one of the voices who counseled St. Joan of Arc through similar difficulties some eleven hundred years later.

Ancient monks called Mary "the philosophy of Christians," and spoke of *"philosophari in Maria."* Obviously philosophy belongs to the housewife as tent-making belongs to St. Paul. It's comprehensive. It's cheap. It requires absolutely no special equipment but wonder. One has to study philosophy and invest in expensive books to be a philosophy professor, but not to be a philosopher. A philosopher is just anyone who's willing to hit head on, with his head, the mystery in what everybody else takes for granted.

Really only housewives have time to grapple in their native habitat with such things as space, time, being, motion, birth, or growth, in order to classify properly why dishes break, or why yesterday can't be lived again, what's up, or just who *is* my five-year-old. Whatever the housewife chooses to study at home, she is in the enviable position of being able to go after knowledge itself, without the encumbrance of degrees. This isn't an inconsiderable advantage, being set free to proceed at her own rate, without grades or classroom, toward what she, and not somebody else, needs to know.

A mother's knowledge can't be just a series of isolated facts to be tabulated later, like a research assistant's. It must be coordinated and unified even beyond the power of philosophy to accomplish. It must be supernaturalized. It must become wisdom. Wisdom can take unto herself any amount of undigested facts and transfigure them, but in this world this happens only through suffering, through pondering them painfully and deeply in the heart.

Few mothers can take it. Their college educations rarely become a part of them to that extent. Ignorant women are the curse of the home, as great female educators like St. Madeleine Sophie Barat and Mother Janet Erskine Stuart saw only too clearly. Educated women, on the other hand, can hardly be made to stay at home at all! They can't waste themselves on a handful of children, and a world greedy for their skills agrees only too readily. Female education today is little more than a way out of the house.

The supernatural education of the young, nevertheless, depends precisely on teachers who are able to "stay home" and transmit to them the painful fruits of their wisdom, the "true knowledge of the things that are." Wisdom knows, says Scripture, "the disposition of the whole world, and the virtues of the elements, the beginning, and ending, and midst of our times, and alterations of their courses, and the changes of seasons, and the revolutions of the year, and the dispositions of the stars, and the natures of living creatures, and rage of wild beasts, the force of the winds, and reasonings of man, the diversities of plants, and the virtues of roots," for wisdom knows everything, keeps track of everything and has everything, like the good housewife she is (*Wis. 7:17-20*).

"Come over to me, all ye that desire me, and be filled with my fruits," she invites her children, in words the Liturgy applies to our Lady, the truly educated housewife (*Ecclus. 24:26*).

And when we hear the Nazarenes ask of Christ, "How did this man come by this wisdom? ... Is not this the carpenter's son? Is not his mother called Mary?" Are we not lost in wonder at the hidden but potent role these holy parents must have played in His formation? Sirach says, "He that instructeth his son shall be praised in him and shall glory in him in the midst of them of his household. He that teacheth his son ... in the midst of his friends he shall glory in him" (*Ecclus. 30:2-3*). From this we can infer what must be St. Joseph's joy in heaven at this very moment, looking on his son, Jesus.

Christ Himself took care to point out the terrible duties of parents. After raising the twelve-year-old daughter of Jairus from the dead, didn't He immediately instruct her parents to see to it that "something be given her to eat?" (*Mark 5:43*).

This action parable makes clear that although God gives and restores life, natural or supernatural, it's the duty of parents to see it fed and sustained. Only the girl's parents and Peter, James and John were allowed to witness this miracle. All others had been sent out, so there's no doubt as to whom it was our Lord addressed the order.

Some of us may be startled to hear that formal catechetics for children in classrooms is a very modern development, indeed, unknown before the eighteenth century. In the primitive church, ecclesiastical catechesis was directed exclusively to adults, and hardly existed at all during the Middle Ages, or any of the great ages of faith, when religion was strongly rooted and transmitted in the home. Today educators are learning again, perhaps, that religious training isn't purely an intellectual exercise, to be indulged in out of the context of daily life— especially by children under twelve, who learn little by abstract concepts, but a great deal by concrete imagery. There are no images more concrete to a child than his parents.

By the time he is twelve, the course of his entire life is ordinarily determined for good or evil. It was a critical age, we suspect, even for our Lord. It may seem superfluous to tell parents to feed their children, especially ones like Jairus, "a ruler of the synagogue," but some parents find great difficulty in doing the obvious. How many children die of spiritual malnutrition with food within easy reach, whose wealthy parents must be reminded like Jairus of what God has commanded them through Moses on Sinai:

> Hear, O Israel, the Lord is our God, the Lord alone! Therefore, you shall love the Lord, your God, with all your heart, and with all your soul, and with all your strength. Take to heart these words which I enjoin on you today. Drill them into your children! Speak of them at home and abroad, whether you are busy or at rest (*Deut. 6:4-7*).

Holy Job, who took his duties as a parent very seriously, went even further, sanctifying his children and offering up holocausts for every one of them saying, "lest perhaps my sons have sinned and have blessed (cursed) God in their hearts" (*1:5*). Today, Job offers Mass for his children, for this is the highest pedagogy. Using the methods of grace, there's no limit to the lessons It imparts, comprehending as it does the fundamental objective of teaching the young anything. The spiritual power for good which parents wield over their children is possessed by no one else on earth in their regard. It's a mystery of grace.

"For them do I sanctify myself!" says the Father of the World to Come concerning His children at the Last Supper, "that they also may be sanctified in truth." As model of all parents, He prays, "Holy Father, keep in thy name those whom thou hast given me ... I do not pray that thou take them out of the world, but that thou keep them from evil" (*Jn. 17:19,11,15*).

A woman in the crowd listening to our Lord preaching was evidently overcome with admiration at the way He himself had turned out. "Blessed is the womb that bore thee!" she burst out, knowing full well where to look for the beginnings of excellence in children. Maybe she was a mother herself.

Our Lord, who knew even better than she did the indispensable role parents play, replied with the famous, "Rather, blessed are they who hear the word of God and keep it" (*Luke 11:27-28*), making plain where His own Mother's power for formation came from.

His hearers must have been well aware that He was in fact quoting another well-known passage from Deuteronomy, wherein Moses promises, "When you hearken to the voice of the Lord, your God, all these blessing will come upon you and overwhelm you: "May you be blessed in the city, and blessed in the country ... Blessed be the fruit of your womb!" (*Deut. 28:2-4*), for good offspring, whether of men or their livestock, are quite clearly the reward of a life lived in God.

The Gospels are filled with the miracles of healing Christ performed when importuned by parents. For His own Mother He was persuaded to change water into wine at Cana. There again later He grants the request of a royal official who entreats Him for the cure of his boy near death at Capharnaum. At Naim He raises from the dead the only son of a widow whose tears alone move Him, just as three centuries later He raises the soul of St. Augustine at the prayer of his mother St. Monica. He cures the daughter of a Syro-Phoenician woman who nags Him mercilessly, begging for "the crumbs from the table."

On reading these stories, it seems He was in a sense compelled to grant parental entreaties, sometimes in the face of serious obstacles, even lack of faith. A skeptical father trying to get help for his demoniac only son pleads, "If thou canst do anything, have compassion on us and help us!" Jesus' disciples had already tried and failed, and the father was desperate.

Jesus tells him he must believe, and for the sake of the child the poor father "with tears" does the very best he honestly can. He cries out, "I do believe!" but adds, "Help my unbelief!"

Accepting this magnificent act of cold faith torn from the man in spite of his strong predispositions to the contrary, our Lord exorcises the spirit. Then, as He did for Jairus' daughter, He took the child "by the hand." Somehow we feel this boy never became a delinquent. Not only was he saved from the power of the devil, but the story seems to indicate that parental salvation itself can hang on concern for one's children. Certainly the miracle wrought in the soul of the father was even greater than that wrought in the body of the boy whose welfare was in question. Whoever won't pray for himself can sometimes be driven to it for his children. Poor children, who suffer for the sins of the fathers!

Pius XII in the encyclical *Mystici Corporis* reminds us:

> This is truly a tremendous mystery which we can never meditate enough: that the salvation of many souls depends upon the prayers and voluntary mortifications offered for that intention by the members of the mystical body of Christ, and upon the cooperation which pastors and faithful, and especially parents, must afford to our divine Savior.

Where to begin? Anywhere. The poorest parents have a wealth of practical experience in which to clothe the truths of Scripture, to prepare food for Jairus' daughters. Like the wise men, everyday practical knowledge opens more and more of its treasures, reflecting God's light from ever new facets utterly unsuspected by the people of our Lord's time. I don't know in what context His hearers explained His parable of the "Single eye," but I understand modern exegetes have a little trouble with it.

"The lamp of the body is the eye. If thy eye be sound, thy whole body will be full of light. But if thy eye be evil, thy whole body will be full of darkness" (*Matt. 6:22-3*).

The general sense is certainly plain enough, but detailed understanding seems to run into trouble with the Greek word ἁπλῦς which can mean *single, simple, candid, sincere,* or, by metonymy, *sound.* Which meaning was actually our Lord's? Well, I don't know, but I must say this parable has been crystal clear to me for some months now, since I began taking our five-year-old to an ophthalmology clinic for a stubborn eye condition.

There on our regular visits I learned about *strabismus*, which is a pretty fancy name for seeing double. A sufferer, it seems, can have either "convergent" or "divergent" strabismus, depending on whether his eyes turn in or out. In housewife vocabulary this means cross-eyed or wall-eyed. The doctor explained to me that victims who go untreated usually end by subconsciously blocking out the vision in one eye by means of a psychological mechanism not yet understood by modern medicine. The vision in the blocked-out eye will eventually disappear entirely, leaving the beholder with the single image he craves. Blind in one eye, he sees flatly what is before him, but never in any depth of focus.

Man just isn't constituted to see double like animals with eyes on either side of their heads, and he'll get out of seeing double in one way or another. This is true spiritually too, and all ascetical theology depends on it.

"No man can serve two masters," said our Lord, pointing up His parable, "for either he will hate the one and love the other, or else he will stand by the one and despise the other. You cannot serve God and mammon" (*Matt. 6:24*).

Some people, however, solve their problem another way. Their plight is extremely common, the doctor informed me, but very hard to detect except by special examination by an expert. Unknown to themselves and to others, they develop a condition which is called *alternating strabismus*. They manage to retain good vision in both eyes, not by focusing them, but by blocking out the vision first in one eye and then the other by extremely rapid and imperceptible alternations. Like the other sufferers, they never see out of both eyes at once and never achieve any depth of focus, but what's worse, they never know what ails them unless a doctor tells them. Spiritually, with twenty-

twenty vision in both eyes, they serve God and mammon by turns, never suspecting that neither is in focus.

"I would that thou wert cold or hot. But because thou art lukewarm, and neither hot nor cold, I am about to vomit thee out of my mouth! is what alternating strabismus gets you in the Apocalypse (*3:15-16*). All the masters of the spiritual life agree that of all ailments tepidity is the hardest to cure, because its victims will never believe they're sick. They see perfectly; it's the doctor who needs glasses!

Yet, as perfect natural vision in depth is "single," using both eyes in focus, so does perfect supernatural vision focus into a single image both this world and the next. It doesn't alternate rapidly between one and the other. If this ideal is impossible to us in our fallen state, our Lord tells us any extreme remedy is better than falling into the fatal alternating strabismus, which lands us in the same pit as the totally blind.

"And if thy right eye is an occasion of sin to thee, pluck it out and cast it from thee! It is better for thee to enter into life with one eye, than, having two eyes, to be cast into hell-fire!" (*Matt. 18:9*).

Well, you may laugh, but this is the exegesis now in use at our house for the parable of the single eye, call it ἁπλ ς or what you will. With children, you need plenty of solid facts at first hand, and writers of commentaries are rarely privileged to take them to eye clinics.

I've always thought it must be comparatively easy to explain the doctrine of, say, Transubstantiation to a roomful of theological students. If you're at a loss with adults, you can always try to take refuge in big words and sometimes even get away with it. But don't try this at the Offertory when the same five-year-old, wearing glasses, tugs at your sleeve and asks, "Mother, what's Father doing?"

"He's setting the table for the Lord's Supper."

"Oh." At the Consecration she asks, "What's he doing now?"

"He's changing the bread into God." (What could be simpler? Only God.) Do be careful. As you know, if you say Father's putting God in the bread, you're teaching heresy.

"Oh," she says again.

That's all she says *now*, because of course, like Eve, she's *thinking*. That means there will come in course of time a long series of questions, and believe me, if you want to save time and avoid trouble, it might be a good idea in the long run just to cuddle up with the decrees of the Council of Trent on the Holy Eucharist. That's the easy way. Let him be anathema who hasn't boned up in time on the simple things like substance, accidents, space, extension, and the other simple things that have tortured philosophers for centuries. Mme. Leseur was right. As that child keeps growing, so do the questions, and Mom and Dad have to know everything. Especially Mom, who can't escape to an office during the week.

When he comes home from school, the nine-year-old will ask breezily, "Mom, how come St. Thomas never got ordained?"

"St. Thomas was ordained, silly!" you answer. "At the Last Supper. And close that door!"

"But he wasn't in the room that other time, Mother." "What room what other time?"

"Remember how he said he wouldn't believe Jesus was alive unless he saw the holes in him? Well, Jesus appeared to the other Apostles that time when He breathed on them and told them they could forgive sins, and St. Thomas wasn't there?"

Oh, dear. I rush to the Gospels and try to find the place in a hurry, because with children you have to check everything, especially when they go to public schools. Clearing up the validity of St. Thomas' orders should be relatively simple. A good two-months research should exhaust the subject, but in the meantime the twelve-year-old has come out with this one:

"Mother, where did our Lord get the clothes He was wearing when He appeared after His Resurrection? The soldiers raffled off His old ones, and He was naked in the shroud!"

Don't think I'm making this up to be funny. It all happened only last week, and it keeps on happening. I've learned, what's more, that if you ever answer offhand, you'll wish you hadn't. I maintain nobody can be sure he knows anything until he's been able to explain it to a child. This morning the five-year-old asked me why God never gave the devil a second chance. Ha! How would you explain in one syllable words the simple nature of pure spirits? Please write, care of the publisher.)

Last week she cocked her head on one side and asked, "Mother, when God died on the cross, He was holding it up wasn't He?"

"Yes, of course," I said.

"Well, I didn't think just the *dirt* could do it," she replied. "It's a mystery!" I offered quickly, hoping she wouldn't go on.

Our library shelves groan with books on prayer, insects, moral, ascetical and dogmatic theology, birds, Scripture, history, astronomy, handwriting analysis, and aviation, all because I can't answer the children's questions. I must say I'm at one with Chesterton, who advised "A Slightly Older Baby" to:

Stand up and keep your childishness:

Read all the parents' screeds and scriptures;
But don't believe in anything
That can't be told in colored pictures!

If it's true, it'll be awesomely simple. That's why you have to be so careful when you're a doctor of the Church. And what parent isn't? By teaching doctrine badly he perverts it; by not teaching it at all he denies his faith. The terrible words of Christ, which the liturgy appropriates to the Common of Doctors, fall heavily on every Catholic parent:

> For amen I say to you, till heaven and earth pass away, not one jot or one tittle shall be lost from the Law till all things have been accomplished. Therefore whoever does away with one of these least commandments, and so teaches men, shall be called least in the kingdom of heaven.

I was asked what a "tittle" was a while back, and before I knew it, I was studying Hebrew. "Now, about St. Thomas. It's true that forgiving sins is part of Holy Orders ... well, but ..."

But what?

(I finally drove thirty miles to ask a theologian.)

No one has the right to tamper with the truths of Scripture, by adding or subtracting; but with young children this is so fearfully easy to do. They're so trusting, so quick to believe. How easy it is to fill their minds with claptrap in the name of religion! This is true especially when telling them Bible stories in our own words. To them the little gray donkey ridden by our Lady on the flight into Egypt assumes the status of defined dogma, although Scripture never mentions him at all and perhaps he never existed. (Maybe our Lady rode a camel.) Any young American will tell you with absolute certainty that there were three Wise Men, although Scripture never tells us that either. The Eastern Church feels that there were in fact twelve Magi, but she'll never convince a little westerner whose mind has already been cluttered and closed to any fresh air, by adults whose own approach to Scripture has always been largely sentimental.

Not long ago I ran across a current catechetical manual wherein is paraphrased the story of Jesus in the Temple. It was with some alarm I read that Jesus, on being asked by his parents what He had been up to, answered in words to the effect that He had been teaching the doctors about God! Not only is this not in the Gospel text at all, but it's absolutely contrary to the message of the story, which stresses the obedience and respect of the divine Boy towards His elders. Actually we are told only that He listened to the Doctors and asked questions.

Being questioned by them in turn, He amazed them by the evident wisdom and grace He unconsciously displayed by His answers. There's no evidence that He presumed at His age to teach His elders anything, let alone brag to His parents about it!

Adults learn to watch out for pious fiction, based on superficial understanding, in "meditations" on Scripture, but innocent children can't be expected to defend themselves against this kind of fakery, call it artistic embroidery or what you will. Until they do, the only remedy is to supply them only with the naked truth, and this can be done only by doctors who never stray too far from it themselves. The responsibility on the lowly doctor who has to learn as he goes along can be pretty burdensome, as I can tell you.

"Preach the word, be urgent in season, out of season," commands the Epistle from the Mass for Doctors of the Church. "Reprove, entreat, rebuke, with all patience and teaching," never letting up for a minute.

Mary, Queen of Doctors, help us.

"You are the salt of the earth," insists the Gospel of the Mass for Doctors, 'but if the salt loses its strength, what shall it be salted with?" You ignorant doctors!

The monks of Maredsous suggest that the "earth" in this analogy is actually potter's clay, and that the "salt" refers to the indispensable salt glaze which must be applied to clay to turn out a first class ceramic. Unglazed clay: natural man; glazed clay: the Christian. Obviously, if the salt's no good, the vessel can't have a proper finish.

How did I happen to run across this delightful interpretation? Well, I suppose the children asked me, and one thing led to another. Somebody has to put a glaze on those kids!

The New Lesbia

CHAPTER 6

L ESBIA est puella. Lesbia is a girl.

There's no use arguing to the contrary. When my first year Latin grammar made a point of this in the very first lesson, I accepted the basic postulate quietly. By this time I had learned not to quibble about two plus two making four, no matter what shape that well-worn formula might take.

I explored Latin further than I did arithmetic, however, and when I began reading the lyric poets there was—not calculus—but Catullus. Catullus led to Sappho, and Sappho led to the amazing discovery that not only was Lesbia a *puella*, but a *puella* might be a lesbian! Semantics, I soon saw, had possibilities all its own, and higher education could lead to almost anything, if you weren't careful.

Sappho, who was herself a lesbian if only because she lived on Lesbos, ran a very advanced school for girl poets on that fabled isle. I gather she fell into the same temptation so many modern educators fall into: she organized the curriculum along lines identical with the boys' academies. This pedagogical error isn't specifically what got Sappho hauled before the magistrates, but it's nonetheless a related aspect of the crime of female homosexuality for which the poetess was examined.

Now shorn of practically all geographical connotations, the beautiful word *lesbian* has become for most of us today no more than a literary euphemism for lady perverts. Generally, it applies to women who have simply given in all the way to one of woman's most morbid inclinations, the desire to be a man. The more obvious ones are given to exceedingly short haircuts and affect neckties and man-tailored tweeds. These by no means easily detected and who, the authorities agree, may be the most numerous and the most dangerous both to themselves and to young *puellae* with like incipient proclivities.

Not that there's anything essentially unfeminine about envying men or learning their tricks. In this world, a man is definitely the thing to be.

They get the space ships; the women get the kitchens. When the kitchens are put into space ships, women will go into orbit too, but probably not until then. That's how it is.

The holy Perpetua, whom the Church remembers every day in the Canon of the Mass, was granted a vision of her martyrdom to take place the next day in the sports arena in Carthage. She sees herself pitted against her opponent, the devil, who appears in the form of a brawny, ugly Egyptian. She says, believe it or not, "I became a man; my fans began to rub me down with oil according to fighting custom." The Egyptian tackled her, and she was thrown into the air, landing on her back, so we know wrestling hasn't changed much since the year 203. She then reports, "But when I saw the fight was going to drag on, I put my hands together, fingers interlocking, and I grabbed his head, and he fell on his face, and I stamped on his head!"

I'm no expert on visions, but I know the experts all allow a strong subjective element in them. All I can say is, if the aristocratic and well-educated Perpetua knew enough to have a vision of the hold she just described, she was a tomboy. She had two brothers, and I'll bet she had had lots of practice. Perpetua, however, was no lesbian, but a real young woman, as the other parts of her story amply prove.

Some years ago, I happened to be motoring peacefully along an Italian road above the Mediterranean, when suddenly I became aware that the traffic seemed to be passing me at unparalleled speed. Wham! Whoom! One after another several low-slung vehicles, whose drivers for some reason all sported enormous crash-helmets, would appear for a split second in the rear-view mirror only to disappear as suddenly from sight in front of me on two wheels around a hairpin turn.

Hugging my side in a world gone mad, I soon realized I must have gotten mixed up in a practice run of nothing less than the deadly and impending *Mille Miglia*. Don't ask me how I get into these situations; I don't know. I do know, however, from reading the papers that this international breakneck racing event kills participants and spectators with equal abandon. I later learned that this particular event that year obliterated a record number of fourteen bystanders who leaned too far forward. Apparently just watching the cars go by fires even the most phlegmatic pedestrian into all sorts of daredevils stunts of his own, tempting death by touching, if possible, the wheeled projectiles as they roar by.

I confess it's catching. Suddenly I felt my tired blood veritably boil with a wild surge to speed up and join in. Try as I would, though, it was no use. I wasn't driving a super-charged Ferrari. To speak plainly, I was in a rented Fiat of four cylinders, which was just nicely making it over the steeper grades. As a matter of fact, I wasn't even driving, because my husband wouldn't let me. He was. To top off the whole revealing situation, I was pregnant, my shoes were off, and there were three helpless children in the back seat. This, I keep telling myself ever since, is Woman's Way.

Fiat! Fiat! Fiat mihi secundum verbum tuum!

Thank God for puns and Scripture at moments like these! Thank God for Mary.

Thank God for God.

I've known women who never at any time in their lives ever wanted to be anything but girls and grow up and get married and have babies, cook, darn socks quietly and keep house. These women have been my envy and admiration for about as long as I can remember, and the present volume wasn't written for them. They are hopelessly well-adjusted and must live in a kind of nirvana. According to my private statistics, gathered from female cronies over some forty years, however, I strongly suspect they're the ideal minority, beyond segments of housewives of my generation will tell the pollsters quite otherwise.

"I didn't mind being a girl so much," one reminisced to me just the other day, "if only being a girl didn't mean never being allowed to do the things boys did!" She's the mother of four. If I know her, too, she's a wing-ding on a hairpin road.

"I use my M.A. in economics to do the marketing!"

"I used to cry myself to sleep night after night," another confided, "because I was a girl. I wanted to hitch-hike, like my brother did, and serve on the Altar." (She's the mother of five, so far.)

I too am the mother of five. As I recall, the first time I realized it might be better to be a boy was when I met up with a roughneck called Heinie. He was built like a small truck; he wouldn't do anything I told him to; and I discovered to my horror that I couldn't lick him. Until I was ten, I could batter down most any boy my own age and weight, and difference in sex seemed utterly irrelevant. After Heinie I began to suspect the worst, and by sweet sixteen I had faced my growing physical inferiority head on. By head on I mean I was betting on my intellectual superiority, determined to outsmart a sex whose only asset seemed to be muscles. This, it seems, ended in marriage, the *Mille Miglia* in a rented Fiat, and so on.

Without piling up a redundance of all too plentiful evidence, I think I can safely speak for a great number of women today when I say that woman's day can often be concluded with the heartfelt cry of the Psalmist in the Lenten Introit said during Passion Week: "Have mercy on me, O God, for man hath trodden me underfoot: all the day long he hath afflicted me!"

He hath sped past me in a high-powered, souped-up Ferrari. He hath been promoted to the supervisor's job I should have had by rights if I had been a man, or maybe he hath just run off to sail a boat because it's the Sabbath and time to recreate, and left me the dinner dishes. Scripture does indeed say "the Sabbath was made for man," and sometimes it takes a lot of faith to believe it was made for woman too.

What keeps us going when these negative thoughts take hold? Certainly it's not the compliments we get. Here's one man's opinion of us:

> You need only look at the way in which she is formed, to see that a woman is not meant to undergo great labor, whether of the mind or of the body. ... The nobler and more perfect a thing is, the later and slower it is in arriving at maturity. A man reaches the maturity of his reasoning powers and mental faculties hardly before the age of twenty-eight; a woman, at eighteen. And then, too, in the case of woman, it is only reason of a sort-very niggard in its dimensions. That is why women remain children their whole life long; never seeing anything but what is quite close to them, cleaving to the present moment, taking appearance for reality, and preferring trifles to matters of the first importance. ... They are dependent, not upon strength, but upon craft; and hence their instinctive capacity for cunning, and their ineradicable tendency to say what is not true.
>
> ... It is only the man whose intellect is clouded by his sexual impulses that could give the name fair sex to that under-sized, narrow-shouldered, broad-hipped and short-legged race; for the whole beauty of the sex is bound up with this impulse. Instead of calling them beautiful, there would be more warrant for describing women as the unesthetic sex. Neither for music, nor for poetry, nor for fine art, have they really and truly any sense or susceptibility; it is mere mockery if they make a pretense of it in order to assist their endeavor to please. Hence, as a result of this, they are incapable of taking a purely objective interest in anything; and the reason of it seems to me to be as follows: A man tries to acquire direct mastery of things, either by understanding them or by forcing them to do his will. But a woman is always and everywhere reduced to obtaining this mastery indirectly, namely, through a man ....
>
> And you cannot expect anything else of woman if you consider that the most distinguished intellects among the whole sex have never managed to produce a single achievement in the fine arts that is really great, genuine, and original; or given to the world any work of permanent value in any sphere. ... They never get beyond a subjective point of view.

These kind words are Schopenhauer's. I keep picking on him, because in him the negative subjectivity that he accuses women of reached about as low as it could, and the extent of his influence in modern times has been as widespread as incredible. In glancing over the foregoing, it helps to remember that his own mother rejected him cruelly, once even kicking him downstairs. A lady author too emancipated to descend to the exigencies of domesticity, she provides an important clue to her son's evident hatred for women. After one brief, youthful try at love, he elected to spend the remainder of his maturity in a boardinghouse, spinning a whole philosophical system around his own pessimism.

We can't blame it all on Schopenhauer, however. To give this tortured soul his due, what he voices about women is simply a vengeful overstatement of the estimation women are so often forced to entertain of themselves, and which subconsciously they have absorbed from time immemorial with the very air they breathe. The sage Aristotle, who didn't mind ranking Sappho with Homer as a poet, no doubt did so because he considered her as good as a man, judged by masculine standards. It's a matter of record he never looked on women generally as anything but unfinished men, useful for reproduction. Inasmuch as he even went so far as to affirm they had less teeth than men, we might be led to suppose he never got close enough to a woman to look her in the mouth, but no matter. All this propaganda has had its effect nonetheless. Women-disparagers and suffragettes alike rarely speak from unbiased firsthand knowledge.

Lest you think, however, that only twisted personalities and unbelieving pagans dwell on female inferiority, I must let you in on what St. Cyril of Alexandria thought of us:

> Cyril insists—often enough to be at once monotonous and indicative of a consistent outlook—that woman is inferior to man. Frequently he contents himself with the sheer enunciation of his thesis: man is superior, woman inferior; man holds the chief place, woman is subject and subordinate; man has the greater honor and glory, even before God, whereas woman is of less esteem. But on occasion Cyril bares a few details. The inferiority is not purely a question of physical size or physical strength. What is more momentous, woman falls short of man in "natural ability." She has not the strength to achieve the virtue of which the male is capable. She is of imperfect intelligence. Unlike her male complement, she is dull-witted, slow to learn, unprepared to grasp the difficult and the supernatural; for her mind is a soft, weak, delicate thing.
>
> Briefly, "the female sex is ever weak in mind and body." Moreover, there is a softness in woman which precludes vigorous purpose. She is a

peaceable creature, with an aversion to war-apparently a regrettable characteristic. She is timid and cowardly, naturally enervated, easily dispirited, with a penchant for insatiable grief and unrestrained tears. "Woman is a twittering, loquacious creature, with a gift for contriving deceit." She is enamored of honor and show, of dress and golden ornaments; she revels in the body's beauty,"[3] and so on.

There's a wide choice of quotations similar to this one throughout history, ancient or modern, ecclesiastical or secular. In later times Montaigne (I think it was) remarked that a woman thinking was like a dog walking on its hind legs. Said he, one didn't wonder that she did it so badly, only that she did it at all! Nietzsche lumped together "shopkeepers, Christians, cows, women, Englishmen and other democrats." Where we live, the worst thing the little boy next door can call another little boy is "girl!"

This is a sad state of affairs, but woman's salvation depends precisely on her recognizing that all these unpleasant gibes are substantially true. In the exterior world, the fallen world of sense, reason, and authority, woman is inferior to man; and even the great St. Teresa admitted in her *Autobiography* that just being a woman was "enough to make my sails droop." After the fall of Adam, Eve suffered terribly, not only sharing Adam's punishment, but bearing a special one of her own:

> I will make great your distress in childbearing;
> In pain shall you bring forth children;
> For your husband shall be your longing,
> Though he have dominion over you (*Gen. 3:16*).

Her great distress brought her even lower than man, whose "glory" she had been created to be. With the withdrawal of God's stabilizing grace, her more delicate, more spiritual, infinitely more complicated nature disintegrated more cruelly than did Adam's, which was more simply constructed. Her perceptive finesse, rich and diffuse emotions, her lavish need to spend herself dwindled into "a gift for contriving deceit," softness of mind, loquaciousness and an alarming penchant for tears at inopportune times. What very great distress!

From the depths, our Lady cried nevertheless for us, "My soul magnifies the Lord, and my spirit rejoices in God my savior, because he has regarded the *lowliness* of his handmaid!" Again, when she

---

[3] *The Image of God in Man according to St. Cyril of Alexandria,* Walter J. Burghardt, S.J., Woodstock College Press, pp. 128-9

praises God because "He ... has *exalted the lowly,* I know that as a woman she knew lowliness as no man can ever know it. If you're a woman this doesn't have to be spelled out to you, When God exalted the lowly, he exalted among others—women. Even Schopenhauer concedes this, dubbing reverence for women "that highest product of Teutonico-Christian stupidity." To women is granted the most powerful-with-God position in the whole universe: the last place! No mere man can ever dislodge her from that, unless she's fool enough to abandon it.

Reporting on her trip to Rome as a young girl, the little Therese of Lisieux remarks with wry but wistful humor:

> I still can't understand why it's so easy for a woman to get excommunicated in Italy! All the time, people seemed to be saying: "No, you mustn't go here, you mustn't go there; you'll be excommunicated." There's no respect for us poor wretched women anywhere. And yet you'll find the love of God much commoner among women than among men, and the women during the Passion showed much more courage than the Apostles, exposing themselves to insult, and wiping Our Lord's face. I suppose he lets us share the neglect he himself chose for his lot on earth; in heaven, where the last will be first, we shall know more about what God thinks. (*Autobiography of St. Therese*, translated by Ronald Knox, p. 176.)

This exaltation of women began in a little town called Nazareth, when one of them accepted woman's lot in the name of all women. "Be it done to me according to thy word," she said.

Believe it or not, the same St. Cyril who held the gloomy views just quoted found them not at all inconsistent with his spirited defense of this young woman as Mother of God, *Theotokos,* at the Council of Ephesus. Defending this dogma against the Nestorian heresy, he produced what some consider the greatest Marian sermon of antiquity. We can hardly believe our ears as he rings out,

> Hail, from us, Mary, Mother of God, majestic treasure of the whole world, the lamp unquenchable, the crown of virginity, the sceptre of orthodoxy, the indestructible temple, the dwelling of the Illimitable, Mother and Virgin, through whom He is called in the Gospels "Blessed who cometh in the name of the Lord." Hail, thou who didst contain Him in thy holy virginal womb, who cannot be contained; thou through whom the Holy Trinity is glorified and adored throughout the world; through whom heaven rejoices; through whom angels and archangels are glad; through whom devils are put to flight; through whom the tempter-devil fell from heaven; through whom the fallen creature is taken. up into

heaven; through whom all creation, held fast by the madness of idolatry, has come to the knowledge of the truth; through whom holy baptism has come to believers, and the oil of gladness; through whom churches are erected throughout the world; through whom the nations are brought to repentance. And what more shall I say? Through whom the only-begotten Son of God has shone forth, a light "to those who sat in darkness and in the shadow of death"; through whom the Prophets foretold; through whom the Apostles preached salvation to the nations; through whom the dead are raised, and kings reign. (Burghardt, *op. cit.*)

Incredible! Is it possible that one of us "twittering, loquacious creatures with a gift for contriving deceit, weak in mind and body," is actually the indispensable channel for all mankind seeking God? What a surprise for the Schopenhauers! How can this be, since women are so unreliable?

Listen closely. Woman restored by grace is anything but unreliable. She is a new Eve, a new creature entirely, who bears the same relation to the women Aristotle and St. Cyril complained of that the sinner bears to the saint. A woman who twitters now just isn't giving grace free play in her soul. Supernaturalized woman is capable of goals undreamed of by the silly, frivolous Eve who was the rule until these days. All her deplorable foibles are due to be recast into the dazzling jewelry they were meant to be originally:

> All glorious is the king's daughter as she enters;
> Her raiment is threaded with spun gold.
> In embroidered apparel she is born to the king.

"The holier a woman, the more she is a woman," said Leon Bloy. God wills her to love "dress and golden ornaments," when she wears them for Him, and has learned their true significance in eternity. Women make wonderful women. And the most wonderful woman of them all is Mary *Theotokos*, who "takes her place at God's right hand in gold of Ophir," after whom are brought to Him "the virgins of her train." She who lived a lifetime as a housewife at grips with the mystery in herself comes to the defense of her daughters, rising in the world's night to prepare food for her household and give victuals to her maidens (*Prov. 31:15*).

The Aristotles, the Nietzsches, the Schopenhauers and the boys next door—even the great St. Cyrils—can't say anything really true about women without first finding an answer to her gentle, "Behold, henceforth all generations shall call me blessed."

Through her, "the gate that looked toward the east" in Ezechiel's temple, must we all enter into God. God himself took the same route as Man, for didn't we note that "the majesty of the Lord went into the temple by way of the gate that looked to the east?" This is the mystery of woman, a mystery so great, no woman is truly a woman who doesn't partake of it and discover it in herself in some way.

Why *should* she excel men in music, poetry, or the fine arts? These belong to the world of sense. Schopenhauer spoke truly when he remarked men acquire *direct* mastery over these things, and that woman's mastery is *indirect*, because her craft, as we keep insisting, is not primarily things, but mankind itself. Through woman mankind enters into life, be it natural or supernatural. This is her role, and any role less than this for her is a perversion.

The mystic Meister Eckhart, glimpsing the towering heights of spiritual womanhood, drew from it a pattern for all humanity seeking God:

> In order to become fruitful, man must become woman. Woman! This is the noblest word by which the soul may be addressed, and it is much nobler than that of virgin. For man to conceive God in himself is good, and in this predisposition he is virgin. But for God to become fruitful in him is better; for to become fruitful by the gift received is to be grateful for that gift. And the spirit then becomes woman through gratitude which generates anew.[4]

In some mysterious fashion, man's spiritual progress is closely allied to his progressive discovery of woman—the figure par excellence of humanity waiting empty for God, and therefore the figure of the Church and every human soul. Bible readers have on occasion taken exception to our Lord's addressing His Mother as "Woman," but I wonder. In the light of Meister Eckhart's words, do we appreciate the full glory of this title He accorded her, first at the wedding feast at Cana?

Woman!

"What wouldst thou have me do, *Woman*?" These were His exact words. For God asks a woman what she desires of Him, and water becomes wine! Do you think this is inconsequential?

But this is nothing, mere preamble. From the Cross He addresses her again, and says, "Woman, behold thy son!" He makes her a gift of all men, at the same time that He gives her to all men. So too, "Woman,

---

[4] *Traités de Sermons*, Aubier, p. 124, quoted in *Etudes Carmelitaines*, Feb. 1952 by Louis Beirnaert, S.J.

why art thou weeping?" the resurrected Christ asks Mary Magdalen in the early dark of Easter morning (*John 20:15*).

This is a mystery so deep, a destiny so high, that only the simple words He used can possibly express it. They are the $E=mc^2$ of feminine spirituality. Small wonder that poor Eve has trouble grasping this simple formula, let alone living it.

The whole world conspires against her to deny herself. "Be a man!" it says. Just the other day our seventeen-year-old daughter received the highest praise possible from one of her brother's friends. "Gee," he said, "when you play baseball, you're just as good as a BOY! Honest, I mean it!" She was quite overcome at the magnitude of the compliment, having learned by now to take such remarks in the spirit in which they are intended. My own husband, when he wants to accord the supreme accolade to some woman in his office, will say, "Oh, she's as good as any man!"

"Gee, Sappho, when you write poetry, you're just as good as Homer!" was pretty much the way Aristotle put it, only in Greek.

There's just one trouble. Our daughter knows that no matter how fast she pitches to second base, some man will always excel her at it, because being a woman, her arm is hung differently from his. It was never really intended for pitching. It was meant for holding. So too, Sappho was a peerless lyricist who excelled at personal poetry; but she wrote no great epics, the impersonal poetry which was Homer's dish. If she tried, she must have discovered her writing arm was hung differently too.

Without the coordinating power of grace and sound doctrine, natural woman is bound to go astray in man's world. Sometimes there are extremely gross manifestations of her aberrations. As a matter of fact, St. Paul inveighed against the Roman women who "have exchanged the natural use for that which is against nature" (*Rom. 1:26*). He was speaking, among other things, of lesbianism. If we read carefully what precedes this accusation in his Epistle, we find he pronounced this vice to be one of the just consequences of idolatry, and no doubt he had in mind some of the sexual orgies practiced in connection with pagan cults, According to St. Paul, the pagan worship of false images, false values, false goals, lead us into such quite ordinarily. Perversion is in itself a terrible punishment for sin, for turning away from God.

Though St. Paul undoubtedly speaks here of the physical manifestation of this unnatural vice, I do believe the passage can be taken in a higher, more spiritual sense; for lesbianism can be not only physical as among the Greeks, or even psychological as is any virago's, but it can be spiritual. Spiritual lesbians don't wear men's neckties and aren't easily known even to themselves, but they are very dangerous to others precisely because they sometimes propagate their vice without even knowing it's vicious. They betray the world Christ gave them by denying it supernatural life and refusing to nourish it, having "exchanged the natural use for that which is against nature."

A spiritual lesbian (to coin a label) is a woman who tries to reach God the way a man would. She practices in her most intimate relations with the Trinity within her own soul a thoroughly masculine spirituality. As St. Paul noted, this sad state of affairs is a direct result of idolatry—in this case, the worship of man's world, man's values, and envy of man's destiny, which are not for woman in this world and never have been.

We must be careful here. There is strictly speaking only one spirituality for all, be they men, women, children, Englishmen, or democrats. "In Christ Jesus there is no male or female." End and essentials are always the same, but individual tactics vary according to the psychology of the person, and this means they vary definitely according to the person's sex, which is bound to color and qualify the whole personality. If this weren't true, the Church wouldn't allocate liturgical functions according to sex. There would be women priests, and little girls could be altar boys.

Edith Stein explored the idea that sexuality was rooted not primarily in the body, but in the soul. Writing to a feminist friend in 1931, she said:

> That the sex difference is due merely to the body is a statement suspect on several grounds. 1. If *anima forma corporis*, then the physical difference is the indication of the difference of soul. 2. Matter exists for form, not vice versa. This makes it probable that the difference of soul is the primary one. Of course it must be thoroughly examined how far growth into the supernatural can and should be an outgrowing of the natural difference.

Women don't do anything like men. They do things men do—they eat, they sleep, they work and they wear clothes, for instance—but when we examine these actions at their deepest levels, we find they do none of these things quite the same way men do. Women don't eat quite like men, or yawn, or sleep like them. Anyone would agree that both men and women have heads, arms and legs, yet their physiology is obviously different, and they don't dress like men. Interiorly, the differences are even more striking.

Above all, *women don't pray like men*. Their sex differences must be taken into consideration every step of the way, and this is particularly true in the crucial beginnings of the mystical life, where sense still plays so important a part in the incipient intimacy with God. Discerning men can see this. For instance, in *The Man Jesus*, Fr. George Bichlmaier, S.J., notes:

> In the first chapter of St. Luke's Gospel there is recorded for us a woman's prayer. When Mary visited her cousin Elizabeth and saw what the Holy Spirit had wrought in her, she was herself moved by the Holy Spirit, and she broke forth into ecstatic prayer of jubilation to which she gave formal expression in the *Magnificat*. If we compare the two prayers of Jesus with the prayer of Mary, it will at once be obvious that Jesus really prayed in a masculine way, while Mary's prayer is a true expression of her feminine nature.
>
> The author of the *Pater Noster* and the high-priestly prayer begins with a clear, definite orientation of his spirit away from himself to God and objective facts: Our Father who art in Heaven ... Father, the hour is come ...
>
> Then he occupies himself with God: His essence, the sanctification of His name, His glorification, His activity, His kingdom. And even where Christ refers to Himself, He sees himself as one who belongs to God: "Glorify thy Son, so that thy Son may glorify Thee."
>
> The woman prays otherwise. She knows, to be sure, that she is in the presence of God, but her glance appears to be directed to herself. It is of herself that she speaks, of the state and activity of her soul, of God as her Salvation, of the great things He has done for her soul, and of what will be done for her in the future.
>
> In the prayer of the Man Jesus the *thou* and *thine* predominate; in that of the woman the *my* and *me*. The prayer of the man sounds objective, impersonal, sharp, pregnant with thought and directed into the distance; even the purpose of being is touched upon: "This is eternal life; that they may know thee, the only true God, and Jesus Christ, whom thou hast sent." The woman's prayer, on the other hand, is subjective and personal; it is expressive of the mood of her own soul, sees the immediate and the proximate, and is confined to her own experiences. The man speaks of what is to happen, of work and activity: "I have finished the work which thou gavest me to do. ..." The woman concentrates on what she had actually received, on her person, on what God intends to do for her—hers is a concrete approach to prayer. Granted that she, too, speaks of the power and might of God: "His mercy is from generation to generation. ... He hath shown might in his arm. ..." her first thought nevertheless is for what God has done in her. The man, likewise, includes in his prayer his personal desires: "Give us this day our daily bread, forgive us our trespasses ...," "for them do I pray," "all my things are thine, and thine

mine: and I am glorified in them," but only after he has spoken of the great essential, the desire of God and his work of salvation (pp. 90-92).

So women are different. Even at the outset of their spiritual life, women's general attitude towards God is normally more subjective, more immediate, more contemplative, given, of course, enormous degrees of individual variation. This doesn't mean women start out from the Fourth Mansion right off the bat, whereas men have to start from the moat; nor does it mean women are holier than men! This means only that as a sex, their psychology from the beginning is more attuned to the formless intuitive ways of "advanced" prayer than the man who directs them might suspect, especially if he has no experience of advanced prayer himself.

Man has dominion over woman. After the Fall, Eve was no longer worthy, or indeed, capable, of maintaining her equilibrium in the responsible working partnership with man in which she was created. Today he exercises authority over her as a sex, but St. Paul says that there will be an end, "when Christ delivers the kingdom to God the Father when he *does away with all sovereignty, authority, and power (I Cor. 15:24)*. Clearly, authority will no longer be necessary to transfigured and beatified beings, of whom we hope a good proportion will be women! What will be their state?

Well, the Little Flower said quite simply the last will be first, and we might just go along with her. In the Holy Family at Nazareth this was already true in reality, for there the head of the house, St. Joseph, stood last in the supernatural hierarchy of grace, second to his wife, with the Child at the head. We forget only too easily that authority is not so much an honor as a heavy burden, a task borne primarily for the benefit of the governed. In the spiritual life, children rank first, as our Lord taught. Women, who learn from children, I do believe are supposed to come next. Then come men, who can learn much, if they will, from both women and children. I don't expect to go unchallenged here, but I'll state my case!

One of my sons solved the whole baffling problem of female spirituality for me once by exclaiming, "But Mom, women don't need spirituality!" I never suspected the boy knew so much. Mulling it over, I've come to the conclusion that what he said is all too terribly true. To become holy, women need only do what comes naturally in a truly supernatural manner. To reach God, all women have to do is be really women.

This is much harder than it sounds, and the greatest obstacle is women themselves and their appalling ignorance of themselves as a sex. Not taking their feminine nature into consideration, their whole prayer life easily becomes masculinized, objectivized, methodized, perhaps beyond repair. I learned the hard way, myself. I could be wrong, but see what you think: We live and compete in a man's world where feminine virtues are despised and where aggressiveness is the one means to success. A woman gets used to hearing the things Schopenhauer said about her. She concludes she's no good unless she can trample down her nature and be like a man: straight-thinking, objective, tough, unemotional, fast-moving, logical, and *aggressive.* (That's what men tell women about themselves.) Woman's tragedy is that she so often succeeds in this self-mutilation.

There's no danger here for the Marys. The danger is for the women who worship the false gods of the exterior world. They never enter into themselves, daring to be personal as Mary was personal. They never discover that all that Schopenhauer said about them is completely untrue when applied to woman in her native habitat—the interior world of grace. Here all her supposed weaknesses and foibles can become decided advantages. When he asserted that women have never "given to the world any work of permanent value in any sphere," it becomes painfully clear that Herr Schopenhauer was not conversant with the literary output of the mystics. St. Mechtilde, St. Gertrude, St. Catherine or St. Teresa, to mention only a few, might have given him a nasty turn smack in the middle of his thesis!

Most women somehow learn to adapt the spiritual analogies from the Boston Red Sox' last game which retreat masters draw out for them; and they manage to enter into a homely speculation on how good, for instance, fresh fish fried on the banks of Lake Genesareth must have tasted to the Apostles after a hard days seining. Though they may hate baseball, fishing, boats, and outdoor cooking altogether, this kind of adjustment to male metaphor is just a normal part of Woman's Day. Even at the Communion rail, woman is expected to say with the priest, "*Domine, non sum dignus,*" though "*Domine, non sum digna,*" is presumably what she must mean, and what Mother Church, herself, would say. This is relatively superficial and harmless, not worth quibbling about.

Real trouble starts when women try to give lip service to masculine activity on their knees, desperately trying to ape prayer techniques which would effect wonders in the soul of a Jesuit novice, but spell utter disaster for his Aunt Minnie. The astute St. Teresa in a letter to a subordinate, M. Maria de San Jose, Prioress at Seville, counseled her convent to obey their Jesuit directors there "although what they may say may occasionally not be so good for us." Men are men.

Incidentally, nobody was more aware of this difficulty than St. Ignatius himself. When he consolidated his Company, he saw clearly that women had no place in his systematized, rigid organization built on military lines, and he has kept them out to this day. He too learned the hard way, by association with the famous Isabelle Roser and her two companions. Affiliated with his Company for two years, these ladies eventually involved the saint in a lawsuit, but they left a wealth of extremely valuable experience behind them to compensate him for his troubles.

In dealing with woman, her proper sexuality must be taken into consideration every moment. In many ways she is more bound up in sexuality than is a man. It colors and shapes her whole life, especially if she's a married woman. Married or not, however, the role of woman in the sex act can be the key to understanding almost everything about her. For instance, a woman doesn't normally reach any objective by striking out at it the way a man does. She makes it hers by *encompassing* it. This is her method in the act of love, and it's her basic technique in all situations.

It illustrates the exasperating way in which she drives a car. Anyone watching a woman driver's roundabout progress towards a destination knows she was made to travel in circles. Her conversation follows the same pattern, whereby every subject must be circled as many times as the walls of Jericho before the walls crumble and she gets to the point. Again, as in the sex act, she's slow. It's fatal to rush a woman in or out of the simplest interview if you want her to tell you anything important,

The reason she acts like this is that woman, as we've said all along, is by nature contemplative. She's made to give by receiving. She has by nature all the attitudes towards God that men contemplatives must learn sometimes with very great difficulty. She is less inclined to acquire virtues one by one by dint of aggressive ascetic effort as a man does. She would rather creep up on them and make them hers in the course of the much larger occupation—attracting God. Men use virtues as they would use their muscles to reach an objective. Women use virtues as they would use jewelry, to attract God as they would capture a man's attention. A spiritually advanced woman, like St. Gertrude, understands well the mystique of clothes and jewelry. Her writings show, furthermore, how God bestows virtues on the soul He loves as a lover gives diamond bracelets.

St. Gertrude also understands that a diamond bracelet a girl has to buy for herself by dint of hard work isn't as precious to her as the one her lover gives her for pure love! Women find the diffuse, grateful, simple look at God more natural to them than any formal, laborious mental exercise performed in His presence, call it meditation or what you will. They know how to wait, pondering in the heart for God's lead; they usually prefer to listen to Him rather than to tell Him about Himself.

Women, driving themselves to make too frequent examinations of conscience, very beneficial to the objective sex (which hates to look inside), usually get nothing more for their pains than a chronic case of scruples, with which to plague the life out of any number of long-suffering confessors. Long-drawn-out particular examens and constantly renewed resolutions on inessential points are the morbid results of interiority gone wrong. They are the special pitfalls of an interior sex which, paradoxically enough, for all its vague intuitions has a genius for details.

Their sense of the immediate, their innate distrust of the purely theoretical make them invaluable in factories, research laboratories, and offices the world over. Gone astray, this trait can strangle the most efficient organization in neatly but securely tied red tape. Ask any man who has to struggle with this problem at home or office. In her house a woman can be a demon housekeeper, never really living in it. That's because she's always cleaning it. She can't stand children, because they make such a mess. Her husband is an unbearable problem. All she can see is dirt and crooked pictures. In her spiritual house, she can't leave off scouring her conscience long enough to let God in the front door.

In other words women have the faults of their virtues. "Incapable of taking a purely objective interest in anything," they fall easily into analyzing others by the light of their own consciences. Endowed with the intuitive insight into the inarticulate that makes them wonders with small children, they can spot the faults of others without even trying. It's an occupational hazard of being a woman.

Like all contemplatives, they must draw everything, even God, into their personal here and now. Mary did this in very fact at the Annunciation, and for many years in Bethlehem, Egypt, and Nazareth, before giving Him to the world. Women are "enamored of honor and show, of dress and golden ornaments and reveling in the body's beauty," because they can't help drawing even material things to their persons. Likewise, preening and adorning themselves interiorly, delighting only too easily in their supposed virtues, they can decorate their interior houses with an awful lot of vain, but flashy and stylish junk!

Priests (God prosper them) must be men. Unless they have progressed spiritually themselves to the point where they pray supernaturally the way women pray naturally, they can't be expected to understand these psychological niceties as a woman would. Listen to the delicacy with which St. Teresa hints at this problem. Speaking of mystical favors, she says:

> In the beginning it is wise to communicate your experience, under the seal of confession, to an experienced priest, for learned men ought to give us light, or you might have recourse to *a very spiritual woman. If you cannot find such a woman,* a learned man is better; if possible, a person both learned and spiritual. (Italics mine.)

After a very high mystical favor indeed—the visit of an archangel who tells her she is to be the mother of the Messias—our Lady runs to the hill country *in haste* to communicate her news and share her cousin's joy. Following the angers hint, she confides, not in the educated priest Zachary, but in his wife Elizabeth who for this eventuality was "filled with the Holy Spirit" (*Luke 1:41*).

Though spiritual direction as such must inhere in the nature of the priesthood, spiritual *counseling* has never been its exclusive duty. That many souls today consider it so is an unfortunate misapplication of monastic practices never at any time intended for the generality of Christians. No wonder there's a shortage of spiritual directors. If only priests could give spiritual counsel, every other man on earth would have to be ordained to fill the need!

In practical problems whose nature only a woman could be conversant with, only a woman can advise. In her highly equivocal position, our Lady well knew this, and Scripture reveals that to supply her need, a woman counselor inspired by the Holy Spirit was duly provided her. St. Paul, who we know was very firm about keeping women quiet in church, and wouldn't have them teaching men, nevertheless clearly defined their role as counselors and teachers of other women younger than themselves. He tells Titus to encourage elderly women "to train the younger women to be wise, to love their husbands and their children, to be discreet, chaste, domestic, gentle, obedient to their husbands, so that the word of God be not reviled" (*2:4-5*). Much of this lies clearly in the realm of spiritual counseling.

Not long ago in a diocesan newspaper I ran across a column in which a Reverend Monsignor attempted to advise a mother writing in to him concerning an acute child-feeding problem! That he heroically tried to answer her thorny question has led me to recognize that the American hierarchy is being driven to sacrifice itself way above and beyond the call of duty, being all things to all men, and women too.

There are all kinds of child-feeding problems, some of them spiritual, which are the special province of an enlightened laity equipped to cope with them at ground level. Let's not expect the impossible of our busy clergy, whose special contribution must always be theological and liturgical. The business world, the marriage bed, and the nursery yield problems for which theology must indeed be developed by them, but these are specifically lay terrain, to be worked by the layman himself if he is to leaven society as he should.

Women have their own special problems. St. Teresa was just now discussing the difficulties besetting a woman very advanced in prayer, in fact, in the Sixth Mansion. Some women, after all, do advance this far, and when they do they advance as women, not as men, Blessed with an extraordinarily receptive psyche as compared to man, woman can find her spiritual life taking turns most men would consider their bounden duty to pooh-pooh at all costs, lest she fall into delusion and lose her soul. By male standards, this diagnosis might be only too correct; by female standards, it could be simply finding fault with the normal.

Speaking of high mystical favors, St. Teresa has this to say:

> Experience is necessary throughout, so also is a spiritual director; for when the soul has reached this point, there are many matters which must be referred to the director. If, after seeking such a one, the soul cannot find him, our Lord will not fail that soul, seeing that He has not failed me, who am what I am. (She's St. Teresa!) They are not many, I believe, who know by experience so many things, and without experience it is useless to treat a soul at all, for nothing will come of it, save only trouble and distress. But our Lord will take this also into account, and for that reason it is always best to refer the matter to the director.
>
> I have already more than once said this, and even all I am saying now ... but I do see that it is of great importance, *particularly to women*, that they should go to their confessor, and that he should be a man of experience therein. *There are many more women than men to whom our Lord gives these graces*; I have heard the holy friar (St.) Peter of Alcantara say so, and indeed, I know it myself. He used to say that women made greater progress in this way than men did: and he gave excellent reasons for his opinion, all in favor of women; but there is little necessity for repeating them here (*Life of St. Teresa*, Ch. XL, 12).

Oh, dear St. Teresa, how we wish you had! After the uncomplimentary truths we hear about ourselves every day, it wouldn't hurt to cheer us up a little and give us hope!

Women, alas, aren't much led by fear and censure, but they respond almost idiotically to love and encouragement, like all people with deep-seated inferiority complexes. Frankly, I think we might be preached more Transfiguration and given less Hell. Man wants, and expects, to achieve. Woman wants, and hopes, to be loved. I learned arithmetic not because I had any respect for the subject, but mostly because I wanted the teacher to like me, and so will most women become saints because they want God to love them, not primarily because they're afraid of Him, or particularly want to possess sanctity.

It does little good to shout at women. This goes over big with men. Shout at a man and call him names, and he'll probably follow you right over the battlements; shout at a woman, and she may shout back, but inside she cringes psychologically. She may be kept out of mortal sin this way, but she will make no real progress spiritually. She would have to be a masochist to respond at all to harshness in religion. This is my opinion, but please don't think I made it up out of whole cloth. As a mother of both girls and boys, who started out thinking all children in a family should be treated alike—my head was crammed with behaviorist psychology—I soon found out that from the womb boys and girls are different. Spank a boy good and hard and he may behave for a full forty-eight hours; spank a girl injudiciously, and her complicated inner mechanism will give her and you trouble for days, maybe years. (I suppose you realize that I generalize dangerously throughout this chapter; but I confidently expect you to make allowances all along for inevitable exceptions and the vast degrees of individual difference.)

Shouting is a form of brutality a man can enjoy, or at least take in stride, like friendly wrestling; but with a woman it's likely to awaken an unhappy past memory of some other brutality she is almost bound to have suffered at the hands of some man at one time or another in the course of her life. It may have been no more than an extra hard spanking from a father who didn't know his own strength, or some cruel teasing from an older brother, or some sexual mistreatment endured in marriage, but whatever it was, it's best not brought into the prayer-life. Against brutality women have no way of fighting back unless they turn vicious. Even Nietzsche allowed that one can never be gentle enough with women.

No man was ever so gentle toward women as the Christ. He shouted at the Pharisees. We know He shouted at St. Peter on one occasion, even calling him Satan; and He certainly shouted at the other Apostles when the showed themselves especially thick-headed or lacking in faith. At women He never shouted.

His "What wouldst thou have me do, Woman?" at Cana seems to have been addressed to all womankind. Her power over Him is such, she shouldn't waste it asking for trifles!

Twice He raised men from the dead at the sight of women's tears. "Don't cry," He said to the bereaved mother at Nairn; and when He saw Mary weeping over her dead brother Lazarus He "groaned in spirit and was troubled," and wept with her. He defended the Magdalene from the contempt of Simon the Pharisee and even from the reproaches of her own sister Martha. He commended a poor widow once who put two mites into the Temple treasury, who "out of her want has put in all that she had to live on."

For the weaker sex He seems always to have had the kind of soft-hearted compassion that is evoked by the sight of fallen grandeur. Knowing so well as man the kind of creature He meant to create as God, He well knew her propensity to give everything, whenever she gave at all. To the adulterous woman who gave everything to the point of breaking God's Law, He said only, "Neither will I condemn thee. Go thy way, and from now on sin no more" (*John 8:11*).

Not that He wasn't stern with women when occasion demanded. He gave the Syro-Phoenician woman a pretty stiff test with His "It is not fair to take the children's bread and to cast it to the dogs"— meaning her. We gather He refused to speak to His own mother and relatives one time it spelled interference with His preaching, nor did He neglect to elicit an embarrassing public testimonial to God's glory from the woman He cured of hemorrhage. Then, too, He squelched Mrs. Zebedee's all too human ambitions for her sons in no uncertain terms.

As far as we know, the only women's group our Lord ever addressed as such were those He saw crying at the sight of Him on the way to Golgotha. Stopping to console them, He gives them the hard-headed advice women need most, exhorting them to rise above mere feeling and come to grips with the larger issues. "Daughters of Jerusalem," He says, "do not weep for me, but weep for yourselves and your children. For behold days are coming in which men will say, 'Blessed are the barren, and the wombs that never bore, and breasts that never nursed'" (*Luke 23:28-29*).

Our Lord never belittled woman's task in the world. Neither did He ever insult women's intelligence, treating them as micro-men; but His approach to women was never the same as to men. His approach to women was, is, and always will be immediately personal. When He wishes to reveal Himself as Messias to the learned Pharisee Nicodemus, He begins in an objective vein. As if opening an impersonal theological discussion, He postulates a premise: "Amen,

amen, I say to thee, unless a man be born again, he cannot see the kingdom of God." Only later does He strike the personal note with Nicodemus: "Thou art a teacher in Israel and dost not know these things?" This is the way one deals with men.

The Samaritan woman, on the other hand, to whom our Lord made a similar messianic declaration, He greets immediately with a request for a small personal service. "Give me to drink," He asks.

She does so, and there ensues a conversation on a very personal level indeed—all about her love life. In the course of it, she comes close to sassing this unknown Rabbi who talks to strange women, and Samaritans at that! After a good deal of palaver, our Lord manages to lead her to a more objective view, telling her that "the hour is coming, and is now here, when the true worshippers will worship in spirit and in truth. For the Father also seeks such to worship Him. God is spirit, and they who worship Him must worship in spirit and in truth."

Notice how, even though objectively stated, the emphasis is always on interiority and on the person. And our Lord ends on the personal note, too, with the astounding, "I who speak with thee am He"—the Messias! Nicodemus was never told so bluntly, so immediately, or so mystically, but led to the same conclusion by way of reason.

Surely there can never be a spiritual director like our Lord, and as St. Teresa said "If after seeking one, the soul cannot find him, our Lord will not fail that soul!" During His life on earth He expected the very best of women, even the bad ones, and I'm afraid He still does. On the way to Calvary He had reason to admire their dogged loyalty in the face of disaster after the men had deserted Him. As the Little Flower painted out, only Veronica found the courage to wipe the blood and perspiration from His face in the presence of His enemies. A man would have had better sense. Even today, wherever faith totters, women are still the last to leave His sacramental Presence in the church.

The giant Samson yielded the secret of his great strength only to the wheedling Dalila, and like His prototype our Lord seems equally prone to sharing His deepest secrets with the weaker sex. According to the account of P. Pedro Ibanez, St. Teresa once asked our Lord, "Are there no other people, especially men and persons of learning, who, if Thou didst speak to them, would do this that Thou commandest me far better than I, who am so evil?"

And our Lord is said to have replied, "Nay, the men and the persons of learning will not fit themselves to commune with Me, and so I come, in need, yet rejected by them, to seek feeble women to whom I can speak freely and with whom I can discuss My business."

As with the Samaritan, He counts on their highly developed capacity for blind faith, their immediate receptivity to the unexplainable. "Blessed is she who has believed," said Elizabeth of Mary. The same angel Gabriel had indeed appeared to both Mary and Zachary. Mary believed him, though she asked how his prophecy would come about.

"How shall this happen?" she inquired, quite sure that it would happen.

The man Zachary, on the other hand, expressed an all too reasonable, but nevertheless culpable doubt, for which he was punished by dumbness.

"How shall I know this?" he asked, meaning *how do I know for sure this is true?* He wanted proof. That's a man for you, and it explains why both angels and women so often find them exasperating.

God-made-man showed Himself first to a woman at His birth on earth; it was to women that He showed Himself first at His Resurrection. One of these women, the Magdalene, ran to tell the men about it right away. "I have seen the Lord," she panted breathlessly, "and these things He said to me."

Naturally, the men didn't believe her or Joanna or Mary, the mother of James, or the "other women who were with them," who were repeating the same tall tale. "But this tale seemed to them to be nonsense, and they did not believe the women," reports St. Luke, because women are notoriously gullible. They never take the trouble to examine solid evidence. They just get excited.

Well, you can't be too careful. As St. Cyril said, women have "a gift for contriving deceit," and are unreliable as witnesses at best, being so twittery. If Eve hadn't believed that serpent so easily, we would all have been saved a great deal of trouble, you might argue.

St. Augustine takes a happier view. His eyes always fixed on the Mother of God, he states:

> Because man fell through the female sex, he is restored by the same sex. Because a virgin brought forth Christ, a woman announced His resurrection. By a woman came death, by a woman, life. ... A woman handed the poison to the man who was to be deceived. A woman hands salvation to the man to be restored. A woman, by bringing forth Christ, compensates for the sin of the man deceived by woman. Hence, also women were the first to announce to the Apostles that Christ had risen.

After seeing the empty tomb for himself, St. Peter still just "went away wondering." St. Thomas wouldn't believe the story even after St. Peter and the other men vouched for it. As I say, that's men!

Just the same, though, our Lord *did* rise from the dead. You can believe it or not, as you please.

Only, if you're a woman, it's easier.

Cherchez la Femme

CHAPTER 7

A WOMAN can spend a lifetime trying to get a little attention. Having learned that no man can look at two things at once, she puts shiny, jiggly jewelry in both ears so he'll have to look into her eyes rather than risk strabismus. She dominates social events by sheer shock, setting on her head hats which may be unfashionable, but never overlooked. The antics that women have to go through to get noticed are appalling. I read somewhere that Cuban women go so far as to chain click-beetles on their best dresses. A sort of jumbo firefly, this beetle can be depended on to give off a very strong green light; but, without dallying in the latent traffic symbolism which may lurk here, I think it's safe to say that Cuban women probably get no more real attention than the rest of us.

Any occasional or superficial success to the contrary, woman inevitably remains the hidden sex. It's not good, says Scripture, for man to be without her, and though he seldom is, he might think so at times, for like the swallowed vitamin, women have a way of disappearing from sight the very moment their influence becomes most potent and pervasive. *Cherchez la femme*, say the French, whenever some man does something totally beyond reason, whether it's setting off the Trojan War or biting into the only fruit in the whole Garden of Eden that happens to be forbidden.

Nobody ever says *Cherchez l'homme*, because a man is always pretty much right where you can get at him. Believe it or not, this often masquerades as "male supremacy," and anybody who doesn't believe in male supremacy hasn't studied grammar seriously. Have you ever noticed how women can disappear in the plainest sentence whenever there's a man in there with them? I'll try to show what I mean.

Many languages aren't as sexless as English—which hardly bothers with male and female genders, preferring to consider most everything neuter—but somehow they all bow to male supremacy in one way or another. The romance languages, for instance, have male words and female words. In France you put *LE crayon* on *LA table*. In France all cats aren't just cats, either, as English might lead us to believe they are in England. In France some are *chats* and others are *chattes*, depending on whether they're toms or the other. Toms are duly referred to as *ils*, females as *elles*.

So far so good. The French, you'll say, have understood such things since before the troubadours,. and are noted for their unwavering, courtly deference to the gentle sex.

Oh?

See what happens when the Frenchman doesn't happen to know the sex of these cats, or wants to refer to cats of both sexes at once. When he wants to say they meow, doesn't he say *ILS miaulent*, using the masculine plural pronoun? Even an Englishman doesn't go that far. He says *they* indiscriminately, which could be male, female, neuter, or any grades in between for all he cares. (I purposely overlook the man who calls any cat she because he doesn't much care for them.)

Unless both cats are incontestably girls, no Frenchman will ever say *ELLES miaulent*. Chivalry goes just so far, *parbleu*! Even if there are seven girl cats and only one tomcat, he still says *ILS* miaulent. Even if he only thinks one of those cats might be a tom, he says *ILS*. So do the Greeks, the Romans, Italians, Spaniards, Hebrews and lots of other nationalities otherwise well aware of masculine and feminine. Those seven girl cats may be making all the noise, but they do it as *ILS*, σφείς, *ILLI*, *GLI*, *ELLOS*, on or whatever else is masculine plural as long as that tom is joining in.

Unless those girls are specifically pointed out, you have no way of knowing from the sentence that they're even there. Majority rule is powerless in situations like this. In any language I've ever run across, there are simply no personal pronouns for a mixed group. So go ahead and put *LE crayon* on *LA table*. If you want to speak of them together, they become *ILS*, like the cats.

That's the way it is.

That's also the way it is in Scripture, which was written in varieties of Hebrew and Greek, and later translated into Latin and a host of vernaculars. There must be women hidden throughout its pages whose presence must remain forever veiled behind Babel's impenetrable grammatical purdahs. We have, for instance, the well-known story of Emmaus, written in Greek by the Gentile St. Luke. In English it goes like this:

> And behold, two of them were going that very day to a village named Emmaus, which is sixty stadia from Jerusalem. And they were talking to each other about all these things that had happened. And it came to pass,

while they were conversing and arguing together, that Jesus himself also drew near and went along with them; but their eyes were held, that they should not recognize him. And he said to them, "What words are these that you are exchanging as you walk and are sad?"

But one of them, named Cleophas, answered and said to him, "Art thou the only stranger in Jerusalem who does not know the things, that have happened there in these days?" And he said to them, "What things?"

And they said to him, "Concerning Jesus of Nazareth, who was a prophet, mighty in work and word before God and all the people; and how our chief priests and rulers delivered him up to be sentenced to death, and crucified him. But we were hoping that it was he who should redeem Israel. Yes, and besides all this, today is the third day since these things came to pass. And, moreover, certain women of our company, who were at the tomb before it was light, astounded us, and not finding his body, they came, saying that they had also seen a vision of angels, who said that he is alive. So some of our company went to the tomb and found it, even as the women had said, but him they did not see."

But he said to them, "O foolish ones and slow of heart to believe in all that the prophets have spoken! Did not the Christ have to suffer these things before entering into his glory?" And beginning then with Moses and with all the Prophets, he interpreted' to them in all the Scriptures the things referring to himself.

And they drew near to the village to which they were going, and he acted as though he were going on. And they urged him, saying, "Stay with us, for it is getting towards evening, and the day is now far spent." And he went in with them. And it came to pass when he reclined at table with them, that he took the bread and blessed and broke and began handing it to them. And their eyes were opened, and they recognized him; and he vanished from their sight. And they said to each other, "Was not our heart burning within us while he was speaking on the road and explaining to us the Scriptures?" (*Luke 24:13-33*).

Who were these two disciples? We're told one was called Cleophas, a not uncommon man's name in that century. Because it's spelled Κλεοπας, in the manuscripts, he was presumably not the same Cleophas (or Clopas) who was the older brother of St. Joseph and father of James the Less, "brother of the Lord." This Cleophas spelled his name differently Κλώπας, —but English can be rather insensitive to the niceties of Greek vowels. The Cleophas who was walking to Emmaus was also a follower of Christ, but this is the only certain mention of him in Scripture.

Who was the other disciple? Some commentators have advanced the opinion that he was St. Luke, but Scripture says merely that "two of them" (in Greek, δύο εξ αυτών) were going to Emmaus. Naturally, the αὐτῶν is masculine plural. If one had been a woman, the Greek text would read the same and leave the reader none the wiser. "They were talking to each other" is rendered αὐτοί ὡμίλον πρός ἀλλήλους and so on through the remainder of the story, all pronouns being set quite properly in the discreet masculine plural. Cleophas' companion is never quoted as a person, but always speaks as one half of "they," and our Lord addresses only "them."

Could this other disciple have been a woman?

As far as the grammar goes, only too easily. We must allow, however, that for centuries it has been taken for granted that these two were both men, and nobody to my knowledge has ever contended otherwise. Rembrandt's famous picture of the occasion shows that he for one had no doubt whatever that these were indeed two men who supped with Christ—though he had no qualms about adding a servant to the scene. I suppose a great many people today in their meditations on Emmaus think automatically of Rembrandt's imaginary representation without question, much as small children always see Mary riding to Egypt on the little gray donkey—who was most likely a camel.

Certainly the first Hebrew Christians knew full well who these two disciples were. In fact throughout the New Testament we are perpetually tantalized by the bare bones of recitals whose details we are no longer able to fill in for ourselves as their first readers were evidently expected to do. St. Mark doesn't even bother to give the full story of Emmaus, but only mentions it in passing, almost as if he might have considered it too well-known to need setting down. St. Matthew and St. John don't include it at all.

Even in St. Luke's version, the identity of Cleophas' companion must have been considered so obvious from the context that specific mention would have been superfluous, or at least out of the ordinary. Now, I can't presume to say who Cleophas' companion was. All I know is that the story opens up marvelously for me when I begin thinking, "Suppose it was a woman?"

Suppose it was Cleophas' wife!

Who is so obvious, and therefore so hidden, as a man's wife? Who could be less worth mentioning? Even today wives are rarely singled out by name where couples are concerned. Don't we in casual conversation speak merely of the Smiths, the Joneses? So why shouldn't Scripture call the Cleophases simply "the two of them" if they were "one flesh" like the rest of us married people? St. Luke may have taken it for granted that mention of Cleophas would automatically include his wife, especially if the Cleophases were a well-known couple. Being taken for granted is the veriest mark of a good wife. Only when a wife acts up are her friends likely to start thinking of her separately. That St. Luke didn't mention Cleophas' companion by name could in fact argue *ipso facto* against this person being another man.

This explanation of the invisible disciple, actually so banal, succeeds in shifting the whole story to a completely different plane. So innocently and sweetly does every detail slip into place within the new context, I can't help wondering. Besides, as a woman, I own to being prejudiced in favor of my sex, and though we must lose our maiden names and remain hidden, I like to think of us as at least present on important occasions.

If the menfolk will indulge us a bit, perhaps we might ponder it all in the heart. Shall we?

Mr. and Mrs. Cleophas, devout Jews and fervent followers of the Christ, had been to Jerusalem for the Pasch and found themselves caught up in the terrible destruction of the Man they had come to accept as Messias. Heavy-hearted and disappointed, they were now returning home to their village, or if not home, possibly to temporary quarters established there for the occasion. Texts differ here, and scholars haven't yet decided whether this Emmaus was sixty or one hundred and sixty stadia from Jerusalem, either seven or eighteen miles. As the Cleophases were walking, and ended by making a round trip the same day, I like to think the village was only seven miles away, but of course I really know nothing about it. (I do hope you read anything I write with this in mind.)

Then, as they walk along, very likely as part of a crowd of others as was the custom, a stranger joins the conversation of this husband and wife "conversing and arguing together." Ah! You really have to be married, I think, to understand this kind of conversation between husband and wife! Mrs. Cleophas—if that's who it was—was a wonderful wife. When the stranger makes overtures to them, she lets her husband talk first. This would, of course, be basic Hebrew etiquette, for the stranger, being a man, would normally address the husband. She does talk, however, because even a good woman can keep silent just so long. After a while we're told "they said to him."

What "they" said is quite revealing, too, for they dwell on what the women reported who had visited the empty sepulchre and seen angels. We can be sure this tale must have made a big impression on Mrs. Cleophas, if not on her husband. This might, indeed, have been the very thing they were arguing about. Certainly she would have been inclined to believe the other women and may have been trying to convince her husband that women aren't always just gullible ninnies. Somehow, women seem to know better than men when to trust other women.

Furthermore, there's the possibility in this case that Mrs. Cleophas may have been herself one of the "certain women of our company who were at the tomb." If Cleophas, on the other hand, was present when "some of our company went to the tomb" later to check soberly the facts of the story and found the tomb indeed empty, but "Him they did not see," I'd say we detect here ample grounds for plenty of "conversing and arguing together" between the Cleophases!

Be that as it may, both disciples are entranced with this stranger who "interpreted to them in all the Scriptures the things referring to Himself," and reaching home at last, what would have been more natural under the circumstances than to invite him in to pursue the conversation? Judged in context, this invitation has all the ring of a casual but warm offer of conjugal hospitality. It's getting late, they said, why not stay with us for the night? It sounds so apt, so utterly commonplace, I wonder whether this interpretation might not be true. Here are three congenial spirits such as sometimes get together, and "at the breaking of the bread," two of them suddenly discover they have been all along in the company of Almighty God. What's strange about that? Doesn't it take three to be married? Wasn't the natural relationship between the sexes raised to the sacramental level revealed to mankind precisely in this fashion?

"The disciples recognized the Lord Jesus in the breaking of the bread. Alleluia. 'I am the Good Shepherd: and I know Mine and Mine know Me.' Alleluia!" sings the liturgy on the Second Sunday after Easter, marveling that birds of a feather Hock together not only naturally, but supernaturally.

Our Lord seems to have taken particular delight in accepting dinner invitations. We gather from the Gospels that He was likely to go to the house of anybody at all; at least no refusal on His part was ever recorded.

"If any man listens to my voice and opens the door to me, I will come in to him and will sup with him, and he with me," He tells us in St. John's *Apocalypse* (*3:20*).

It stands to reason He still accepts invitations to dinner and would reveal Himself to any devout couple who liked to discuss Scripture and dispense hospitality. At Emmaus He "reclined at table with them," and "took the bread and blessed and broke and began handing it to them. And their eyes were opened, and they recognized Him."

Overcome with joy, the Cleophases rush immediately back to Jerusalem in spite of the lateness of the hour to tell the good news. (If they weren't a young couple, I do hope it was only sixty stadia.) As we might expect, St. Mark tells us they weren't believed by the Apostles any more than the women had been, and I guess poor Cleophas might have been judged to be just another married man who allowed his wife to subvert his better judgment.

If the other disciple was in fact Mrs. Cleophas, this story takes on infinite layers of meaning for millions of married Christians. I for one do wish it could be proved so. There's something so eminently congruous about the Christ manifesting Himself after His Resurrection specifically to a married couple, besides to His Apostles and men and women generally. There might be here something of the fullness of grace prefigured for marriage at Cana, another dimension added to the mystical reinstatement of Adam and Eve. The redeemer first promised to a married couple in Eden, emerging from earthly obscurity as a provider of wine when the supply gave out at a wedding, reveals Himself in His full risen Humanity "at the breaking of the bread" at a married couple's own table. This bears pondering in both heart and head, if it be so.

He converses with them. He *goes into their house* with them. Then He blesses, breaks, and hands back to them their own bread. Whether or not He was in fact distributing Holy Communion to them as He does at Mass is a matter about which exegetes are not agreed, but no matter, for certainly in the broad sacramental sense this action of Christ's takes place daily in every Christian home. There's little need to wonder how it happened at Emmaus.

Christ waits to be invited, but once invited, He accepts. On first reaching Emmaus, "he acted as though he were going on," and indeed He acted this way where marriage was concerned, for Scripture relates no separate institution of marriage as a sacrament on His part. We know that for centuries marriage wasn't clearly defined as a sacrament at all. Now modern theology has proved that the sacramentality of marriage is inherent in the baptism of the contracting parties. This truth has long been recognized in practice, as it is today, for the Church doesn't require an unbelieving couple who later become Catholics to remarry according to the canonical rite. The elevation of marriage to Marriage has already taken place, when they invited Christ to "stay with us," as did the disciples at Emmaus.

"He went in with them," says Scripture, for as they said, "it is getting towards evening, and the day is now far spent." This has an apocalyptic flavor. We sense that humanity here treads in the latter days, when everything and everyone must be made holy, even married people! No sooner is He recognized than He vanishes from their sight, for as He explained before His Passion, "It is expedient for you that I depart" (*John 16:7*). He leaves them exclaiming, "Was not our heart burning within us while He was speaking on the road?"

A married couple is one flesh. These disciples didn't say "our hearts," but our heart was burning as the Christ spoke to them, for Christians can have only one heart between them, and especially those who are united to each other in holy matrimony, into whose house Christ has entered. Somehow, I just can't feel that Cleophas and his companion were brothers, or cousins, or father and son, or just friends. Christ explains the Scriptures to us married people in a special way, as indeed He must have done at Emmaus. It's remarkable that St. Luke takes care to tell us that our Lord chose a later, separate occasion to enlighten His Apostles—"to open their minds that they might understand the Scriptures." Actually, He appears to His Twelve for this purpose just as they were discussing Cleophas' amazing story! Isn't it likely that this second exegesis was more slanted to men who would have special, priestly duties, unlike those of the married layman Cleophas? That to Cleophas our Lord had something special to say too?

I hesitate to make too much of the hidden and perhaps fictitious Mrs. Cleophas, but if she does move behind the scenes at Emmaus, we can't be surprised at finding her traces in St. Luke's Gospel, rather than in the other three. The Gospel according to St. Luke often goes by the name "Gospel of Mary," or again, "Gospel of the Holy Women." If it hadn't been for St. Luke, we might be tempted to believe God had little serious interest in women as such under the New Dispensation. To him we're indebted for all the familiar "homey" stories of the Annunciation, the Visitation, the shepherds, the Child Jesus in the temple—in fact just about all the glimpses we have of the hidden life at Nazareth.

It has been obvious to Scripture scholars for centuries that only our Lady herself could have supplied much of this information. To Luke, the Gentile convert, writing sometime before the destruction of Jerusalem, it would seem she had a care to leave "victuals for her maidens," for many of his passages speak especially to women. He mentions many women who would otherwise be unknown to us today: the widow of Nairn, the widow who gave the mites, the stooped woman, the daughters of Jerusalem, the "woman from the crowd" who praised the Mother of Jesus, and even the penitent woman who anointed our Lord's feet at the house of Simon. (Whether or not this last was actually Mary Magdalene I leave to you as he does.) He also tells us about Martha's censure of her sister Mary, about the women who ministered to Christ "of their substance," and records the especially feminine parables of the woman and the leaven, and the lost coin.

Furthermore, St. Luke's is in many ways the most "interior" of the Gospels from a human standpoint, for it dwells heavily on the prayer life of our Lord's Humanity, His nights on Olivet, and contains His most fulsome instructions on how to go about praying. He also records for us the three great Canticles of the New Church: the *Magnificat*, the *Benedictus*, and the *Nunc Dimittis*, all intimately bound up with the presence of our Lady.

In all this we may detect the all-pervading hidden influence of Mary, who may be hiding behind St. Luke as Mrs. Cleophas may be hiding behind Cleophas. Perhaps it's to her we're indebted for the inclusion of the whole detailed story of Emmaus, with all its subtle implications. What actually may have been the relationship between Mary and the alleged Mrs. Cleophas? Suppose Cleophas and Clopas were really the same man, their separate identities existing after all merely in spelling? As St. Joseph's older brother, his wife stood with Mary herself on Golgotha! Wonderful vistas open here, but we must leave fancy aside to adhere to truth in poverty of spirit. Until corroborating evidence turns up, there are enough apocryphal little gray donkeys around as it is.

Whether or not our Lady insisted on including the story of Emmaus in Scripture, God certainly did; and it vibrates with subtle overtones for the most humble listener. One sentence that strikes a sympathetic chord at our house is the one which reads: "And it came to pass, *while they were conversing and arguing together, that Jesus himself also drew near and went along with them.* Whether Cleophas and his companion were a married couple, old cronies, or total strangers matters little. Just by itself that sentence is staggering. It should be written in letters of fire and waved under the noses of all namby-pamby Christians who think holiness consists in never disagreeing with anyone, and that any difference of opinion among the people of God is automatically sinful.

"Conversing and arguing together" are not synonymous with "envy and contentiousness" (*Phil. 1:15*). On the contrary, they are human means to truth. The Greek word here translated by "arguing together" is συξητείν, which contains the idea of *inquiring*. It's our Lady's "How shall this happen?" asked of one another by any number of persons. Where nobody knows the answer for sure, two heads are better than one. This necessarily implies a fruitful difference in points of view, otherwise one head would certainly be far more efficient than two heads thinking identically.

Arguing together is inextricably intertwined with the mystery of individual vocations, so often apparently contradictory, and yet ordained always to God's one and holy Will. It's the mystery of parallel lines which meet only in the Godhead. The whole of human history proves that God's providence develops precisely from pitting opposites one against the other, destinies of nations and individuals evolving from conflicts of all kinds on all levels of society. The apparent contradictions of common and private good, science and religion, Church and State, grace and free will, justice and mercy, are familiar to all of us; yet dogma is defined as a result of them, for truth arises from conflict, and dogma itself rests secure only on paradox. Even material evolution takes place so, scientists would have us believe; and Scripture reveals that this state of affairs pertains to the unseen spiritual world as well.

It's clear that God's creation, like music, is built upon two principles which, when viewed separately, often appear contradictory: order and movement. Order alone is static; movement alone is disorder; yet the product of the two is peace or, if you will, harmony. The four living creatures in Ezechiel's revelation, whose wings were joined together in such a manner that they stood to form a perfect square "turned not when they went," but still "everyone went straight forward" (*Ezech. 1:9*). Impossible physically, this operation isn't at all impossible spiritually, but it's a great mystery all the same, which is why it had to be revealed to us and why we must take God's word for it.

This divinely ordered movement, stable yet "running and returning like flashes of lightning" (*Ezech. 1:14*), expresses itself in apparently contradictory striving of all kinds among creatures. Though often misdirected, in itself it's always good. It's only because of fallen nature that it takes on the ugliness we have come to believe is integral with it, the horrors of war and bloodshed, the spite and venom of malicious verbal combat, unwholesome rivalry between husband and wife, or the debilitating struggles between deep forces in our own souls, not to mention the cataclysms of opposing forces in the material elements. Volcanoes, lovers' quarrels, and hiccups spring from one and the same primal disorder. Dare we forget that the Law itself was propagated from Mount Sinai by Moses, who had actually. killed a man through passion for justice?

Lest we overlook the excellence of strife, God in later times permitted warrior monks like the Knights Templar, and saints like St. Louis and St. Joan of Arc, to grace the world of physical conflict. These were fighters, whose particular vocation was combat, who well knew that turning the other cheek is no virtue where others are left to suffer the consequences. In the belligerent world of mental action, God has presented us with masters of polemic like St. Paul, St. Cyril, St. Augustine, St. Catherine of Alexandria, St. Bernard and countless others. Among exegetes, He has given us St. Jerome, whose canonization has been a scandal to pastel pacifists ever since, who rigorously class him as a "Saint to Be Admired but Not Imitated."

Indeed, imitating St. Jerome in all things could be dangerous for souls not equaling him in purity of intention. A dip into his letters today is like a bath in champagne and red pepper, so much and so exclusively did he love truth. Did you know he called St. Ambrose "that oracular little crow?" Well, I understand he did. St. Ambrose! Both being now canonized doctors of the Church, it's unlikely either has abandoned his declared position in heaven, for which the earthly striving was the merest preparation. We can be sure St. Ambrose loves St. Jerome all the more for having been so concerned about his supposed errors, and that both these doctors continue to present their points of view to us still on earth.

Besides, St. Jerome had other targets. Referring to a letter from St. Augustine on the exegesis of a passage in Galatians, he berates this other doctor of the Church with equal vigor. Here's a sample:

> Therefore, if it really is your letter, write me frankly that it is, or send me a more accurate copy so that we may discuss scriptural questions without more petty rancor. Then I may either correct my own error, or demonstrate that another has without reason exposed me in such a reprehensible fashion. Far be it from me to presume to attack any book composed by your blessed self. It is sufficient for me to articulate my own views without tearing to pieces what others maintain. But it must be obvious to a man of your discernment that one is satisfied with his own opinion, and that it is but puerile braggadocio to seek prominence—as young men in all times have done—by attacking famous men. I am not so stupid as to feel insulted when your explanations differ from mine, because you are not provoked if my views contradict yours. But true reprehension occurs among friends when each, not observing his own wallet, observes, as Persius has it, the wallet carried by the other. Furthermore, love one who loves you, and just because you happen to be young do not challenge a veteran in the field of Scriptural commentary. Each of us has his allotted time, each runs the race to the utmost of his endurance. Now is your time to race and achieve great distance for our side; it is no more than fair that I rest, and while I am reposing I may, with your indulgent permission, quote from the poets, lest you seem to be the only one around who is able to refer to them: remember the contest between young Dares and ancient Entellus, and the common proverb,

"The weary ox treads with a firmer step." With melancholy I have dictated these words. If only I could receive your embrace! If only we could participate in a mutual conversation, instructing and learning from each other! (*Letters of St. Jerome*, Paul Carroll trans.)

Isn't he wonderful? Only saints can carryon like this, "instructing and learning from each other" as the disciples "argued together" on the way to Emmaus, knowing that only in the truth can they really love each other. Sinners naturally prefer half-truth or outright falsehood. It's generally more polite, and causes far less disagreement. Wouldn't you say the great bulk of lies told every day stems precisely from a desire to avoid pain?

"Do you not know that the friendship of this world is enmity with God?" asks St. James (*4:4*).

After Satan entered into him, Scripture tells us Judas sought to betray our Lord "without a disturbance" (*Luke 22:6*) and used for his purpose a *kiss*. Somehow we usually think of evil in connection with uproar and confusion, these being its frequent visible effects; but evil at its deadliest, just before it strikes a real coup, works smoothly and with as little fanfare as possible, alarming no one. This was the slithering serpent's tactic with Eve, and it was so successful he's hardly found reason to use a better.

"Woe to you when all men speak well of you!" (*Luke 6:26*).

"Love should be full of anger!" writes St. Jerome to his friend Heliodorus, preparing to tell him a few things straight out for his own good in some four thousand well-chosen words.

A spiritual cliche has it that God perfects saints as jewelers polish diamonds, by rubbing one against another. Because diamonds are about the hardest substance there is, it stands to reason that anything softer than another diamond would hardly do the trick. We read with some surprise in the Acts of the Apostles that on St. Paul's second missionary journey,

> Barnabas wanted to take with them John also, who was surnamed Mark. But Paul asked that he, inasmuch as he had deserted them in Pamphylia instead of going on with them to their work, should not again be taken along. And *a sharp contention sprang up* so that they separated from each other, and Barnabas took Mark and sailed for Cyprus (*Acts 15:37-39*).

Commenting on this famous disagreement in a spiritual conference on private judgment, St. Francis de Sales asks, "Ought we then to be disturbed and surprised at seeing such a fault as this among ourselves, when even the Apostles committed it?" Certain it is that every St. Paul has his St. Barnabas, and in modern times every Cardinal Newman has his Fr. Faber.

We might go so far as to say every husband has his wife, for there's nothing so universally sanctifying, or so crucifying, as being disagreed with, and man and woman are bound to disagree. If his wife loves him, she's bound to bother him at least as much as he bothers her. St. Teresa often remarked that you couldn't know what persecution really was until you found yourself persecuted by good people with the best intentions. This kind of torture God reserves for His elite, and St. Teresa herself was warned by good people that she was being directed in her reform by the devil. They even threatened her with the Inquisition!

Our Lord predicted this would be the lot of anyone who truly undertook to follow Him. "Yes," He said, "the hour is coming for everyone who kills you to think he is offering worship to God" (*John 16:2*).

Believe it or not, this fruitful friction is the corrupted human counterpart of angelic struggle, of the scope of which Scripture gives only the barest hints. At the risk of destroying the reader's faith, let it here be stated that if I read Scripture right, even good angels don't agree among themselves on everything by any means. As might be expected, this shattering truth peeps out at us in the Book of Daniel, who asked so many questions and got so many answers.

A good angel, perhaps Gabriel himself, let slip to Daniel that good angels *fight* against one another if necessary. "Fight" was the word he used, and there's no glossing it over. It's not his fault, after all, that since the Fall this perfectly good word has become encrusted with all sorts of ugly barnacles. If we were to tell it, we would probably say angels "strive" against one another, but the net result is the same: angels sometimes get in each other's way in their service of God. Telling Daniel, as we have seen, that "from the first day thou didst set thy heart to understand ... thy words have been heard and I am come for thy words," the Angel explains why he's a little late arriving:

> But the prince of the kingdom of the Persians resisted me one and twenty days: and behold Michael, one of the chief princes, came to help me, and I remained there by the king of the Persians. ... Dost thou know wherefor I am come to thee? And now I will return, to fight against the prince of the Persians. When I went forth, there appeared the prince of the Greeks coming. But I will tell thee what is set down in the scripture of the

truth: and none is my helper in all these things, but Michael your prince (*10:13;20,21*).

These "princes" are almost unanimously recognized as the guardian spirits of nations, the warrior Michael being the special protector of God's chosen people. In acquitting themselves of duties God assigns them, it's evident that angels run into conflicts of interest as a matter of course. Not only do they oppose each other as a consequence, they even form coalitions against each other! Naturally, I hardly expect you to take my word in such a matter, so here is a theologian's explanation.

Fr. Pascal Parente explains that when Gabriel,

> ... says he is going to fight against the prince of the Persians, that means, he is going to fight against the national Guardian Angel of the Persians. In going forth he saw the national Guardian Angel of the Greeks coming, but it seems that he did not succeed in obtaining help from him. The only one who had helped and assisted him in his holy battle was St. Michael the Archangel, the Guardian Angel of the Jewish nation of those days.
>
> This charming revelation by one of the great heavenly spirits, the Archangel Gabriel, may disconcert us a little. After all. how can we reconcile the unchangeable charity and harmony and peace existing among heavenly spirits with fighting and wars, which usually imply enmity and discord?

How indeed?

> Yet, there is no doubt that this talk of war and fighting refers to love and zeal for the salvation of the people committed to their care. Each national protecting Angel sought the spiritual advantage and the salvation of the people of his territory, as duty demanded. The Archangel Gabriel (to whom Daniel had prayed for the liberation of the Jewish people from the captivity in which they were still being kept by the Persians) had secured the assistance of the Archangel Michael ... in promoting the liberation of the Jews from captivity, but he had found a powerful opponent to his efforts in the national Guardian Angel, or prince, of the Persians, who resisted all attempts of Gabriel and Michael with the purpose of keeping the Jews in captivity much longer. This great Angel of the Persian people, who were a pagan nation that did not believe in the true God, had noticed the many blessings that the presence of those faithful captive Jews had brought to the Persians, whereby many of these had found the way of salvation. He, therefore, wanted that those blessings should continue for the good of his wards, and resisted with all his love and might the efforts of the other Angels, who were concerned with the interests of their nations. It was a battle of love perfectly compatible with

peace and charity. Each Angel knows what God wants him to do for the people of his territory, but without special revelation he does not know what God expects from the Angel of another nation, hence their differences (*The Angels*, pp. 112-3).

Utrum inter Angelos possit esse pugna seu discordia, says the Angelic Doctor himself, putting it all in a nutshell.

Whoever wants to be any different is just trying to be holier than the angels. They present us with an ideal to be followed in conflicts of all kinds, be they cold wars, political arguments, pest control, card games, theological controversy, or a divided apostolate. They teach one-track devotion to whatever or whoever is entrusted to our care, regardless of consequences. No housewife with her eye on the angels could ever leave her husband and children eating warmed over hash at home while she bustles out to feed the needy at the corner mission. She couldn't even bustle out to save the whole world if it meant letting the housework go. If necessary, she must fight the world to stay home!

The angel strives always in God's presence, his sale object the accomplishment of God's will *for him* by the means at hand. He's not concerned with God's will for other angels. His motive power is entirely love; there's no malice toward his opponent. St. Jude tells us that even when "fiercely disputing with the devil about the body of Moses," St. Michael "did not venture to bring against him an accusation of blasphemy, but said to Satan, 'May the Lord rebuke thee'" (*9*).

"If you have bitter jealousy and contentions in your hearts, do not glory and be liars against the truth," admonishes St. James (*3:14*).

We must be pure to fight well, for tenacity in conflicts can be said to be a special characteristic of the elect. Jacob, who had the unique distinction of wrestling with an angel "until the break of dawn" is our teacher here.

The angel, "when he saw that he could not overcome Jacob," had to be content with dislocating his thigh. "Then he said, 'Let me go; it is dawn.'"

But Jacob answered, "I will not let you go till you bless me."

Then he asked Jacob, "What is your name?" And he answered, "Jacob."

He said, "You shall no longer be called Jacob, but Israel, because you have contended with God and men, and have triumphed" (*Gen. 32:26-29*).

And the limping Jacob got his blessing, because that's what a good fight, fought in the proper spirit, gets you.

"I have fought the good fight ... there is laid up for me a crown of justice," corroborated that scrapper St. Paul shortly before his death (*II Tim. 4:7,8*).

Said the Messias Jacob prefigured:

> Do not think that I have come to send peace upon the earth. I have come to bring a sword, not peace. For I have come to set a man at variance with his father, and a daughter with her mother, and a daughter-in-law with her mother-in-law; and a man's enemies will be those of his own household. He who loves son or daughter more than me is not worthy of me (*Matt. 10:34-37*).

How fortunate for us the holy Angels don't love each other more than they do God. They would forget all about our conflicting interests and heaven would fall on our heads! Certainly the argument on the way to Emmaus could never have come to flower. We don't know exactly how heated it became, but we do know it reached the point where the heart of the two disputants was "burning within them" at the words of the Stranger.

It was precisely when they were "conversing and arguing" that He had drawn near to them and joined the discussion, and if I read the story correctly, we can expect Truth to draw near an honest argument, engaged in through love by people who really want to know. Isn't this trinitarian? Wasn't incarnate Truth, sprung from the Father as an act of pure knowledge, manifested in Hesh through the power of the Spirit of Love? As the generation of the Son within the Blessed Trinity is a purely intellectual generation, so do we humbly re-enact it in our own souls when the Godhead begets within us Its own Truth, who is Christ. Whoever bears false witness of any kind sins, not merely because he lies, but because he doesn't reflect the Blessed Trinity.

Christ is the proper end of all arguments. This goes even for arguments between husband and wife. If the two disciples at Emmaus were in fact a married couple, we know for sure the subject under discussion got a comprehensive raking over. We might go so far as to say that no argument is argued in depth unless both sexes engage in it! Arguments between men can get entirely too objective and cerebral, those between women too personal and affective. Neither quite hits the whole truth, but each complements the other marvelously. Husbandly order wedded to wifely movement produces, believe it or not, *peace*.

An outstanding example of what I'm trying to say occurs in the Church's modern presentation of mystical theology, where through the Order of Mt. Carmel she gives us the combined teaching of a man and a woman on prayer and the spiritual life. St. John of the Cross, the objective theologian, and St. Teresa of Jesus, the practical psychologist, mutually illumine each other's teaching to the point that taking one without the other can lead inexperienced souls into gross error. What God has joined together here is sundered at your own risk, if you are seriously seeking truth, say those who know.

"Yet neither is man independent of woman, nor woman independent of man in the Lord. For as the woman is from the man, so also is the man through the woman, but all things are from God" (*I Cor. 11:11-12*).

The same principle holds, it seems to me, in any discussion between man and wife humbly seeking the truth about anything. Indeed, it isn't good for man to be alone. In the sacrament which is marriage, it takes two to produce Christ, who is Truth. A man who looks on his wife as little more than a legalized servant-prostitute supplying his sensual and emotional needs is far from living a fully Christian life. He forgets "woman is the glory of the man," just as a bad wife forgets that "woman is from man" (*I Cor. 11:7-8*). Marriage is a union of souls endowed with intellects and free wills, and the community it creates can't exist on a purely animal level and retain its proper character.

In marriage, two mysteries try to comprehend each other within another Mystery greater than themselves. If this doesn't lead to argument, call it συζητείν or whatever you like, there's a dead cell somewhere. "Conversing and arguing together" in love is divinely ordained and normally fruitful. At Emmaus Christ himself sanctioned it, indeed *crowned* it.

If "the holier a woman is, the more she is a woman," she must be so in order to fulfill her role in the Church alongside man, "a helper like to himself." That means it's also true that the holier a man is, the more he is a man, that holiness for him can never be effeminacy, no matter how "feminine" his soul may be before God in a certain sense. Each sex must play fully the role God assigned it, come what may.

About the time He drew near, Cleophas might have been summing up his side thus: "But how could He have walked out of that tomb? Look at the *facts*, dear. It doesn't stand to reason. Just because a bunch of silly women get so worked up that they saw things doesn't prove anything. You know how women are!"

"I certainly do," his partner might have replied. "And I know these women. Take Joanna, for instance. She has good sense, she wouldn't lie. Neither would the others."

"I didn't say they lied. I just said they got worked up."

"Well, you could be right, but I've got a feeling there's more to it than meets the eye. In fact, I just *know* there is."

"Having a feeling and just *knowing* is no proof of anything!"

And so on.

Mrs. Cleophas couldn't have told Cleophas how she "knew." Like all people whose particular product is wisdom rather than knowledge, a woman can scarcely prove anything by rational argument that will hold up in court. A man would be ashamed to offer the kind of evidence she stoops to, as he would be ashamed to wear his hair as long as hers. St. Paul points out, "For a man to wear his hair long is degrading," and that's that. Nevertheless, it was with her glorious hair that Mary Magdalene wiped the feet of Christ. No man could or would have done such a thing!

St. Paul also points out, however, that for a woman to wear her hair long is not only not degrading, but a glory. She is made to shine in ways that would disgrace a man, and this analogy can be applied to her intellectual deportment too. Her "hair," says St. Paul, was given to her as a "covering." Are we forgetting she is the hidden sex? She is mankind's tabernacle, whose coverings protect the Holy of Holies.

As Chesterton remarked, women are often silly, but they're always wise. "The sagacity of women, like the sagacity of saints or that of donkeys," he conceded, "is something outside all questions of ordinary cleverness and ambition." Sad to say, women can hardly convince themselves even of this, unless some man tells them. They must be constantly supported from reason, as St. John of the Cross supports St. Teresa. What women have to offer is so unapprehendable, it's no wonder they tend to disappear at the most dramatic moments.

Take Zebedee's wife, Salome, for instance. Now there, you might say, is a forceful woman, one who can be depended on to stay right out in front. Our Lord himself found her rather pushy in asking preferment in His Kingdom for her two sons, James and John.

He said, "You do not know what you are asking for. Can you drink of the cup of which I am about to drink?"

Whom was our Lord addressing as "you?"

"They answered," records Scripture, "'We can!'"

Who were "they?" And who's "we?" Just James and John?

Or did Mrs. Zebedee chime in here like the girl cat among the toms?

To "them" Christ then says, "Of my cup you shall indeed drink: but as for sitting at my right hand and at my left, that is not mine to give you, but it belongs to those for whom it has been prepared by my Father," though He doesn't deny Mrs. Zebedee's request outright. We know in fact He granted at least a large part of it. When He asked her, "What dost though want?" there were strong echoes of His statement at Cana, "What wouldst thou have me do, Woman?"

But did you see how by this time Mrs. Zebedee has disappeared? Right in the middle of what must have been one of the greatest moments of her life, she disappears. Was she given a share in the cup our Lord speaks of? Who knows? We are left to wonder as much as we please what hidden suffering may ultimately have been hers, not just as a natural mother, but as the spiritual mother of two bishops, both great saints.

The spiritual parenthood of natural children opens up a very big subject I'm not in the least prepared to pursue, but I suspect it's rooted in the mystery of the Presentation in the Temple. When the Messias' parents first "took him up to Jerusalem to present him to the Lord" in infancy, the holy Simeon tells His mother, "Thy own soul a sword shall pierce" (*Luke 2:22,35*). Surely, as an exemplar for all women, there's significance here for any mother who seriously and unobtrusively brings up children for God. Their destinies, good or bad, are inescapably bound up with hers, if only because she rears them.

The world, of course, need never know, but when a woman disappears behind any man, he may as well expect developments. Consider briefly how the blessed Mary disappeared behind our Lord, and *Cherchez la femme*! You can search for her all through Scripture. And that uncovers another facet of the subject: If the books of the Bible are just so many ways of saying Christ, is it too outrageous to suppose that some of the ways of saying God's Word are feminine? That woman was created to speak Him in a special way, reflecting God as no one else can? Is it logical to suppose that she was denied the opportunity in Scripture? Were some of the sacred authors in fact women?

We know many incidental parts are quite openly ascribed to female utterance, if not outright composition. Aside from our Lady, women like Miriam, Debora, Anna and Judith are credited with some of Scripture's most beautiful passages. It's not surprising, furthermore, that these productions are all canticles or lyrics, rich in emotional content and intensely personal in outlook. If men wrote them and placed them in the mouths of these heroines, I can only say these men were geniuses at interpreting feminine psychology.

The Bible must have had thousands of unknown authors, compilers, and editors. We have no idea who besides Moses put together Genesis, let alone all the historical and sapiential books. How many of these may have been the work of a woman only God knows,

Who must have inspired her, and Who created her in the first place to be to man "a helper like himself."

In these latter days, it's a matter of record how much St. Jerome depended on scholarly women of the caliber of St. Paula, St. Eustochium, or Fabiola to help him in the redaction of the Vulgate. One modern Protestant scholar is of the opinion that St. Paul's controversial Epistle to the Hebrews was actually from a woman's pen! I don't know about that. For my part, I'll readily concede to men the authorship of the historical books and commentaries, though women may easily have done much of the hack work involved. Sometimes I wonder whether the Book of Tobias, so set in "family situation," might not have been hatched in the head of some Jewish Frances Trollope divinely inspired. Maybe a woman put together the sensitive story of Ruth. Perhaps some parts of the Bible were of joint husband and wife authorship. Who knows?

History and theology aren't woman's literary oyster, but religious poetry is. I strongly suspect the Canticle of Canticles—which Rabbi Akiba called the Holy of Holies of the Old Testament—may be largely, if not entirely, the work of a woman. Wasn't the Holy of Holies herself a woman—the Immaculate Mary? Certainly the sublime lyricism of the poem would point to a sort of Hebrew Sappho very close to God, who knew human love and what it was meant to represent. Uniting holiness and poetical skill, its symbolism betrays an intimate knowledge of female psychology and physiological reaction which could scarcely be known outside the sex, or expressed from so truly a feminine viewpoint.

Furthermore, the descriptions of the Bridegroom are very much ones which would occur to a woman, especially if she were well acquainted with heroic messianic terminology. Without going into details too delicate to treat summarily here, it's safe to say it would be nobly congruous for the Canticle to have been written by a woman, if only because this heavenly poem is the quintessence of the love song of the Church and human nature for her God. Bearing in mind Meister Eckhart's comment that every human soul must become "woman" in order to receive God, why shouldn't she write this long song for humanity?

If she did so, that she did it anonymously is only proper. We don't need to know who she is, if she is Woman. Hers is the hidden sex, figure of the chosen Bride of a hidden God.

> Truly you are a God of mystery,
> O God of Israel, O Savior! (*Isa. 45:15*)

Created in His image and likeness, woman conforms to God most specially in His hiddenness. More than man's, her life on earth can be "hidden with Christ in God."

But, "when Christ, your life, shall appear," God promises her, "you too will appear with him in glory!" (*Col. 3:4*).

In the meantime, there's the housework to do.

The Derider of Majesty

CHAPTER 8

"OF COURSE atheist existentialism leads squarely into the Catholic Church.

Small talk can take desperate turns at times, and I remember tossing this off to an unsuspecting philosophy professor at lunch once, just as he bit into some very sticky macaroni and cheese.

"Good heavens!" his eyes said helplessly. He should have known about housewives, because it turned out he was married to one. He had the edge on me, for with philosophers I had, and have still, very little personal acquaintance.

Before he could swallow, I thought it might help to add, "You must admit, it's a very direct route!"

"Dear lady," he managed at last to rejoin, chewing fast, "that's perfectly true, but it's like saying the most direct route from here to China is straight through the earth!" Pointing downwards into his plate through the remaining macaroni, he added, "Few people go that way."

Well, I did. Through lots worse than macaroni and cheese I did. And I still can't see why everybody who reads, say, Jean-Paul Sartre, doesn't eventually run for instruction in the Faith.

Yes, I've heard M. Sartre is on the Index.

I remember reading him way back when he wasn't, when he didn't even appear in hard cover, but mostly in philosophical quarterlies. I was trying hard to be an atheist at the time, not knowing any better, but I had to abandon that position as resting entirely too much on faith. It was even harder, I discovered, to postulate the non-existence of God than His existence, for atheism depends rather much on being able to close one's eyes to such trivia as cause and effect, not to mention nest-building and migrations of birds, and the phenomenon of human heroism.

Like many other searchers, not being able to prove anything conclusively one way or the other for myself, I decided to stick with Socrates for the time being and admit I didn't know anything. I had had to part with Kant, who seemed so sure I *couldn't* know anything. My reasoning went something like, "Immanuel Kant, but maybe I Kan." After all, if you knew you never knew, you never knew you never knew. Philosophers, it seemed to me, didn't always play fair.

This made me what polite society calls an agnostic, a very uncomfortable and unsatisfying thing to be, but the best I could honestly manage. To relieve the tedium of not knowing anything about anything—leading quite naturally into not doing anything about anything—I read philosophical quarterlies. Other housewives who caught me at it tried to interest me in bridge. There were several clubs they said I should get interested in, because if I didn't I would get queer. Well, life is risky.

Quicker than you can say Heidegger-Jaspers-Kierkegaard, I soon became so epistemologically wound up no suburban group would have me. Luckily about this time we moved to the country. When I got around to M. Sartre and his "total engagement," I was already totally engaged; but here, to my consternation, was a thoroughgoing, convinced atheist who believed, of all things, in *free will*. Not only did he believe in free will, he believed in exercising it to the hilt, grappling in lethal combat with the tenuous thing he plainly called the *present*.

I hadn't whole-heartedly used my will for years, for I had been advised in school that, practically speaking, all human actions are completely determined by heredity, environment, and current events utterly beyond my control. Unluckily for me, I was a serious student who made good marks, so none of this poison went unassimilated. Free will was a palpable illusion, on a par with the "order" the human mind persists in discerning in the chaos of nature. Take a handful of pennies, my professor suggested, and throw them on the rug. You'll always see some pattern in the way they land, he promised, but the pattern will be mine, not the pennies'. This goes by the name of "higher education," and the other side of the question had quite simply never been presented to me beyond the grade school level. My professor couldn't explain to me why my mind so persistently sought order and insisted on finding it, if only within itself, so he just didn't try to explain it. But then, as I've already confessed, make-believe never had much attraction for me, and if free will didn't exist either, well, there was nothing left but to face up to the fact and forget it.

But M. Sartre didn't agree. Descending as low as possible into human existence to prove his point, namely, that any conscient creature can act freely according to his capacity no matter how far down he descends, he includes in one novel a hospitalized war casualty, of the class termed "basket cases," who keeps himself going by telling himself that he is no longer a man but a thing. Abdicating free will, he resigns himself to utter passivity, to being picked up, carried about, set down, and acted upon only by others. Even in these circumstances, however, he finds he must and can still act, and that heroically, for one day on a train journey in a baggage car he discovers he has a terrible choice before him: to restrain or not to restrain a bowel movement in the presence of a young lady.

I don't think the little way ever got more little than it does here, and unfortunately M. Sartre draws many wrong conclusions from the human potential for nobility in desperate humiliation, but truth is truth, wherever you find it. Frankly, I thought M. Sartre had got on to something.

I decided to give the idea a fling, and believe me, the results were amazing. I can't say they were always good, but they certainly happened. With little ole me at the controls again at last, dull days sometimes became rather exciting. I had been driving for years, of course, but suddenly there was hope that I might actually head in some direction I wanted to go, instead of blindly following the car and the direction of traffic!

Still, I was skeptical. Probably using this so-called "will" was just another predetermined action, predetermined by having run across the predetermined works of the predetermined M. Sartre. Heh, heh, you couldn't fool me! Besides, how did he know his will was free? Somehow he seemed to be using his will "as if," the way little girls pretended to feed their dolls. Because I found him curiously unbothered by problems of contingency, I was forced to read more and more of M. Sartre just to find out what it was he hung his free will on. Quite unaccountably, characters in his plays would toss off epigrammatic repartee to the effect that people create themselves as they go along, that their choices determine their being—or words to that effect.

"A man is what he wills himself to be," pontificates Garcin, a character in *No Exit* who finds himself in Hell.

"You are—your life, and nothing else," offers a lady companion called Inez.

Both being dead and damned, these were the conclusions of their lifetimes, not just aimless conversation. *Faire, et en faisant, se faire,* seemed to be something of a first premise with these existentialists, who, whatever else may be said about them, didn't seem to mind accepting responsibility for whatever happened to them. As some wags put it, they were bent on making a transitive verb out of "to be." At the lengths atheistic existentialism goes, existence does seem to thumb its nose at essence, and ultimately it makes of man his own creator, responsible to himself. This is why M. Sartre and associates are unhappily on the Index today, apparently unaware that it is God who hath made us, and not we ourselves.

Am I boring you?

Well, this is a conversion story—not the whole story, but a part of the intellectual part of it. The truth is, I got rather fascinated with deliberately using my free will, sometimes just for the heck of it, for even random use could liven up a drab afternoon. Often a *moral* choice was inescapably involved, and that brought up the whole question of what to hang morality on. One does have to have rules to play. If one day you decide to tell your husband the truth about how the car battery was suddenly found dead on Tuesday morning, you have a right to know why this is such a good idea, especially as he would never suspect a thing if of your own free will you managed to rush out in time and turn off the offending headlights you left on all night.

None of this seemed to bother M. Sartre, who gave the impression that he handled his will at all times with the skill of a virtuoso. There must, I decided, have been some article of his I had missed—namely, the one in which he explained how he knew his will was free, and the rules for using it.

My curiosity finally got the better of me, and I wrote him a letter, addressing it, I do believe, in care of a favorite haunt of his, the café *Deux Maggots*, Left Bank, Paris. (He had appeared in hard cover by now.) I can't remember what I said, but it was probably along the lines of, "I am a housewife in the American provinces far from philosophical milieux. On what do you base free will?" This I couched in the most erudite French at my command, but if he ever got the letter, he must have sized me up as a female rube way out of her depth. I finally gave up expecting an answer, and by now I suspect he couldn't answer a simple question like that. If he could, why would he be on the Index?

Free will *is* a knotty problem to all of us. Jacques Maritain says the trouble lies in the fact that,

> ... the act of free will as such is not of this world. Even in the natural order it does not belong to the world of creation, to the world of that which has been made. That is why the angels, although the knowledge of all that belongs to the world of creation is due to them, do not know the secrets of hearts. The free will transcends the world of creation. Hence it can produce an act of direct or nonmediated love for God above all, by which the person, passing beyond this world and without intermediary, crosses the abyss between the created and the Uncreated to give himself to the Uncreated (*The Sin of the Angels*).

But I'm getting ahead of my story.

Meanwhile, back at the ranch, I began thinking M. Sartre's system would work just fine if there were a God standing at the apex or the base of his philosophical edifice. I was sorry, but I couldn't see a random universe in which the individual was a law unto himself as "free." My mental constructions of it always degenerated into either mechanism or chaos. If there were a God to guarantee freedom, however, and to qualify its exercise, I could see free will was dynamite. Under these conditions, I could see that in a certain sense a little ole housewife might really create herself.

Setting to, I discovered that some people agreed with me. One of them was St. Thomas Aquinas. He was the first real philosopher I ever ran across who didn't consider answering a housewife's questions beneath him. Somehow, he was bothered by all the same problems I was. What a coincidence!

I was leary of him at first. I had been warned in school that he was *medieval*, a word roughly synonymous in secular institutions with "benighted," or at least "mid-evil." To hear them tell it, he spent most of his life worrying about how many angels could stand on the head of the proverbial pin. He was also concerned about the predicament of the cannibal at the general resurrection whose body could hardly be said to be his own, having fed off other people's bodies all his life. Naturally, after such recommendation I hadn't wasted time reading St. Thomas; but certain existentialists quoted him a good bit, and I began reading him, just for kicks between loads of diapers.

I was astounded.

Even in my abridged edition, his answers made an awful lot of terrifying sense. The way he would run head on into dilemmas and come up with something convinced me this was no ordinary pedant. It soon became clear that he didn't believe in the same kind of free will M. Sartre did. In fact, I was much relieved to learn that strictly speaking, he didn't believe in free will at all, but only in free *choice* between offered alternatives.

There was, I discovered, a perfectly legitimate place in the universe for what I had learned to label "determinism." Saints called it Simply "God's Holy Will," and found it liberating in the extreme, for human will is free to the extent that it conforms to God's. A wonderful thing about any given circumstances in this context is that they aren't necessarily inexorable. Prayer can change circumstances, people, or both, and the highest exercise of free choice lay in conforming to God in the continuing act of creation called "sanctification," whether of oneself or others. Suddenly, in God's determinism lay the whole plan of man's salvation, to be accepted or rejected by him, *freely.*

"God made man from the beginning, and left him in the hand of his own counsel. ... He hath set water and fire before thee: stretch forth thy hand to which thou wilt!" (*Ecclus. 15:14,17*).

Then St. Thomas told me, "*Love resides in the will.*"

Just like that, in five words. Love resides in the will—not in the intellect, or in the feelings, or in the imaginations. In the will. If that's true, love is the one thing a man has complete control over.

If you've been a believer all your life, you may think this is pretty obvious, but believe me, it isn't. In the vast world of paganism where *l'amour est enfant de Bohème*, love and will seldom enter any permanent alliance. A human being who discovers that love is an act of the will, independent of sensuality or sentiment, is on the way to real free love, for suddenly he is free to love anything he wants to love, as much as he wants to!

He can love even people he dislikes.

He can love his enemies, or his wife. Atheists can often not do this. No wonder they find the conventions irritating.

A Christian, most of all, can love God. Thank God for God! Only God can stand the amount of love a human will is capable of giving.

Ubi casitas et amor, ibi Deus est, for God is Love.

I ask you, is there any freedom to compare with this freedom to touch God with one's *will*—at will?

Hello, China!

"For I make doctrine to shine forth as the morning light, and I will declare it afar off," promises Holy Wisdom (*Ecclus. 24:44*).

As Jeremias declares, "The Lord hath raised us up prophets in Babylon!" (*29:15*).

Even among the sins and errors of Babylon can God be found, for the devils themselves become witnesses of His Truth. At the presence of Christ "devils also came forth out of many," says St. Luke, "crying out and saying, 'Thou art the Son of God!'" We are also told, however, that "He rebuked them and did not permit them to speak, because they knew that he was the Christ." Apparently He doesn't want us to take their word for anything, not even Himself; and Christ hereby warns us that evil doesn't lead us to truth by what it says.

Evil leads us to truth by ultimately giving itself away under pressure as the impotence that it is, often bursting in air. We don't come to the true Church by listening to the words of heretics, but we come to her very surely by dogging heretics into betraying the truth to us. This principle is known to every good convert-maker, who advises his quarry first of all to try to practice to its fullest any religion he may hold at the moment. False religion progressively reveals every hole in its structure to a determined searcher of majesty who insists on answers.

The more evil tries to deceive, the more it falls into telling the truth. So often does Scripture drive this point home, it constitutes a dominant theme beginning with sin itself in Genesis.

"No, you shall not die," purrs Satan into Eve's shell-like ear, tempting her to that forbidden fruit, "for God knows that when you eat of it, your eyes will be opened and you will be like God, knowing good and evil." It's clear Satan believed this to be complete falsehood, for our Lord himself designated him "father of lies."

As some of us know, Eve ate. And in Satan's prophecy now stands revealed the most baffling, the most glorious-to-God of evil's mysteries: Sinners find falsehood in evil; saints find only truth. Sinners *shall* die, their eyes shall *not* be opened, but blinded; they certainly do *not* become like God, for they know only evil. For them Satan's every word to Eve was false. To the redeemed, however, "death shall be no more." Their eyes do indeed open on everlasting light, for their Redeemer is one who makes the blind see. Conformed to Him, they "shall eat butter and honey," and "know to refuse the evil, and to choose the good" (*Isa. 7: 15*). Indeed, being so like Him, they are told, "Ye are gods," just as Satan predicted. For saints, everything Satan said to Eve turns out to be true. What torture this must be to his malicious spirit, straining to lie, and not being able to!

Balaam, Scripture's famous false prophet, had the same trouble. Hired by king Balac of Moab to curse Israel, every time he opens his mouth to curse, he ends by uttering a blessing. He piles four of them one on top of the other, each better than the last and culminating finally in a messianic prophecy:

> I see him, though not now;
> I behold him, though not near:
> A star shall advance from Jacob,
> And a staff shall arise from Israel,"
> predicts the frustrated Balaam.

To Balac's exasperation, Balaam can only reply, "Did I not warn the very messengers you sent to me, 'Even if Balac gave me his house full of silver and gold, I could not of my own accord do anything, good or evil, contrary to the command of the Lord'? Whatever the Lord says, I must repeat" (*Num. 24:12-13*).

This sort of thing happens all the time. False teachers, says St. Jude, "deride majesty." They "deride whatever they do not know; and the things they know by instinct like the dumb beasts, become for them a source of destruction. Woe to them! for they have gone in the way of Cain, and have rushed on thoughtlessly into the error of Balaam for the sake of gain" (*10-11*).

Like Balaam, however, not being able to do anything of their own accord, good or evil, contrary to the command of the Lord, the more they deride majesty, the more do they reveal it to those who humbly search for it. The cunning Caiphas, laying down the dogma that "it is expedient for us that one man die for the people," unwittingly spoke the whole truth of Redemption. When the Sanhedrin asked our Lord, "Art thou, then, the Son of Man?" He answered, "You, yourselves, say that I am" (*Luke 22:70*).

Evil is terribly useful to good people, otherwise the good God wouldn't permit it! Holy Tobias was taught by the angel Raphael how to turn parts of the ferocious fish that tried to devour him into food for his journey, medicine to heal his father's blindness, and matter for exorcising the demon troubling his fiancee. This beautiful allegory applies to all the just, by whom evil itself can be used to conquer the flesh, the world, and the devil as Tobias did.

I once saw a lovely Riminese painting of our Lady with the Child Jesus sitting on her lap, much like many other such pictures except for one detail. The divine Boy was clutching in His chubby hand a very unusual toy—an outsized, fiercely armored, but utterly helpless, bright green locust! Whoever painted this ancient masterpiece knew enough to keep one foot in the Old Testament, where this insect figures as a telling symbol of death and destruction. A more vivid pictorial representation of evil as the sport and plaything of Holy Humanity, I never have seen. I do wish painters would paint this way again.

Thank God, to the pure all things are pure.

While we're on the subject, there's a delightful story from the desert Fathers which perfectly illustrates the point. As James the Deacon tells it, he was attending a bishops' convention in Antioch once:

> And as we sat, certain of the bishops besought my master Nonnus that they might have some instruction from his lips: and straightway the good bishop began to speak to the weal and health of all that heard him. And as we sat marvelling at the holy learning of him, lot on a sudden she that was the first of the actresses of Antioch passed by: first of the dancers was she, and riding on an ass.

Like Balaam!

> And with all fantastic graces did she ride, so decked that naught could be seen upon her but gold and pearls and precious stones. The very nakedness of her feet was hidden under gold and pearls, and with her was a splendid train of young men and maidens clad in robes of price, with torques of gold about their necks. Some went before and some came after her, but of the beauty and loveliness of her there could be no wearying in the world of men.
>
> Passing through our midst, she filled the air with the fragrance of musk and all scents that are sweetest. And when the bishops saw her so shamelessly ride by, bare of head and shoulder and limb, in pomp so splendid, and not so much as a veil upon her head or about her shoulders, they groaned, and in silence turned away their heads as from great and grievous sin.

These were evidently very good bishops, but perhaps not quite saints. Nonnus' reaction, says James the Deacon, was quite different:

> The most blessed Nonnus, did long and intently regard her and after she had passed by still gazed and still his eyes went after her. Then, turning his head, he looked upon the bishops sitting round him. "Did not," said he, "the sight of her great beauty delight you?"

Nonnus, you see, was a saint. When he looked, he saw what was, and he didn't see what wasn't.

The bishops wouldn't answer him, continues the story.

> And he sank his face upon his knees, and the holy book that he held in his good hands, and his tears fell down upon his breast, and sighing heavily he said again to the bishops, "Did not the sight of her great beauty delight you?"
>
> But again they answered nothing. Then said he, "Verily, it greatly delighted me, and well pleased was I with her beauty: whom God shall set in presence of His high and terrible seat, in judgment of ourselves and our episcopate!"

This, I guess, is humility.

It doesn't surprise us to learn that the beautiful harlot soon finds herself in church for the first time in her life, listening to Bishop Nonnus preach. Struck to the heart and begging to be allowed to speak with him, she is sent the following uncompromising reply:

Whatsoever thou art is known unto God, thyself, and what thy purpose is, and thy desire. But this I surely say to thee, seek not to tempt my weakness, for I am a man that is a sinner, serving God. If in very deed thou hast a desire after divine things and a longing for goodness and faith and dost wish to see me, there are other bishops with me: come, and thou shalt see me in their presence: for thou shalt not see me alone!

And here again is sanctity speaking. Although Nonnus freely admits the woman is very beautiful, he takes no chances with his own weakness. Holy pusillanimity, you might call it, and a wonderful virtue it is. It never yet lost a conversion. Needless to say, the harlot went to see Nonnus on his terms, and she wound up as the celebrated St. Pelagia of the desert solitaries, just to show us what can happen.

It seems to me brilliant authors on the Index, "the very nakedness of their feet hidden under gold and pearls," should be treated as Nonnus treated Pelagia. Admire them, learn what you can from them in the presence of chaperones, and then by God's grace convert them if possible! If seeking good amid evil infallibly leads to God, they have as good a chance as St. Pelagia or any of the rest of us. I suppose a fairly comprehensive and orthodox course in dogmatic theology could actually be worked out by careful analysis of condemned propositions in books on the Index, if nothing else were available. Systematically it would be as easy as going to China straight through the earth, but theoretically it would not be impossible.

Because the Christian has been liberated to love everything that is, he can throw out only what isn't—sin and error. By persistently loving only what is, wherever he finds it, he finds evil robbed of all power over him. "They shall take up serpents; and if they drink any deadly thing, it shall not hurt then," promised Jesus to those who believe in Him (*Mark 16:18*).

What is this search far truth but doggedly separating what is from what isn't? Truth is only knowing what's what, that's what. As St. Thomas readily concedes, God is the cause of evil. (Isn't that a terrific shocker?) This has to be true, of course, because evil can maintain itself only as a disordered relation to something good. Destroy the Church and all heresy would disappear overnight. If Satan could destroy God, he would destroy himself, for God alone keeps him in existence.

There are prophets in Babylon, and they will point the way. Even pagans have no excuse for not finding God, as St. Paul says,

... seeing that what may be known about God is manifest to them. For God has manifested it to them. For since the creation of the world His invisible attributes are clearly seen—his everlasting power also and divinity—being understood through the things that are made. And so they are without excuse, seeing that, although they knew God, they did not glorify Him as God or give thanks, but became vain in their reasonings, and their senseless minds have been darkened (*Rom. 1:19-21*).

This is a terrible passage, full of the awful responsibility of having free choice. It leaves us no quarter. Who can overlook a God Who is everywhere and revealed in everything? The voodoo woman intent on producing the pains of lumbago in her neighbor by sticking pins in a wax effigy is dreadfully close to Him, for even fetishism yields up a distorted truth of the first magnitude. Every good luck charm, rabbit's foot, or amulet is corrupted evidence that somehow spirit can be contained and conveyed through matter. As the entire sacramental system of Holy Mother Church proves, God's power can and does sometimes flow through matter in obedience to the will of man!

When our Lord cursed a fig tree outside Jerusalem before His Passion and caused it to wither as a terrible prophecy of the fate decreed for obdurate Judaism, no devotee of voodoo would have found the sequel surprising. Perhaps prophesying the Antichrist, St. John in the Apocalypse says cryptically, "Here is wisdom. He who has understanding, let him calculate the number of the beast, for it is the number of a man; and its number is 666" (*Apoc. 13:18*). Can quack numerology be far behind? If only we knew the true mystique of numbers, so tantalizing to St. Augustine and many other giant intellects! And so with augury, palmistry, and all the "black" arts, which ultimately boil down to so many forms of perverted sacramentality.

As they can lead to God's truth, so can every other error, once grace enters the mind of the beholder. I suppose we might even go so far as to say an Electra complex might get you there eventually, if that's really all you had to start with. After all, every girl wants to marry her father, when her father is God and her destiny is nothing less than an eternal nuptial union with Him. Seems to me any perversion can be turned to good account once you find out what it's a perversion of. Nothing makes you yearn for "immortal diamond" like finding out you've been stuck with a cheap zircon!

Freudians are really incredibly naive. Every woman looks for a father in her husband, just as every man instinctively looks for a mother in his wife. Scripture put the Oedipus complex in proper perspective once and for all when it reported in a perfectly natural tone of voice in Genesis that "Isaac led Rebecca into the tent and took her to wife.

Because he loved her, Isaac was consoled for the loss of his mother," the deceased Sara (*24:67*). What is there to get so excited about?

Dark perversions are simply black shadows inevitably testifying to the blinding light which casts them; and it's interesting to note in passing that the verb "to cast a shadow" and the verb "to clarify" in the intuitive Hebrew language are one and the same. God is the cause of evil. Every so-called Oedipus complex is constrained to give evidence of the blinding theological truth which is Mary—not only the Mother of the Word in time, but the Bride of the Word in eternity.

Satan is the diabolic calculator who tries to eliminate whatever is, by multiplying it by zero. What he can't destroy he travesties and caricatures. Of St. Nicholas, the holy virgin Bishop who loved children, he has made a carnival buffoon known as Santa Claus, whose gluttonous belly shakes like jelly with every guffaw around Christmas time, thereby obscuring the significance of the feast for many a tender Christian. Rape is akin to rapture as a holiday to a holyday, and in hocus-pocus the traces of the divine *Hoc est enim Corpus Meum* never quite fade. Isn't even diabolic possession a cheap imitation of the Divine Indwelling? Satan used the same tactics during our Lord's passion, not only instigating the mockery in Pilate's courtyard, but suggesting to the crowd the release of the murderer Barabbas in place of the Son of God the Father. Believe it or not, the name Barabbas means the "Son of the Father," because such, too, is man, and that's the point of it all.

I suspect that the devil may ape God with a sort of antigrace, assigning his evil spirits to material things or to the words of false doctors, as God attaches grace to holy objects and to the words of His saints. It may be that a culpably prurient inquirer into the condemned works of Schopenhauer, say, may well end up saddled with the spirit of that philosopher's "absolute unconscious evil." Who knows? I suppose you've noticed by now that I quote an awful lot of holy people. Perhaps you feel I do this to avoid the unnecessary exertion of saying it in my own words. Well, of course, you're right, but who could resist slipping such powerful sacramentals into a book that just anybody might pick up? Even second hand the words of the Bible, of St. Augustine, of St. Teresa can convey grace. As for my stuff, well, the publisher and I can only hope the evil spirits don't creep in.

If they do, anyone who begins to suspect their vile parodies can pick up the thread in them that leads to God. In the corrupted "bedlam" one can always discover Bethlehem as the origin. If the proper clues are followed, even druidic tree worship leads quickly past the elves and mistletoe to the Christmas tree and thence to the foot of the Holy Rood, the Cross. Say, "Gosh!" or say, "Goodness!"—both are disguised ways of saying, "God!"

King Assuerus, a figure of our Lord, asks his beautiful bride, "What is thy petition, Esther, that it may be granted thee? And what wilt thou have done? Although thou ask the half of my kingdom, thou shalt have it" (*Est. 7:2*). And she obtained the deliverance of Israel.

Satan, acting through the reprobate King Herod, asks Salome the same question. "Ask of me what thou willest, and I will give it to thee. ... Whatever thou dost ask, I will give thee, even though it be half of my kingdom" (*Mark 6:22-23*). In this case, however, Satan engineers the death of the last of the prophets, John the Baptist.

Need we remind that the original four-letter word has always been the holy Tetragrammaton, the unpronounceable Name of God? And that Moloch leads inevitably to Abraham, to Christ, and to the Mass—which is the zenith of human sacrifice? Need we stress that this transcendent sacrifice makes of us Christians nothing less than holy cannibals?

If this is a hard saying, we needn't wonder. The Jews also found it so, for when they heard it for the first time, they asked, "How can this man give his flesh for us to eat?" And "from this time many of His disciples turned back and no longer went about with Him" (*John 6:67*). They were properly horrified.

Maybe you think this is all a bit overdrawn, but people have to start from wherever they are, and some people may be pretty far afield. If there weren't good in *everything*, most of us would be sunk. As the car radio blared out only this morning, "My heart belongs to Da-a-a-ddy, so I simply can't be ba-a-a-a-d!" This is a far cry from *jam lucis orto sidere*, but it may have to do as a morning hymn for lots of us commuting Babylonians. After all, even the Daddy in this jazzy classic derives from the God from whom is all Fatherhood. Seems to me interpreting the lyrics in the light of this great truth is all that may be wanted to set us on the high road to perfection, if not confirmation in grace. Who will deny that a girl whose heart belongs entirely to God simply can't be bad? Babylon's air waves are full of these little quickie spiritual conferences for listeners in the know.

You think this is silly? Starting from where she is, you may ask how a strip-tease artist, for instance, would pick up at close range the trail to God. Her way may be long, but it might be considerably shortened if some holy Nonnus could explain to her on the spot the mystical significance of her art. The strip-tease in public may well be sinful, but the act itself is pure to the pure, especially when viewed under its spiritual aspects by those who understand that the enticement of God by progressive denudation and despoliation of the soul is the art of great saints. Virtue is very much a matter of perspective!

"You shall seek me, and shall find me: when you shall seek me with all your heart. And I will be found by you, saith the Lord ... because you have said: the Lord hath raised us up prophets in Babylon!" (*Jer. 29:13-15*).

If God plants His witnesses in evil, as Scripture affirms, then we can expect to find vestiges of the Blessed Trinity there too, if only in reverse. I'm not prepared to explore this aspect at full depth, which would take us into the very core of Hell, but I can't resist pointing out a few of the clues that are scattered about us. As we have seen, the flesh, the world, and the devil are negative poles of faith, hope, and charity; and if we can find vestigial reflections of the Blessed Trinity even in material nature, we can certainly hope to find them in error and evil. Satan tempted our Lord three times in the desert, first according to bodily appetites, then to human glory, and finally to power, for he is constrained to oppose the God-Man by the three trinitarian theological virtues.

I hope you won't think me facetious if I offer humble corroboration from botany; but I've just learned that all forms of poison oak and poison ivy grow leaves in groups of threes. If Satan were looking for a substitute for St. Patrick's shamrock to teach his own version of theology, he might well make use of poison ivy-and maybe he did. (He often gives us bats for doves.) The Blessed Trinity, Exemplar of all that ever was, is, or shall be, is bound to leave more or less perfect traces on all that exists; but It can also be said to leave traces on what doesn't exist. Evil, being a kind of mirror-writing of what is good, still bears witness to the Triune God by the character of the reverse form it happens to take.

Like Alice Through the Looking-Glass, even sober, materialistic scientists today are finding themselves, I'm told, up against the dilemma of the probable presence of a "non-something" in physical nature which they can so far only describe as "anti-matter." Should such be defined, there must be metaphysical repercussions all down the line, but to a Christian, it will be merely welcome confirmation of what he has known all along. He knows that St. Peter denied Christ not once, but three times, for his sin was against a Triune God. In giving external form to his repentance, St. Peter likewise protested his love three times to our Lord's triple query, "Simon Peter, lovest thou me?"

This is no superficial tale, but a lesson that goes too deep to be explained merely by words; it goes straight to the heart of the problem of evil, lodged in the heart of man made to God's image and likeness.

Christ suffered at the hands of a human anti-trinity of Herod, Caiphas, and Pilate, acting for the same Adversary who tempted Him in the desert with a three-fold temptation.

Baudelaire, a poet drawn to give lyric articulation to the agony of the damned, apotheosizes Satan under the title *Trismégiste*, "thrice-greatest," proving right there his uncanny insight into the nature of evil:

> *Sur l'oreiller du mal c'est Satan Trismégiste*
> *Qui berce longuement notre esprit enchanté,*
> *Et le riche métal de notre colonié*
> *Est tout vaporisé par ce savant chimiste,*

he croons, presenting Satan in terms of the ancient god Thoth, inventor of magic and alchemy, who "vaporizes our wills." Satan must wrest "thrice-greatest" homage from his worshippers if he is to deride fully a God who is thrice-praised in heaven as "Holy, Holy, Holy." Satan has no choice, poor devil.

Far more profoundly than Baudelaire, the Apocalypse also takes due cognizance of this ontological necessity, for it symbolizes evil precisely as an anti-trinity whose "persons" are the Dragon, the Beast, and the False Prophet. Carrying the analogy further, it speaks also of an "image" of the Beast, who, no doubt aping the saving action of Christ, imprints "the mark of its name" upon its followers. In Hell, "the smoke of their torments goes up forever and ever; and they rest neither day nor night, they who have worshipped the beast and its image, and anyone who receives the mark of its name" (*Apoc. 14:11*).

In his vision of the end of the world, St. John tells us:

> I saw the beast, and the kings of the earth and their armies gathered together to wage war against him who was sitting upon the horse, and against his army. And the beast was seized, and with it the false prophet who did signs before it wherewith he deceived those who accepted the mark of the beast and who worshipped its image. These two were cast alive into the pool of fire that burns with brimstone. ... And I saw an angel coming down from heaven, having the key of the abyss and a great chain in his hand. And he laid hold on the dragon, the ancient serpent, who is the devil and Satan, and bound him for a thousand years. ... And when the thousand years are finished, Satan will be released from his prison, and will go forth and deceive the nations ... and will gather them together for the battle. And they went up over the breadth of the earth and encompassed the camp of the saints and the beloved city. And fire from God came down out of heaven and devoured them. And the devil who deceived them was cast into the pool of fire and brimstone, where are also

the beast and the false prophet; and they will be tormented day and night forever and ever (*Apoc. 19:19-20; 20:1-2, 7-10*).

So much for the anti-trinity.

On the human level, the arts and mythology have always roiled with intuitions of this truth, some conscious, others not. Just as the pagans of classical antiquity recognized not one, or twenty, but three Fates, so with sure instinct Shakespeare set not one, nor four, but three witches over the bubbling kettle in Macbeth. (Women, good or bad, are always cooking!)

In our own day, the avowed Communist Picasso painted what I do believe is the most heart-rending picture of human misery in the history of modern art. It belongs to his famous "blue period" and hangs in the National Gallery in Washington, D.C. It's the blues in pigment. There are three figures on the canvas, a man, a woman, and a child, whose face is prematurely aged by deprivation and hunger. All stand together barefoot beside a limitless blue sea, each gazing at his own personal emptiness.

Anyone who might wonder what a spiritual negative of the Holy Family must be has only to look at this picture. Called simply "Tragedy," it's a work of such powerful genius, I confess I find it hard to look at without clutching my throat. It speaks of fallen trinitarian humanity in terms that only a creature made in the image and likeness of the Trinity could find at his disposal; for the trinity in the human psyche manifests itself symbolically with explosive force in the world of art, whether the artist is a believer or not. Who has control over his deepest intuitions? Certainly not the artist, who is often more surprised than the critics at what his work insists on saying. Even Balaam, confronted by his talking mule, ended by listening to her!

(Picasso's picture hangs in a room adjoining the one in which Salvador Dali's "Last Supper" is displayed. Going from one to the other of these masterpieces is like commuting between Heaven and Hell. Blue predominates in both, but at the Last Supper it is shot with gold, and Judas Iscariot is incognito, for like Picasso's, Dali's picture also deals with reality in human dress. Whoever is responsible for placing these two canvases in such near proximity must have been directed by angels.)

There's another modern work that sends me into similar paroxysms of admiration at the trinitarian testimony it yields in spite of itself. It's a one-act play. Besides being what critics call sensational "good theater," it's on the Index, for the aforementioned philosopher Sartre wrote it. I had to obtain my Bishop's permission to re-read it at this juncture, and

I must say I can see why a chaperone is needed. I had forgotten how wild Babylonian prophets could get.

Played to English-speaking audiences under the title *No Exit*, it opens to our view an atheist intellectual's well-constructed idea of Hell. The plot is quite hellish and well constructed, as well as devilishly theatrical. Three persons (I guess that gives it away right there!) find themselves in a hotel room hellishly furnished in French Second Empire, sporting three sofas whose hellish colors clash, and a bronze chimney ornament that can't be budged. (To get the full flavor of this decor, one must understand how Frenchmen feel today about Second Empire, but this isn't quickly explained. The point is, they don't like it, for various deep psychological, historical, and esthetic reasons.)

As we might expect, there are no windows on the set. As the dialogue progresses, we learn also that the room keeps getting hotter and hotter and the occupants can never sleep, because their eyelids won't even blink, let alone close, from now on. Unless they jump into the orchestra pit over the footlights—which wouldn't be cricket—the *dramatis personae*'s only contact with the outside is a valet who sometimes comes in answer to a bell that sometimes rings when pressed.

These are only minor inconveniences, however, for we soon learn that the real hell of it lies in the eternal interplay of the three personalities, now just beginning. One of these is Garcin, who is a lecher and a vainglorious coward, shot for desertion in wartime. The second is Estelle, a narcissistic nymphomaniac who murdered her illegitimate baby, and finally there's Inez, a lesbian, who also happens to be a sadist, and who died the victim of murder. With this pungent cast, a kind of dreadful morality play soon gets going. Anyone finding it all pretty disgusting and shocking will certainly not like Hell, as these are presumably the kind of people to be found there.

After telling one another various lies about how they happened to land where they are, they settle down to the serious business of each two torturing a third for eternity, In the ringaround-the-rosy of perverted and selfish desires, each applies to one other person for gratification of sense, vainglory, or pride of power, only to be frustrated by the third member. Meanwhile, the room gets stuffier and stuffier, and, though Garcin finally manages to get the door open, no one will leave without taking with him the one other from whom he seeks self-realization. So they just close the door again.

"Wherefore, thou hast also greatly tormented them who in their life have lived foolishly and unjustly, by the same things which they worshipped" (*Wis. 12:23*).

This, you'll admit, is Hell; I do believe only a French intellectual could have conceived it in just these philosophical soap opera terms. Though the characters are not so much people as ideas, they make their point.

They are the closed corporation of the damned, whether viewed as persons, or as the three. trinitarian powers of the damned soul, doomed to hopeless conflict. Though to M. Sartre his Hell must be a little more than a literary device, I for one suspect the real thing must be very much like this when viewed from within; this play alone would be enough to make me pause and consider the price of the primrose path.

What intrigues me most of all, however, is the trinitarian form in which M. Sartre freely chose to cast this torment. Whether or not a blasphemous parody of the Most Holy Trinity is intended, with the valet perhaps aping the role of the Holy Humanity of our Lord, I can't know. Happily, such judgments don't come within the province of literary criticism. What is remarkable is that an atheist existentialist should write a play along such lines, and that it should show forth such sound doctrine.

(Pelagia, you're beautiful!)

Hell, being essentially a condition contrary to God, must like Satan oppose Him in a manner somehow trinitarian in order to oppose Him completely. So must society, so must the individual within his own soul, where the natural trinitarian operation is reversed. The will, directed by the passions and senses, dominates the intellect, and error inevitably results. With dragon and beast behind him, the false prophet speaks. Whether conscient of the Most Holy Trinity or not, man is essentially formed in Its image and can't act without reference to It. As Scripture says, even when we sin, we are His! (*Wis. 15:2*). The Lord is God not only of the hills, but also of the valleys (*III Kings 20:28*). The devils are His, too. The spirit who tormented Saul was "from the Lord," and Satan, who despoiled Job, did so only by God's permission.

When, round about curtain time.tthe hero of No Exit finds himself stroking the eternally inert bronze chimney-piece, he muses:

> This bronze. Yes; now's the moment; I'm looking at this thing on the mantelpiece, and I understand that I'm in Hell. I tell you, everything's been thought out beforehand. They knew I'd stand at the fireplace, stroking this thing of bronze, with all those eyes intent on me. Devouring me.

Then he swings abruptly around and asks, "What? Only two of you? I thought there were more; many more!" Laughing, he adds, "So this is Hell. I'd never have believed it. You remember all we were told about the torture-chambers, the fire and brimstone, the 'burning marl'? Old wives' tales! There's no need for red-hot pokers."

Finally he concludes, "Hell is—other people!"

Isn't it marvelous that Garcin and M. Sartre should know that? It certainly must be so, for so is Heaven. Heaven, too, is other People. Heaven is Three Divine Persons, and all who share Their society.

"Where can I go from your spirit?" cries, not Garcin, but David. "From your presence where can I flee? If I go up to the heavens, you are there; if I sink to the nether world you are there!"

So Hell, too, is God's. And so are M. Sartre, Pablo Picasso, and Balaam. So are the voodoo woman and Garcin and Estelle and Inez the lesbian. And so is the beautiful harlot who was really St. Pelagia.

For Babylon is full of prophets, says Jeremias.

"For I say to you that God is able out of these stones to raise up children to Abraham," warned John the Baptist.

"And I will be found by you," saith the Lord. Even in the Index— "when you shall seek me with all your heart."

God the Good Mother

CHAPTER 9

I HAVE a Mormon friend who is a housewife. She told me a story once about another housewife she knew who was always puzzling over the riddle of the universe. Not that there's anything strange about that. Good housewives who stay home where they belong have to come to grips with the big problems sooner or later. Nobody can dust day after day without wondering now and then what dust is, be it stardust or the other kinds. But this housewife, it seems, ran across the key to the whole confounding mystery at one swoop.

Thinking hard, she went to bed one night as usual, slept and dreamed, and saw it all, plain as day. She was so overcome at the simplicity of the solution that occurred to her, she got up in her sleep, ran for pencil and paper and jotted down the salient points, fearing she might forget them by morning. Then she returned to bed, pleased and happy at knowing everything at last.

Wondering on waking whether this marvel had really happened to her, she straightway looked for the slip of paper, because sure enough, she couldn't recall what she had written. It was in plain sight on the night table, and it said, in her handwriting:

Daisies are white and yellow.

No doubt of it, there must be some peculiar affinity between daisies and housewives. And there it was, the clue to everything that is, but she couldn't remember how it fitted. It made no more sense to her than it does to me. I understand she was terribly let down, knowing it all in the middle of the night, only to see it irrevocably gone. There was nothing to do but start thinking all over again. As they say, back to the ole ironing board!

I do like this story. Without probing unduly into the whys and wherefores of garden variety mysticism, I think it's safe to accept as pretty solid fact that daisies are white and yellow. (Please, Professor Kant, now now.) Anyway, I *guess* it's safe to accept daisies white and yellow as pretty solid *phenomena. ...*

I'll even go so far as to say that anybody who understands why and how daisies are white and yellow could easily unlock all the other secrets of the natural universe. Unfortunately data like white and yellow daisies are much too simple to be understood by finite minds. The theory of relativity, now, or some other man-made logical construction can be easily grasped with sufficient effort and I.Q., but not daisies!

It's the same with women. The whole mystery of Eve, what she is, what she does, and why God created her, is bound up in facts as simple and obvious, and as little understood as white and yellow daisies.

For instance, women have wombs and breasts.

Explain me *that*!

Scripture keeps dwelling on these characteristics of females, and we may believe it's not just to teach us humility by embarrassing us. That we often find such references embarrassing just shows how far we are from grasping the real significance of feminine physiology.

Please don't think I grasp it, but my suspicions are aroused when I hear that the angel called Gabriel was sent from God to a young girl in a house in Nazareth to tell her, "Behold, thou shalt conceive in thy womb and shalt bring forth a son."

Running to share her extraordinary news with her old cousin in the hill country, this same young girl is greeted by Elizabeth with, "Blessed art thou among women, and blessed is the fruit of thy womb!" When Elizabeth, filled with the Holy Spirit, takes care to add that the child in her own womb leapt for joy on this occasion, we may well wonder at the unseen drama taking place within two pregnant women.

My suspicions are even more aroused when I hear the whole Catholic world today pray over and over, *Hail Marry, full of grace, the Lord is with thee. Blessed art thou among women and blessed is the fruit of thy womb!* echoing endlessly the words of the Angel and Elizabeth, with little enough concern for modern prudery.

Natural delicacy would no doubt have it, "Blessed art thou among women, and blessed is thy *Son*," blandly overlooking the vertiginous mystery involved, in an effort to maintain propriety, but the Church will have none of that.

"Blessed is the womb of the Virgin Mary, which bore the Son of the eternal Father!" chants the liturgy without euphemism, singing the glories of this same Mary, whom the unknown woman praised on earth by addressing to her Son the words, "Blessed is the womb that bore thee, and the breasts that nursed thee!" (*Luke 11:27*).

I don't pretend to understand this, but any fool can see there must be more here than meets the eye. Perhaps the time has come for women to stop being embarrassed about being women, and be women. Perhaps the time has come for us to ask plain out why we have wombs and breasts.

Well, why?

The full answer can lie only in God, in whose image and likeness woman is made. That she is made in His image every true believer must maintain, and this goes for St. Cyril of Alexandria, too, all Schopenhauers notwithstanding.

God says, "Let us make mankind in our image and likeness; and let them have dominion over the fish of the sea, the birds of the air, the cattle, over all the wild animals and every creature that crawls on the earth." Then, says Scripture,

God created man in his image.

In the image of God he created him.

Male and female he created them (*Gen. 1: 26-27*) .

Not only are we created in the image of God, but we are created male and female. This is terribly important. Daisies, let's say, are all daisies, but they're white and yellow. White and yellow daisies together must somehow reflect better the perfections of the Godhead which daisies are meant to reflect than would daisies all white, or all yellow—or blue, or black. (Honest, I think that housewife had a mystical intuition of the first magnitude!)

All due proportion kept, it must be the same with men and women. To reflect God as God wills it to, humanity must be both male and female. Complementary to each other, both sexes reflect God truly by image and likeness, but each in its special way. Made like God, woman is commanded to be perfect as He is perfect, not as man is perfect.

Poor women, taking their cue from Mary, we might ask, "How shall this happen, since God is so awesomely masculine?"

He is the King of Kings, the Judge of all, the one whom our Lord instructed us to address as "Our Father." Then, too, when God came to earth in our flesh, He came as Man, not as woman. (The fiercest suffragette has never been able to get around this one.) Because He is our Head, this could hardly be otherwise without reversing the order of creation. Any woman undertaking to imitate Christ as closely as a man might find herself a full-fledged spiritual lesbian in no time, maybe even preaching in pulpits with her hat off, not to mention spending whole nights praying in the woods alone.

To make our dilemma worse, God is the Husband of Israel, the Bridegroom of the Church, before whom all chosen souls are spiritually feminine. Though it's true this gives woman great psychological advantages in the ways of prayer, it's extremely difficult for her to "identify" with God, whom man, on the other hand, finds a ready Model. How could a woman ever be like Him and still be a woman? Seeking to be perfect as her heavenly Father is perfect may well give her moments of confusion.

But is God really so uncompromisingly masculine?

In spleruloribus sanctorum, ex utero ante luciferum genui Te, sings the Church at Christmas, applying the words of the Psalm at the Communion. "Amid the splendors of heaven, from the womb before the daystar I begot Thee," says God the Father of His Son, the Word.

When God the Trinity speaks of begetting from the womb, for Him alone this is no mixed metaphor. "God speaks of his womb," says St. Basil, "to confound the impious!" He adds that it is necessary that they learn by a consideration of their own nature that the Son is the genuine fruit of the Father, who both begets and produces. In Ecclesiasticus, the just man is promised, "Thou shalt be as the obedient son of the Most High, and he will have mercy on thee more than a mother" (*14:11*).

Although the Church has yet to define in what man's image and likeness of God consist, perhaps I had better quote St. Thomas before it's too late. He warns that Genesis does not mean to say that mankind was created to God's image according to distinctions of sex: *Sed quia imago Dei utrique seu est communis, cum sit secundum mentem, in qua non est distinctio sexuum* (*Summa Theol.* Pars I, Q93, A6). Unquestionably there can be no sex in God properly speaking, but this does not prevent our acknowledging Him as both Father and Mother. Theologians, as a matter of fact, often speak of the *nativitas in utero Patris*, with perfect propriety.

> For there is, indeed, generation in God. ... For the First Person of the Trinity, himself living, is the origin—not in time, but in the order of being—of another Person who is joined with Him and who is of the same divine nature.
>
> "Shall not I that make others to bring forth children, myself bring forth?" says God through the prophet Isaias (*66:9*).
>
> "Thou art my son; this day have I begotten thee" (*Psalm 11:7*) "From the Father alone is the Son, not made, not created, but begotten" (Athanasian Creed).
>
> "The Father begetting, the Son begotten. The Father, begetting the Son from all eternity, communicates His substance to Him, as the Son has testified," says the Lateran Council.
>
> This is not merely real generation, but generation that is uniquely perfect. So perfect that the Son remains within the Father for all eternity; so perfect that the case is not one of mere similarity between two numerical examples of the same nature, but of a same identical nature that

both Father and Son possess; so perfect that there is no distinction between conception and birth, and no distinction between maternity and paternity.

... The Father has the womb and there is no distinction between the womb and Himself, between his act of generation and himself. The Father is an eternal act of generation. There is thus no distinction of sex in God, but that which sex differentiates—the function of generation—exists in God undifferentiated, eternal, perfect, infinite ...

Now it is from this perfect generation, this single and infinite point of being, this divine mystery at the heart of all causation, that sex divides and derives: "From whom all paternity in heaven and in earth is named" (Vincent Wilken, S.J., *The Image of God in Sex*, pp. 15-16).

Women are inevitably caught up into this transcendental mystery, for it requires two human beings of different sex to reflect the perfect generation of the one Generator in the Blessed Trinity. Though the woman is secondary to the male principle, she still performs an essential role in the representation of the divine act. On earth the Blessed Virgin reproduced most closely the divine production of the Son in the Blessed Trinity, in fact producing the same Second Person in flesh, Though the rest of us stand incalculably farther from the single perfect production in the Godhead, we are never allowed to forget the essential unity of the sexes. Man and wife, to be man and wife, must be *one flesh*. It follows that we are commanded to "Honor thy father *and* thy mother," for this unity must be respected. Who can honor one who dishonors the other, both parents being representative of the one Generator? It's so easy to overlook the obvious!

Fr. Wilkin continues:

The man is the active sower of the seed; the woman is the fertile soil on which it germinates. The difference is not merely physiological. Body and soul are so one together, soul is so much in the body for the sake of the body, to elevate its sensibility, that a man is a man with the whole of himself, and womanhood likewise penetrates and embraces the whole personality. Nature, allotting different roles, provides different points of view and characteristic reactions to sustain them (Wilken, *op. cit.*, p. 51).

Writing under the vigilant eyes of St. Cyril, who keeps reminding me my female brain is "a soft, weak, delicate thing," I have understandable hesitancy about launching off into what we might describe as an exploration of the theological roots of womanhood, an area still uncharted by the most intrepid male theologians. Still, I have to live, today, as a woman. That means I have to do some thinking, whether I like it or not.

"In the beginning God created the heavens and the earth; the earth was waste and void; darkness covered the abyss, and the spirit of God was stirring above the waters," whereupon the world as we know it soon came forth. I suspect that only a housewife with a womb which has borne children can really understand certain aspects of this primordial revelation *in the flesh*, in the here and now, at eye level.

For instance, the waters mentioned are easily recognized by exegetes as the prototype of the waters of baptism, as indeed they are. Men, however, who have no wombs, are inclined to think of water here exclusively as a washing agent, and it's possible that as small boys with dirty ears they may even have learned to associate water with pain. Baptism, they will tell you, "washes" away original sin by the redemptive suffering of Christ, and this is an eminently true analogy, but only as far as it goes. Any mother—especially one who has been privileged to deliver children without anesthesia—can be led to see that these waters in Genesis at the beginning of the world are more than just lustral.

They are *birth* waters.

They precede the birth of the world as breaking amniotic waters must precede each normal human birth, or any damp, hatching chick. Water is important to the birth of life, as any mother who has undergone the agony of a "dry" birth can tell you. This is mystery unutterable into which every creature possessing a womb either physically or spiritually is caught up.

So, too, baptism is no mere springing out of a font as one would pop dripping out of a bath-tub. Baptism is nothing less than being shot from the womb of Mother Church on the facilitating waters of divine grace. Thereare no dry births unto eternal life! Baptism doesn't just "wash" sin off the sinner; it actually re-creates him, reproducing him in the likeness of God as if his sins had never been.

When the Church was drawn from the side of Christ on the cross, "immediately there came out blood and water" (*John 19:34*). Since that time, she prays on Holy Saturday over her baptismal fonts: "May He by a secret mixture of His divine power render this water fruitful for the regeneration of men, so that a heavenly offspring, conceived in sanctification, may emerge from the immaculate womb of this divine font, reborn a new creature; and grace as a mother may bring forth everyone, however distinguished either by sex in body, or by age in time, to the same infancy!" The Church is a holy mother who understands such things.

"Amen, amen, I say unto you, unless a man be born again, he cannot see the kingdom of God," the Christ tells the man Nicodemus. "Unless a man be born again of water and the spirit, he cannot enter into the kingdom of God"(*John 3:1,5*).

Nicodemus, being a man, found this pretty hard to believe, but every woman has the clues to these spiritual marvels in her own flesh. "If I have spoken of earthly things to you, and you do not believe, how will you believe if I speak to you of heavenly things?" (*John 3:12*).

How indeed? Men are at a great disadvantage in some areas! In these days of hospitals, antiseptic puritanism, and narcosis, even women can hardly get close enough to the marvels of earthly birth to suspect, let alone ascertain the marvels of spiritual birth. Modern society apparently feels that mothers themselves best begin their careers totally or partially unconscious. This attitude, I do believe, has had repercussions.

Well, first things first, especially "in the beginning." What's in a womb?

Life.

Wombs produce life. They don't beget life, for surely this is the masculine prerogative, but they form it once begotten. The Latin word *matrix* reveals best this deep truth of motherhood, for it means both womb and mold, and the meanings are interchangeable. Woman forms and molds mankind, not only physically, but intellectually and spiritually. St. Paul won't allow her to "exercise authority over men," but he does allow they will nevertheless "be saved by child-bearing" (*I Tim. 2:12,15*); she will bear men!

She is the shape of culture as she is the shape of history. As Schopenhauer saw only too clearly, she "has never managed to produce a single achievement in the fine arts that is really great, genuine, and original," but what he didn't see was that she has produced every single one of the great artists! A woman, let's face it, was the mold of Schopenhauer, I'm afraid it was the mother who kicked him downstairs because he interfered with her career. Woman is the shaper of men. *They* are her achievements.

"A woman shall compass a man," says Jeremias (*31:22*).

Hail, Mary, full of grace, blessed is the Fruit of thy womb, Jesus. Mary, the mold of the Sacred Humanity, is inevitably the mold of all His members. To imitate her at all, the Christian woman must form her children, natural or supernatural, in His likeness and give Christ to the world, as Mary gave Him. From the beginning, the womb of woman was never meant to produce anything but what the "womb" of the eternal Father produces: again, Christ.

The womb is therefore not only the mold of life, but the mold of eternal life. Any woman who doesn't know this, doesn't know the most important thing about being a woman. This brings the mystery and purpose of the Divine Indwelling very close.

"Hail, full of grace; the Lord is with thee. Blessed art thou among women!" Mary, in whose womb the divine Word dwelt not only spiritually, but in the flesh for nine months, comprehended the mystery as no man will ever comprehend it, but her daughters who have borne children of flesh, may, I think, have an inkling!

Once begun, life either natural or spiritual is a progress from the womb to the tomb. Certainly the author of Job saw that tombs and wombs are simply different aspects of the same truth, for Job laments, "Naked came I out of my mother's womb, and naked shall I return thither" (*1:21*). Obviously he can't be referring only to the womb of his human mother, for as Nicodemus said, "Can he enter a second time into his mother's womb and be born again?" (*John 3:4*).

For natural man this is, of course, impossible; but for supernatural man this is a condition of life. The Resurrection is birth from the womb which is the Holy Sepulchre, where our souls and bodies will be joined again as they were at our first conception. All the elect are now being formed in the womb of Mother Church, which is also the tomb of the old Adam and Eve. The baptismal font is tomb as much as womb. "For we were buried with him by means of baptism into death, in order that, just as Christ had arisen from the dead through the glory of the Father, so we may walk in newness of life" (*Rom. 6:4*). The mystery of the Incarnation is inalterably bound up in this paradox. Even in speaking of our Lady, St. Jerome said, "Although the doors were shut, Jesus entered within; in the sepulchre that was Mary, which was new and hewn in the hardest rock, no one either before or afterwards was laid" (*Letter to Pammachius*).

"Amen, amen, I say to you, unless the grain of wheat falls into the ground and dies, it remains alone, But if it dies, it brings forth much fruit" (*John 12:34*).

Viewed in this light, proper burial assumes importance equal to being born! "If a man beget a hundred children, and live many years, and attains great age, and his soul makes no use of his substance and he be without burial," said Ecclesiasticus dourly, "of this man I pronounce, that the untimely born is better than he" (*Eccles. 6:3*). I guess he knew a thing or two!

Any housewife who has watched at the bedside of the dying knows how similar the death agony is to the pangs of birth; and for the redeemed, the last agony is indeed the labor which finally ushers in eternal life.

But women not only have wombs. They have breasts, and that's very mysterious, too.

What's in a breast? Well, milk.

(Please don't think I presume you ignorant of the facts of life. To come to grips with mystery, one must ask and then answer the most obvious questions.)

Breasts produce milk, for the nourishment of the child that the womb has formed and produced. It's really amazing how many people don't seem to know this. Certainly a lot of Hollywood directors have never given it second thought. More often than not, breasts are only for beauty queens or to entice unwary males into procreating children the mothers don't know what to do with. They're only part of a beautiful figure.

The truth is, they aren't just part—they *are* a beautiful figure. Like the womb, the breast reflects an attribute of God, who not only generates and creates, but feeds and sustains what He has brought forth. His providence doesn't leave His creatures to die, once they have been given life.

Can a woman forget her infant, so as not to have pity on the son of her womb? And if she should forget, yet will I not forget thee! promises God, the Good Mother, by His prophet Isaias (*49:15*).

Scripture would have us know the care and nourishment afforded by earthly mothers are most powerful reflections of an activity proper to God.

"Our Father, who art in heaven ... give us this day our daily bread" we pray, knowing full well where sustenance is to be gotten. "For your Father in heaven knows that you need all these things," He tells us (*Matt. 6:32*).

"How often would I have gathered thy children together, as a hen gathers her young under her wings, but thou wouldst not" (*Matt. 23:37*), lamented a God whose mother-love was sadly rejected, and whose children refused to eat.

This tender, maternal solicitude on the part of a "masculine" God need hardly startle us, for classical antiquity was aware of it even without revelation. Mythology, which can be depended on for a firm grasp of natural first principles, had long fostered in Rome the cult of the male father-god Jupiter under the title *Jupiter Ruminus*. Believe it or not, this means "Jupiter who offers the breast." It would seem that even in pagan Rome a woman with breasts could hope to be like a god, so we may wonder why Christian women have so much trouble.

Believe it or not, in Greek the very word *pater*, or father, is derived from an ancient verb meaning "to feed," just as our own "pastor" is allied to *pascere*, which conveys the same notion. God is, indeed, the Good Mother, who feeds and tends all creation, and of whom all other mothers are merely pale, though true, reflections. In the guise of a housewife, His Holy Wisdom "sets forth her table" and calls, "whosoever is a little one, let him come to me!" (*Prov. 9:2,4*). Greater than any earthly mother, who nourishes her infants with food from her own being, He gives His little ones *Himself* to eat.

THIS IS MY BODY, TAKE AND EAT.

Manducat Dominum pauper et humilis.

Any woman who would be perfect as God is perfect must conform as closely as she can to this one model of divine Motherhood, so marvelous and yet so terrifying to nature. Women, who have breasts, have the inestimable grace of knowing in a small way what it means to be eaten, as God is eaten, who is Love. This was His "gift of self," and it must be hers, in one way or another.

The Middle Ages seem to have been much closer than we to an understanding of the "womanly" attributes of God. At least they weren't so squeamish about speaking of "Jesus our Mother" or the "Motherhood of Mercy" and the like. Dame Julian of Norwich didn't hesitate to place the Most Blessed Trinity itself in such context. Speaking of a vision on the subject, she says:

> I beheld the working of all the blessed Trinity, in which beholding I saw and understood these three properties: the property of the Fatherhood, the property of the Motherhood, and the property of the Lordhood, in one God. In the Father Almighty we have our keeping and our bliss as anent our kindly substance, which is to us by our making, without beginning. And in the Second Person in wit and wisdom we have our keeping as anent our sensuality: our restoring and our saving; for he is our Mother, Brother, and Savior. And in our good Lord, the Holy Ghost, we have our rewarding and our restoring for our living and travail, and endless overpassing of all that we desire, in his marvelous courtesy, of his high, plenteous grace.
>
> For all our life is in three: in the first we have our Being, in the second we have our Increasing, and in the third we have our Fulfilling: the first is Kind, the second Mercy, and the third is Grace.
>
> For the first, I saw and understood that the high Might of the Trinity is our Father, and the deep Wisdom of the Trinity is our Mother, and the great Love of the Trinity is our Lord: and all this have we in kind and in making of our Substance (*Revelations of Divine Love*, Ch. 58).

Speaking of her Lord and Savior, the "devout *Ankress*" finds nothing untoward in saying:

> He might no more die, but he would not stint of working: wherefore then it behoveth him to feed us; for the dearworthy love of Motherhood hath made him debtor to us. The mother may give her child suck (of) her milk, but our precious Mother Jesus, he may feed us with himself, and doeth it, full courteously and tenderly, with the Blessed Sacrament that is precious food of very life; and with all the sweet Sacraments he sustaineth us full mercifully and graciously. ... The mother may lay the child tenderly to her breast, but our tender Mother, Jesus, he may homely lead us into his blessed breast, by his sweet open side, and shew therein part of the Godhead and the joys of Heaven, with ghostly sureness of endless bliss ...
>
> This fair lovely word *Mother*, it is so sweet and so kind itself that it may not verily be said of none but him; and to her that is very Mother of him and of all. To the property of Motherhood belongeth kind love, wisdom, and knowing; and it is good: for though it be so that our bodily forthbringing be but little, low, and simple in regard of our ghostly forth bringing, yet it is he that doeth it in the creatures by whom that it is done. ... And in this I saw that all our duty that we owe, by God's bidding, to Fatherhood and Motherhood, for (reason of) God's Fatherhood and Motherhood is fulfilled in true loving of God; which blessed love Christ worketh in us (*Op. cit.*, Ch. 60).

Really, I think this is all very beautiful, and if you're a woman, it brings the imitation of God within the range of our powers at last! If the men can't see it, I'm sorry.

Women have wombs and breasts. Furthermore, physiology teaches us these are interdependent organs. Breasts cannot produce milk unless the womb has first conceived; and the womb is most properly restored when the breasts nurse. The womb itself, like the breast, is essentially a nourishing organ, for it too sustains the child whose generation the male principle has inaugurated, with nutriments from the mother's body. This is very, very significant, for it reveals woman totally for what she is: *the nourisher of society*. Her whole life is bound up in this function, on whatever level she may choose to live it.

Men nourish too, but we must stress that women don't nourish as men nourish, providing food directly from the outside, like Daddy bringing home the bacon. Women feed society as they feed their babies. They assimilate food from the outside, but digest and transform it within themselves before offering it, in a form suited to the recipient. This analogy holds true not only in the nursery, but it continues all through life. It operates in the kitchen, where Mother is the one who prepares, cooks, and transforms the dinner Daddy provides. It isn't eaten raw, but must be rendered digestible by Mother.

> Fishy, fishy in the brook,
> Daddy catch him with a hook;
> Mommy fry him in the pan,
> Baby eat him like a man!

runs the nursery jingle, full of high truths and trinitarian vestiges at the pre-school level. The best cooks may be men, but women do most of the cooking!

I'm sure it has occurred to others besides me that the home library where the minds of the family are fed is a room analogous to the dining room where their stomachs are filled. Religious orders, which for centuries have read aloud to those eating in their refectories, know any kind of food is food. The mother has intellectual cooking to do, too, for teaching and feeding are aspects of the same divine attribute. Upon the mother devolves the duty of adapting raw knowledge to the digestion of children. It does little good to be a crackerjack dietician whose children are crammed with balanced meals, if mentally and spiritually they are living skeletons, doomed to eternal death by starvation, unless some spiritual wet-nurse comes to their rescue from elsewhere. How many natural mothers wouldn't think of letting their child skip a meal, yet never buy them a book, let alone fast and pray for them, as Job did, feeding them spiritually from their own being!

Throughout Scripture woman is represented as a nourisher, in fact, the bread-baker of the world. "Quick, three measures of fine flour! Knead it, and make loaves!" Abraham commands Sara, preparing to entertain the three mysterious strangers under the tree outside his tent.

A loaf in the oven, a child in the womb—are women's business. This delicate promise of trinitarian life, in the production of which woman plays so vital a part, rises to higher pitch in the New Testament. "The Kingdom of heaven is like leaven," said our Lord, "which a woman took and buried in three measures of flour, until all of it was leavened" (*Matt. 13:33*).

What a destiny!

Of the Valiant Woman, Scripture says she gets up in the middle of the night to feed her household and give "victuals to her maidens," who are, I believe, the young souls for whom she is responsible, whoever they may be. Offhand, I can't think of any woman I know who sets out "victuals," though I do know some who wouldn't be above setting out *vittles*. The Vulgate, however, uses a word here I consider truly beautiful, not only in sound, but in meaning. It's *cibaria*. *Cibaria* isn't just food; it's food in the sense of a continuing ration, like breast-milk, which can be depended upon to appear when needed, in necessary quantity. If we take our cue from the Vulgate, we can see the Valiant Woman fed her family not just intermittently or when she felt like it, but constantly and regularly, setting the pace to appetites.

Women can explain things to their children in ways theologians can't. Women adapt doctrine, filtering it through their being, much as they prepare food for all the household. This talent of woman is what makes her like Mother Church, *Mater et Magistra*, the mold, nurse, and teacher of little ones. Writing, too, is analogous to preparing dinner for others to consume. So why shouldn't women have written parts of the Bible, eminently the Book for "little ones?"

"Crave as newborn babes pure spiritual milk," advises St. Peter, "that by it you may grow to salvation, if indeed you have tasted that the Lord is sweet" (*I Pet. 2:2*). St. Paul also speaks of his "little ones in Christ," whom he has fed with milk, for milk is a figure of the rudiments of doctrine, the first food of the soul. It's what every spiritual mother, be she Mme. Martin or St. Peter or St. Paul, must give her children—who can't be expected to digest the Apocalypse at birth any more than they can eat meat right off.

Like Mother Church, women are always pregnant and always nursing in the sense that they never cease to form and nourish, once life has been begotten in them. The fifth Joyful Mystery has already been called in evidence of the fact that the Blessed Virgin nourished our Lord in this way not only physically, but intellectually and spiritually, and we have no reason to assume she ceased on His becoming of age. She is forever the one we address as *Alma Redemptoris Mater*, *Dei Mater Alma*, Nourishing Mother of God the Redeemer. Only in heaven will we get some adequate notion of the part her silent prayer must have played behind the scenes of His exterior ministry, what strength she was perhaps responsible for supplying His anguished Humanity during the Passion. We can ask here again, too, what may have been the nourishing role played by the mother of the sons of Zebedee, the "sons of thunder." I wonder what our Lord meant by that. From where, we may ask, did they steal that thunder?

In these terms, motherhood is the work of a lifetime, both here and hereafter. Let's admit it. Women are spiritual cows. It has been my good fortune to live in the country for many years, where I can watch cows at close quarters, and believe me, they fill me only with admiration. Call me bovine, and I'm flattered! For me, "Holy Cow!" has become a truly ecstatic expression, for any cow is a delightfully homely figure of feminine contemplative life. Whoever wants to understand "pondering in the heart" should watch cows. Into the milk they produce go endless, patient hours of cud-chewing, and their calves find dinner easily. Not to be overlooked is the fact that to keep producing, cows must be milked regularly; otherwise they go painfully dry. They secrete milk by the same process holy souls secrete wisdom which must be given out if the supply is to continue. It's all done inside, with what comes in from the outside, and it's not done in a hurry.

God told Ezechiel to "set thy *heart* upon all I shall show thee," because wisdom doesn't spring from the mind alone, but from the whole being. To meditate on God's law day and night means to ruminate it, to mull, to cud-chew, to fill the breast with it. Naturally the very word *meditate* has its roots in *madh-a*, the Sanskrit word for *wisdom*, its source and its product.

Os justi meditabitur sapientiam, "The mouth of the just shall meditate wisdom," says the Church of her Confessors, speaking of the knowledge of God which can be tasted. This text must be pondered in bovine terms before it really comes clear! With such meditation, "his tongue shall speak judgment: the law of his God is in his heart."

The ancient "Epistle of Barnabas" urges us:

> Now grasp fully also the teaching about food. Moses says again: "Eat of every animal that divides the hoof and chews the cud." What does he mean? That whoever receives food recognizes him who feeds him and, relying upon him, seems to rejoice. He spoke well in regard to the commandment. What then does he mean? He means: Associate with those who fear the Lord, with those who meditate in their heart on the meaning of the word they have received, with those who speak of and keep the commandments of the Lord, with those who know that meditation is a work of joy, and who ruminate the word of the Lord.

I've often marveled that St. Luke, the Evangelist who dwells most on prayer and the interior life, should be symbolized by the ox, a ruminant. I don't suppose this is purely casual. What is? While we're on the subject, I might interject here that the third stomach of the ruminant is actually called, of all things, the *psalterium*. I can't resist mentioning it. Ever since I found out, any psalm reminds me.

St. Francis de Sales, a confessor-bishop who understood the true Significance of the human breast, called milk "the wine of the breasts." He says:

Milk, which is a food provided by the heart and all of love, represents mystical science and theology, that is, the sweet relish which proceeds from the loving complacency taken by the spirit when it meditates on the perfections of the divine goodness. But wine signifies ordinary and acquired science, which is squeezed out by force of speculation under the press of divers arguments and discussions. Now the milk which our souls draw from the breasts of our Savior's charity is incomparably better than the wine which we press out from human reasoning; for this milk flows from heavenly love, who prepares it for her children even before they have thought of it (*Love of God*, Bk. V, Ch, 2).

"Come over to me, all ye who desire me, and be filled with my fruits," invites God, the Mother, through Holy Wisdom and the blessed Mary (*Ecclus. 24:26*).

To be like God, woman must produce Christ, as Mary did. "The motherhood of Mary," says Matthias Scheeben, "is the most perfect image of the paternity of God the Father with regard to the Son of God in His humanity" (*Mariology*, I, p. 179). Like Mary, then, every woman must also nourish Christ, and the food she offers Him can only be this milk of Wisdom, which is nothing other than Himself. It is secreted from her spiritual "breasts" by first ingesting the Food which is, again, Christ the Word. She must be one Christ, loving Himself.

"Blessed is the womb which bore Thee, and the breasts which nursed Thee!" Spoken by "a woman from the crowd," these words apply to every chosen soul.

And Christ rejoins, "Whoever does the will of God, he is my brother and sister and mother" (*Mark 3:35*).

Our Lady's *fiat* consisted precisely in receiving the Word of God, allowing Him gradually to take on her flesh and then suckling Him that He might be known to the world. Since that time, *Verbum caro factum est* in every Christian who accepts this "motherhood."

The prophet Joel predicted a joyful time to come when "the hills shall flow with milk," when God shall dwell with His people in the long promised land characterized in patriarchal times as "flowing with milk and honey." Milk throughout Scripture is a figure of God's abundance and goodness, and it doesn't take a freudian to see that the "hills" of which Joel speaks are poetic metaphor for breasts.

This is the time for which the world waits.

Since the beginning, woman together with man was given dominion over "the fish of the sea, the birds of the air, the cattle, over all the wild animals and every creature that crawls on the earth" (*Gen. 1:26*). We must never forget that one of the creatures which crawls on the earth is Satan himself, whom God cursed by decreeing: "On your belly shall you crawl, dust shall you eat, all the days of your life" (*Gen. 3:14*). God also decreed that Satan's ultimate defeat would come about through a woman, that there would be irreconcilable enmity "between your seed and her seed." In other words, it's precisely by her maternal functions that woman destroys evil. These are in fact her only means.

In the previously mentioned martyrdom of the tomboy St. Perpetua, it's interesting to note that she dwells prominently in her recital on her joy in nursing her child in prison. When the child was brought to her, she says the dungeon became a palace. "Immediately I recovered my strength," she says; for, as the Chinese say, in some mysterious way feeding the child makes the mother full. Perpetua's companion in martyrdom, St. Felicitas, actually gave birth in prison, rising from labor just in time to enter the arena. Tertullian, an eye-witness, speaks of her going "from blood to blood, from the midwife to the gladiator with the net." Years later, St. Augustine, who never overlooked a good pun, delivered a sermon about these two women who, as women, overcame the devil and won for themselves "perpetual felicity."

In the Book of Judges, the evil Chanaanite general, Sisara, was also doomed to "fall into the power of a woman." Fleeing on foot from the rout of his army, he reaches the tent of the housewife Jahel, a prototype, of course, of our Lady and Mother Church.

> Jahel went out to meet Sisara, and said to him, "Come in, my lord, come in with me; do not be afraid." So he went into her tent, and she covered him with a rug. He said to her, "Please give me a little water to drink. I am thirsty."
>
> But she opened a jug of milk for him to drink, and then covered him over.
>
> "Stand at the entrance of the tent," he said to her. "If anyone comes and asks, 'Is there someone here?' say, 'No.'"
>
> Instead, Jahel, wife of Heber, got a tent peg and took a mallet in her hand. While Sisara was sound asleep, she stealthily approached him and drove the peg through his temple down into the ground, so that he perished in death (*Jud.4:18-21*).

Invited to Jahel's tent—a universal folk symbol of the womb, Sisara asks for water, but is given milk. Of course, he perishes as a consequence, as inevitably as Satan perishes through baptism and the nourishing milk of the sacraments and prayer, the wombs and breasts of Mother Church. Our Lady destroyed him the same way. Thinking to find a natural ally in weak woman, Satan now finds a deadly enemy armed with the "tent peg" of the Cross—the divine support of motherhood.

The prophetess Debora, herself a mother, "at this time ... was judging Israel" (*Judges 4:4*). She finds it proper to celebrate Jahel's victory with a beautiful, barbarous canticle. "Blessed among women be Jahel," she sings, "blessed among tent-dwelling women!"

(Ah, that reminds me of someone.)

> He asked for water, she gave him milk;
> in a princely bowl she offered curds.
> With her left hand she reached for the peg,
> with her right, for the workman's mallet.

Not mincing matters, she continues,

> She hammered Sisara, crushed his head;
> she smashed, stove in his temple.
> At her feet he sank down, fell, lay still;
> down at her feet he sank and fell;
> where he sank down, there he fell, slain.
>
>   * * *
>
> May your enemies perish thus, O Lord!
> but your friends be as the sun shining in its might!

An Issue of Blood

CHAPTER 10

THE shaded light of the Old Testament, so gentle to unredeemed humanity's weak eyes, becomes blinding in the New. Until we become accustomed to it, we can hardly see at all, so clearly and obviously is every truth revealed. Sometimes what we apprehend first are actually not the truths themselves, but the dark, reversed after-images they inevitably project in one way or another. These, perhaps, the soul used to darkness grasps and interprets first.

"Blessed is the womb that bore thee and the breasts that nursed thee," spoken by that unknown woman from the crowd is only the light side of the female sex. To understand well the role of woman in the world, we must also come to grips with her dark side: her enormous potential for evil through *denial* of her maternal functions.

They cast a powerful negative shadow at the very outset of the Way of the Cross. On His way to crucifixion, our Lord stopped to console the "daughters of Jerusalem" who wept for pity at the sight of Him, and we remember He said, "Do not weep for me, but weep for yourselves and for your children. For behold, days are coming in which men will say, 'Blessed are the barren, and the wombs that never bore, and breasts that never nursed'" (*Luke 23:28-29*).

No doubt He refers proximately to the destruction of Jerusalem due to take place some thirty years later, when there would be "woe to those who are with child, or have infants at the breast in those days," but the prophecy holds for all generations of women and all those to be born of them in the last days. It would seem that when men say barren women are blessed, we must know that great evil is come upon us. We may rely upon this sign, guaranteed by God, and we recognize it in the exterior world today, where whole nations take it upon themselves to destroy unborn life as a matter of public policy. It's an inevitable reflection of what is even truer in our interior world today, where women who are spiritually barren are called "blessed,"—women who are so taken up in man's world they no longer have time to transmit and nourish supernatural life.

"Then they will begin to say to the mountains," foretells the divine Prophet, "'Fall upon us!' and to the hills, 'Cover us!'" for such a state of affairs is not the will of God. Our Lord, of course, was quoting his predecessor Osee, who predicted in like terms the punishment of Israel. "Give them a womb without children and dry breasts!" he also quotes the divine wrath as saying (*Os. 9:14*). On the road to Golgotha, He who gave the command to increase and multiply, both physically and spiritually, compassionated in His humanity the women and children who must be victims of the infringement of divine law.

About three weeks ago, my husband handed me the following article from one of our most respectable newspapers. The story it tells speaks much louder than anything I could invent, so here it is:

> Contraceptive services, therapeutic abortions, and sterilization are the best weapons against illegitimacy, a psychiatrist told a Regional Conference on Unwed Motherhood today.
>
> Dr. Walter Stokes told a panel session, "We ought to toss aside our horror of abortion." Therapeutic abortion should be used in cases of extreme economic and social stress, he said. Many of the cases in which children will be under welfare care had best be aborted, he noted.
>
> Dr. Stokes also recommended "full and wise use" of available contraceptive services as well as full use of voluntary sterilization of men and women. Dr. Stokes was a pioneer in medical preparation for marriage. The second generation of college-graduated couples he counseled is now coming to him, Dr. Stokes said. Ninety-nine percent of almost 400 girls who are daughters of his first patients were not virgins at the time of their marriage, Dr. Stokes reported.
>
> "This could sound scandalous," the doctor said. But most of the girls had had relationships only with their fiances. These parents had tried to face up to the reality of children's erotic feelings and emotions. The percentage of frigidity is extremely low. "There has not been one illegitimate pregnancy among this group," Dr. Stokes said.
>
> He addressed an all-day conference at Mount Vernon Place Methodist Church, sponsored by the Social Hygiene Society of the District and the Commission on Christian Social Concerns of the Church. Dr. Stokes contrasted the way in which upper middle class white girls and lower class negro girls handle unwed motherhood. He said he has had considerable experience with both types of cases in full time private practice and in hospital clinics. Unlike the former, he said, the lower-class girl generally has her baby and the baby is likely to become a public charge in the care of the mother. Again unlike the middle-class girl, her chances of a second unwed pregnancy are relatively high.

The article closes with a wealth of depressing statistics, in the midst of which a Unitarian minister by the name of Wilkes is quoted as remarking, "Somewhere along the line advice about contraceptives as well as moral platitudes should be given!" Well, advice about moral platitudes, anyway.

"For behold, days are coming in which men will say, 'Blessed are the barren, and the breasts that never nursed,'" in which morality will consist merely in platitudes, and in repressing the ugly evidence of immorality. We may well wonder at the consequences, and ask with Christ, "If in the case of the green wood they do these things, what is to happen in the case of the dry?"

Alas, physical aspects of moral disease always point to much deeper, more serious spiritual aspects of the same problem. With the help of the Holy Spirit perhaps we can see more clearly where the real trouble lies. All three synoptic evangelists tell us a story of an unknown woman with a female complaint, which apparently they considered of prime importance, so we might do well to study it.

On His way to restore to life the daughter of Jairus, a young girl on the threshold of womanhood, the following incident occurs:

> And there was a woman who for twelve years had had a hemorrhage, and had suffered much at the hands of many physicians, and had spent all that she had, and found no benefit, but rather grew worse. Hearing about Jesus she came up behind him in the crowd and touched his cloak. For she said, "If I touch but his cloak, I shall be saved." And at once the flow of her blood was dried up, and she felt in her body that she was healed of her affliction.
>
> And Jesus, instantly perceiving in himself that power had gone forth from him, turned to the crowd, and said, "Who touched my cloak?"
>
> And his disciples said to him, "Thou seest the crowd pressing upon thee, and dost thou say, 'Who touched me?'"
>
> And he was looking round to see her who had done this. But the woman, fearing and trembling, knowing what had happened within her, came and fell down before him, and told him all the truth. But he said to her, "Daughter, thy faith has saved thee. Go in peace, and be thou healed of thy affliction" (*Mark 5:24-34*).

What pathos in this story! I think these ten verses must contain the whole of woman's misery in this world, her sad degradation, frustration and helplessness, meant nevertheless, to culminate in her glorious renewal. They are an apt companion piece to the Lord God's curse in the beginning, when He said,

I will make great your distress in childbearing;
in pain shall you bring forth children;
For your husband shall be your longing,
though he have dominion over you,

and yet promised at the same time that her progeny would destroy the devil.

It may be significant that our Lord addressed the woman He healed as "Daughter," and not "Woman," the respectful title He was in the habit of according older women, even His own Mother. We are told this afflicted woman suffered from her ailment twelve years. If she was, say, in her early twenties at the time she accosted our Lord—as His mode of address might lead us to believe—then it's quite likely she had suffered ever since puberty, and had therefore never known life as a normal woman.

This type of physical debility had far-reaching repercussions which Christians today, not conversant with Judaism, can hardly appreciate. The great hidden lesson in her story resides in the fact that according to strict Mosaic Law, a menstrous woman is legally unclean. Motherhood for her is out of the question from a legal, let alone a clinical standpoint. The Torah states categorically to the men of Israel, "You shall not approach a woman to have intercourse with her while she is unclean from menstruation" (*Lev. 18:19*). If indeed her ailment dated from puberty, even marriage was out of the question. For her the title "Daughter" may well have been equivalent to "Miss," and for Israelites, to live without hope of children was to bear a special curse of God.

Nor was this the only difficulty she faced. The Law also states: "When a woman is afflicted with a flow of blood for several days outside her menstrual period, or when her flow continues beyond the ordinary period, as long as she suffers this unclean flow she shall be unclean, just as during her menstrual period" (*Lev. 15:25*). This means that "Anyone who touches her shall be unclean until evening. Anything on which she lies or sits during her impurity shall be unclean. Anyone who touches her bed shall wash his garments, bathe in water, and be unclean until evening. Whoever touches any article of furniture on which she was sitting," shall do likewise, and so on (*Lev. 15:19-22*).

What imagery! This is a powerful parable in daily reality of the kind of influence a woman in sin exerts on others. Using quite innocent bodily misery, the God of Sinai taught his primitive chosen their first moral ABC's in ways the most ignorant could understand, and we do well to keep in mind the same essentials. The Jews learned so well and took the lesson so literally, one of the worst problems of the early Church lay in weaning them from legal figures onto the accomplished reality of the New Covenant. Even for us, though the legal prescriptions are indeed superseded, the import of the lesson is decidedly not .

Still operative for our friend, the prescriptions of the Law rendered any normal community living well nigh impossible. Her lot was almost as bad as a leper's. Today it's hard for us to ascertain just how rigidly these regulations were enforced in our Lord's time, but we may be sure at least the Pharisees insisted on the letter. A perpetually menstruous woman who adhered to the Law literally was automatically cut off from the full practice of her religion:

"You shall warn the Israelites of their uncleanness, lest by defiling my Dwelling, which is in their midst, their uncleanness be the cause of their death," states Leviticus (*15:31*). Not allowed to go near sacred things or even enter the Temple precincts, she could of course take no part in public worship. This was tantamount to excommunication.

With these facts before us, we can see what courage our heroine displayed in forcing her way through a crowd to reach our Lord, and we see, too, why she touched Him surreptitiously, hoping in the dense, milling crowd to get away with it, without His knowing what she did. This accounts for her "fear and trembling." It wasn't just natural embarrassment due to the nature of her ailment, but fear of serious scandal and censure, perhaps of arousing our Lord himself to righteous indignation. As a pious practicing Jew, He would be rendered unclean at her very touch.

I feel that somehow to muster the courage to do what she did, this poor woman must have heard stories of His disputes with hair-splitting Pharisees and have banked on His taking a larger view of ritual uncleanness than they did. As it was, she dared touch only His cloak, and that from behind. St. Matthew says she touched only "the tassel of his cloak," a detail that may not be unimportant. In the Book of Numbers we find:

> The Lord said to Moses, "Speak to the Israelites and tell them that they and their descendants must put tassels on the corners of their garments, fastening each corner tassel with a violet cord. When you use these tassels, let the sight of them remind you to keep all the commandments of the Lord, without going wantonly astray after the desires of your hearts and eyes" (*15:37-39*).

If our friend was a good religious woman, as we have every reason to believe she was, touching this tassel certainly reminded her of God, and may have been in the nature of a daring sacramental action, a special, desperate appeal to the divine power residing in this Just Man. Christ himself tells her, "Thy faith has saved thee," making sure we wouldn't think that sacramentals are fetishes, supposed to work of themselves.

From the moment of her cure, life in all its plenitude opened up for her, both as an Israelite and as a woman. To learn what her story really teaches, we must see this woman in the role in which Scripture first presents her: a figure of physical and spiritual sterility resulting from impaired womanhood. A woman in name only, she is a curse both to herself and everyone with whom she comes in contact. Because neither womb nor breasts can function properly, she can neither bear life. nor nourish it.

Echoing the Lord God in Eden, St. Paul told the young bishop Timothy, "And Adam was not deceived, but the woman was deceived and was in sin. Yet women will be saved by childbearing, if they continue in faith and love and holiness with modesty" (*I Tim. 2:14-15*).

I'm afraid it follows that a woman must somehow be a mother to be saved at all. Apparently, for her there's no other way. This isn't always true physically, but it's always true spiritually, as Pope Pius XI pointed out. Certainly a woman must be fully a woman to be a saint.

With spiritual growth, attraction between the sexes doesn't decrease, but increases, *in a spiritual manner*. (Let's not misunderstand here.) In the Church there's a very mysterious, supernatural interplay between the sexes, quite transcending physical sexuality. It can certainly never be completely understood in this life, but we can glimpse darkly that in propagating the life of grace women somehow second the role of man by producing or sustaining the Christ life he begets or provides for. If this were not so, if men and women performed exactly the same spiritual tasks, here again we might ask why men and women are assigned different liturgical roles in the Church.

Keeping in mind what Edith Stein suggested on sexual differences in the soul, we can't escape the fact that in the supernatural order, an overwhelming number of great saints have come, as it were, in pairs, one a man and the other a woman, each the mysterious complement of the other. As we might expect, this is especially true of founders of great religious families. There come to mind St. Augustine and his mother St. Monica; St. Chrysostom and St. Olympias; St. Benedict and his twin sister St. Scholastica; St. Francis of Assisi and St. Clare; St. Francis de Sales and St. Jeanne de Chantal; St. Vincent de Paul and St.

Louise de Marillac; St. Teresa of Jesus and St. John of the Cross; and indeed the list seems endless.

Even crusty old St. Jerome had his St. Paula, and the supposedly all-male Jesuits had *one* female member in full standing—Juana of Spain, daughter of Charles V, who kept her vows secretly and faithfully, abiding by the rule all through her court life! (Today it is recognized that Jesuits do indeed have their spiritual female counterparts like their prototype Juana.) The close cooperation of our Lord and His own blessed Mother in the re-creation of fallen mankind would seem merely to be the divine capstone on the whole edifice, begun in like manner by Adam and Eve.

Perfection isn't sterile, sexless neutrality. The sexes were designed to cooperate to produce Christ, and never anything else, on any level whatsoever. Woman plays an essential and vital part in this scheme. If she suffers in her female functions, physical or spiritual, she must be cured as quickly as possible, and not left to "spend all she has," or to "suffer at the hands of many physicians" whose ministrations only make her condition worse. Women must be allowed to be *women*, not what men think women should be to suit their convenience, or what women themselves might like to be.

Literally hundreds of books are being written today on what ails women. I think Edith Stein stated the problem about as well as any:

> Many of the best are almost crushed by the double burden of professional and family duties; they are always on the go, worn out, nervy, and irritable. Where are they to find the interior calm and serenity in order to be a support and guide for others? In consequence there are daily little frictions with husband and children despite real mutual love and recognition of the other's merits, hence unpleasantness in the home and the loosening of family ties.
>
> In addition, there are the many superficial and unstable women who want only amusement in order to fill the interior void, who marry and are divorced, and leave their children either to themselves or to servants no more conscientious than the mothers. If they have to take a job, they regard it only as a means to earn their living and to get as much enjoyment out of life as possible. In their case one can talk neither of vocation nor of ethos. They are like dry leaves blown about by the wind. The breaking up of the family and the decline of morals is essentially connected with this group and can only be stemmed if we succeed in diminishing its number through suitable educational methods.

The virtuous wife and mother fares almost the worst. With the best will in the world to stay home and do her duty she finds that everything that might give her life meaning and real importance has been taken from her. She is no longer allowed to educate her children beyond the age of six except in the most desultory and supplementary way. She isn't allowed to nurse them when they are really ill, having been led to believe that anything worse than a bad cold can be treated only by so-called professionals in a hospital's cold, clinical atmosphere. She isn't allowed to bear her children or layout her beloved dead in the warmth of her own love in her own home. Even her cooking is done for her in crisp packages.

Everything she needs is placed just beyond her reach, driving her to leave her hearth to spend hours in stores and supermarkets, and find her recreation in public places. She's no mother, but an itinerant. Needless to say, the vivifying solace of the Blessed Sacrament in her own home—once accorded to responsible housewives in the early Church—isn't even to be hoped for, I'm told.

The sanctuary is often miles farther than the nearest bowling alley. So is the school, yet it often happens that her little children must be chauffeured there to be prepared for their first Holy Communion, not by her or her husband, in the warmth of the home, but by outsiders in the artificial atmosphere of a classroom. Not infrequently it happens that these outsiders are simply other mothers—whose own children are being prepared in turn by mothers not their own, in other classrooms! I do find this confusing, being allowed to teach other people's children, but not mine! One must know a young child so intimately and individually to speak to him of a God who is Love. This is a matter so private, so fundamental, and, it seems to me, so little to be undertaken in public.

Well may our Pope John XXIII ask of Our Lady of Guadalupe, as Mother of America, "May sanctity flourish in all homes—sanctity of the family in whose midst Catholic education may receive in your sight a healthy increase."

Yet, conditioned always to run out for whatever she needs, it's no wonder the modern housewife does the same spiritually, never thinking to stay home and run in for the sustenance of her family's spiritual life, as well as her own. Forgetting the ever-present source of grace which the sacrament of matrimony supplies her at her own kitchen sink, the spiritually hungry woman as often as not engages in a chronic desultory search among pious societies, book clubs, or libraries—far from home—for what lies under her nose in her own house. Even God, it seems to her, can be reached only by car on free afternoons. (May He forgive us!)

She is given to understand, furthermore, that to hold her husband she must spend precious time in the beauty parlor, running to the gym in between visits, or he will leave her for the *tavern*. Is it any wonder that at the end of her frazzled day her delicate, autonomous nervous system inevitably rebels, and she finds herself hysterically unable to pay the marriage debt? Believe me, I use the word *hysterical* advisedly, deeply aware of its derivation from the Greek for "womb."

At her Saturday night confession she may well accuse herself of what she may have been led to believe (by well-meaning persons unacquainted with inexorable female ryhthms) is a mortal sin: inability to react to her husband's lovemaking with the reliable responses of an automaton. Trembling at the dire consequences of her selfishness, she may well panic with guilt, become more frigid, and her state of "sin" may become permanent.

Gritting her teeth to avoid "mortal sin" at all costs, she erupts into repeated hysterical outbursts that seriously disrupt the equilibrium of the whole family, and for which she feels increasingly guilty. Perhaps, she reasons, a career on the outside might actually help.

But those of us who have worked in offices know that there the same horrible drama develops, only in different forms, for the woman is meant to be a woman everywhere. Modern men don't seem to be able to get it through their heads that women are different from men, that they are creatures of cycles and rhythm. No matter how much you rail at a woman, she can't escape these, much as she might like to.

A case in point is the naive assumption that birth control is a modern invention. Certainly the much publicized "Rhythm Method," following natural female cycles, was well-known to the ancient Jews. It escapes our notice in the Bible only because there we find it practiced as what to us seems to be the method in reverse. Well-acquainted with the occurrence of infertile periods in women, the Hebrews, in fact, legislated so that intercourse between the sexes would take place only when conception was a definite possibility. A child was the greatest benefit to be produced in a marriage, and fertility was not a handicap to be overcome, but a condition to be rejoiced over. Children, natural or spiritual, are women's special, and indeed only real contribution to society.

Women today, living in a world that says, "Blessed are the barren," find themselves with a product nobody wants. Is it any wonder they rush into man's precincts by the droves trying to find some purpose for existing? It follows, of course, that when the womb doesn't produce, the breasts cannot nurse, either naturally or spiritually. Sterile women have nothing with which to feed the world.

As we noted, single women working in the world are Joans of Arc, Jesuit female counterparts, who must extend themselves exteriorly in man's world in order to do God's will. They are wholly in the world, and they're wonderful there. The married woman, however, is *a cloistered woman*. As Gertrud von le Fort pointed out so perspicaciously in *The Eternal Woman*, the married woman is one who doesn't serve the world directly and actively through a profession; she vitalizes, forms, and transmits to others who do these things.

No matter how active she may be in her proper sphere, the wife and mother's life is fundamentally an enclosed one of prayer, service, and suffering. The spirituality that most approximates hers today might be that of a Dominican, a Carmelite friar, or a Benedictine monk, who may indeed have much contact with the world, but whose methods remain primarily contemplative, and who always keep at least one foot in the cloister, where the mode of life is both secluded and cenobitic.

From what I see about me, married women who see themselves in any other terms wind up crucified in all directions, spiritually more out of the home than in it. If they are fervent, they become easily embroiled in techniques proper to their husbands or other "activities" for spreading the Kingdom, and may end by running homes which are little more than madhouses of indoctrination. There, as often as not, everything is done with an eye to impressing "true married spirituality" on any hapless guests, who soon suspect they've been invited in for that purpose alone. If you've ever wandered onto one of these hearths, need I say more?

The truth is, vast treasures of contemplative prayer must lie locked up in millions of homes throughout the world, waiting only to be awakened. The home is, after all, *the* cloister, the original cloister designed by God in Paradise to be the pattern of all convents and monasteries, destined to pour its grace abroad on all those issuing from it, that is, the whole world.

Isn't it clear from the Acts of the Apostles that the first convents were private houses? Witness, e.g., Philip the Deacon, who had staying at home in Caesarea "four daughters, virgins, who had the gift of prophecy" (*21:9*).

Such a place can be devoted to works of the exterior apostolate only in a most secondary and casual way, for its primary business is the nurture of souls. (For this reason the home is also the minor seminary.) Like every cloister, it is a school, a love nest, a shelter, and an *ecclesiola*, as well as an arena for spiritual combat where the fiercest interior devils can be engaged!

We live in the fullness of time, when every virgin must blossom into a mother, and every mother become truly a virgin completely consecrated to God in motherhood. These vocations are highly complementary. Even so, like the housewife, not all persons living in religious cloisters are "contemplatives" in the narrowed sense of the word, but they lead the contemplative life, and do its work. Although the married woman may not be necessarily committed to it till death, it can be at least her normal preparation, painful perhaps, for a real exterior apostolate after her children are grown. Wasn't this pattern followed by Mary the Mother of Jesus?

St. Francis de Sales saw in widows and older women a rich field of recruits for the Visitation, which he first envisaged as an order devoted to active charity in the world. Strange to say, however, contrary to its founders' ideas, it soon became enclosed and exclusively contemplative! To the contemplative Visitandine St. Margaret Mary were granted the revelations of the Sacred Heart. I wonder. The housewife is the natural figure of wisdom. Could it be that the more perfect housewife would naturally gravitate to the contemplative ideal by the very force of her vocation?

After some twenty-five years of trial and error, I have been forced to the conclusion that we married women ultimately profit more from the works of St. Teresa and St. Bernard, or the Rule of St. Benedict, or even Cassian, than from the annals of foreign missionaries and settlement workers. If I have no vocation to the home cloister, do I have a vocation to marriage? After all, not everyone has!

I've admitted to learning a lot from watching cows. Well, I've learned even more from watching the dairy farmers who tend the cows. What impresses me most about these farmers is the heroic lengths to which they are prepared to go to keep a cow settled and happy. Her food is the best he can afford. Her routine is never upset, and she is never confronted with problems she can't solve easily. To soothe her nerves, music is sometimes piped into her stall.

She is of course never allowed to run around loose, frittering her energies; and in the pasture she is encouraged only to amble around like any other contemplative and chew her cud peacefully, unmolested by anything animal, human, or insect. She is dusted and sprayed with antibiotics and assured of the services of the best veterinarian the farmer can afford. I'm told that the more advanced dairyman with psychiatric training is wont to approach each cow personally during the day and tell her he *loves* her. If there's anything at all upsetting his cow's psyche, hell move heaven and earth to eliminate it, knowing full well that if he doesn't, her milk production will decline in direct proportion to what's bothering her. It's useless to lay before her eyes the milk quota to be met, because he has learned that her autonomous nervous system is completely beyond her control anyway.

For the purpose of this study, let's assume that a woman's nervous system is far more complicated and sensitive than any cow's. Modern psychology teaches that only very indirectly is it governed by the will—clearly a result of original sin, which dislocated Eve far more seriously than it did Adam. Yet modern women are expected to nurse their children in the face of the most nerve-wracking tensions, most likely while battling traffic in station wagons loaded with their older children and others'. They're lucky if they aren't shamed into campaigning for political office between feedings.

From what I've seen in the pasture, no self-respecting Holstein would stand for this a minute. She'd go dry in twenty-four hours, and so do women. Untold numbers of modern western women can't nurse their babies adequately with the best will in the world. This wreaks havoc with natural child-spacing designed by God, for a non-nursing mother can become pregnant again almost immediately. Believe it or not, Hebrew children were most commonly nursed until the age of three, providing the mother with the natural restorative action breast-feeding exerts on the womb, not to mention the salutary effect on the child! "The weaned child," says Isaias, "shall thrust his hand into the den of the basilisk," for the home training that protects him against evil begins at the breast.

Many women are ashamed to nurse their children, having forgotten what breasts are for, and what they represent spiritually, if their mothers ever told them. Many more can't be bothered with such bovine activity in the face of a really important career, say, pounding a typewriter all day for extra money the family doesn't need, but can't do without. (Somebody will have to explain to me why dusting a desktop in an office or serving meals to strangers on an airplane qualifies as a "career," whereas doing the same thing at home for those one loves is drudgery. I'll admit I don't know the answer to this one.)

So much for the physical statement of the feeding problem. If that were all, worldly science could soon overstep it. It has already installed artificial heart-beats in cribs to fool the hapless infant into feeling his absentee mother is near. Unfortunately, this is only a revelation in physical terms of the fact that women are forsaking, or being badgered into forsaking, their vocation as *dispensers of wisdom*, which is what breast-feeding represents.

The times our Lord predicted are upon us, when men would say, "Blessed are the breasts that never nursed!" Women no longer nourish their young spiritually as they should, any more than they nourish them physically, from their own being. To heck with the milk production, let the cows provide! Mothers are all too prone to let anyone who will do so nourish and teach their children, relegating their nursing to cows and hired help, their schooling to public servants, their social life to schools, and even their religious education to those who, with the best will in the world, can never possess the grace a mother possesses for the spiritual formation of her own child.

Is it true that "we are become as one unclean, and all our justices as the rag of a menstruous woman," as Isaias repined? Have we all "fallen as a leaf and our iniquities, like the wind ... taken us away?"

"The house of our holiness, and of our glory, where our fathers praised thee, is burnt with fire, and all our lovely things are turned into ruins. Wilt thou refrain thyself, O Lord, upon these things; wilt thou hold thy peace, and afflict us vehemently?" (*Isa. 64:6,11,12*).

I feel terribly sorry for women. I'm one of them.

What to do?

Well, let's not suffer at the hands of physicians any longer, be they Doctor Walter Stokes or any other. I don't know about you, but I've spent all that I have. Let's run to Christ, "come up behind Him," in the crowd and get help for ourselves. This can be done only as our friend in the Gospel did it, directly and secretly, and with great faith.

Our Lord is God, isn't He?

Well, *noblesse oblige*, if we can just get to Him. There are no rules for this kind of desperate action; it's every woman for herself. You pray for me, and I'll pray for you.

Our blessed Mother wasn't exempt from the ritual effects of our curse; she fulfilled the days of her purification according to the law of Moses at the time she presented the Child of her womb to the Most High in the Temple. The Lord said to Moses,

> Tell the Israelites: when a woman has conceived and gives birth to a boy, she shall be unclean for seven days, with the same uncleanness as at her menstrual period. On the eighth day, the flesh of the boy's foreskin shall be circumcised, and then she shall spend thirty-three days more in becoming purified of her blood; she shall not touch anything sacred nor enter the sanctuary till the days of her purification are fulfilled. ... When the days of her purification ... are fulfilled, she shall bring to the priest at the entrance of the Meeting Tent a yearling lamb for a holocaust and a pigeon or a turtledove for a sin offering. The priest shall offer them up before the Lord to make atonement for her, and thus she will be clean again after her flow of blood (*Lev. 12: 1-4,6,7*).

When our Lady did this, she did it in the name of all women, and therefore of all humanity before God, that Christ our Pasch might atone for us once and for all. *Salve Regina*, Mother of mercy ... to thee do we cry, poor banished children of Eve! To thee do we send up our sighs, mourning and weeping in this vale of tears. Turn then ... thine eyes of mercy towards us, and ... show unto us the blessed Fruit of thy womb, Jesus!

> Give praise, O thou barren, that bearest not: sing forth praise, and make a joyful noise, thou that didst not travail with child: for many are the children of the desolate, more than of her that hath a husband, saith the Lord.
>
> Enlarge the place of thy tent, and stretch out the skins of thy tabernacles, spare not: lengthen thy cords, and strengthen thy stakes! ... thy seed shall inherit the Gentiles, and shall inhabit the desolate cities. For the Lord hath called thee as a woman forsaken and mourning in spirit, and as a wife cast off from her youth. ... For a small moment have I forsaken thee, but with great mercies will I gather thee. In a moment of indignation have I hid my face a little while from thee, but with everlasting kindness have I had mercy on thee, said the Lord thy Redeemer (*Isa. 54:1-7*) .

This Redeemer promised we must expect days in which men would say to the mountains, "Fall upon us," and to the hills, "Cover us!"

> For the mountains shall be moved, and the hills shall tremble; but my mercy shall not depart from thee, and the covenant of my peace shall not be moved: said the Lord that hath mercy on thee. O poor little one, tossed with tempest, without all comfort, behold I will lay thy stones in order, and will lay thy foundations with sapphires. ... All thy children shall be taught of the Lord: and great shall be the peace of thy children (*Is. 54: 10,11,13*).
>
> Rejoice with Jerusalem and be glad with her, all you that love her: rejoice for joy with her, all you that mourn for her: That you may suck and be filled with the breasts of her consolations: that you may milk out, and flow with delights, from the abundance of her glory! (*Isa. 66:10,11*).

That being the case, let's follow the prophet's advice and enlarge the place of thy tent ... if you know what I mean.

The Mirror of Majesty

CHAPTER 11

YOU may consider me excessively sheltered, but I think the Eternal Triangle in this life is found mostly at home, in the human family. When it comes to real triangles, it's the goodtime girl in the mink stole who's more likely to be sheltered from the awful Truth than the one in the housedress with soap in her eye. The kind of triangle the latter is involved in is hardly in the nature of casual extra-curricular alliance, for she soon wakes up to find herself tangled up in the wellsprings of creation. These relations aren't broken off easily.

I'll try to explain what I mean.

Without ascribing sex to God in any way, theologians have long applied the obvious analogy of the human family-father, mother, child—to the Blessed Trinity. Admittedly highly defective, as any analogy applied to the Triune Godhead must necessarily be, still it supplies our feeble minds with some vestigial symbols to think with. The transcendence of the mystery of three divine Persons in One is such, believes Matthias Scheeben, that it comprises a mystery supernatural even to the nature of the Godhead itself as such. Drawing conclusions in Its regard from the structure of the human family is somewhat like trying to reconstruct a thousand miles of sunlit seashore by poring over a grain of sand. If a grain of sand, however, is the only palpable trace of seashore available at the moment, I say it's better than nothing; and that's about all many of us women have, who boast neither wide education nor deep theological training.

So let's think about the Family we call the Most Blessed Trinity and ask God to help us search His majesty.

"With labor do we find the things that are before us," prayed Solomon, "but the things that are in heaven, who shall search out? And who shall know thy thoughts except thou give wisdom, and send thy Holy Spirit from above?" (*Wis. 9:16-17*).

Like the cheery Dame Julian, theologians for the most part allocate the role of "wife" within the Trinity to God the Son, inasmuch as through Him and in Him all things were made, Who is "form" or "matrix" of all that exists. Also, together with Him, the Father sends forth the Holy Spirit, or "child" in this construction. Later theologians also tend to identify the Son with the Wisdom so often presented in feminine guise in Scripture's sapiential literature.

Because of the sexual overtones liable to misapplication, and the clumsy deficiency of the concepts, this family paraphrase is rarely developed very deeply. If more married people read theology, however, I have a feeling it might be, because it strikes into the very heart of our own human "trinity." Identifying with the Son, as we have noted, is difficult for a woman. Is there no other way to find her a place in the Blessed Trinity, *as a woman*? I wonder.

Believe it or not, Fr. Scheeben (with commendable diffidence) envisaged a family construction in which the Holy Spirit, and not the Son, played the role of "wife"—always, of course, by appropriation. From what he tells us, he may have taken his cue from some of the early Fathers of the Church, who understood Wisdom to be not the Son, but the Holy Spirit, and from later Fathers who assumed mother Eve to be a natural ectype of the Holy Spirit.

This is no territory for us housewives to run around in unchaperoned, so I'll let Fr. Scheeben speak for himself. In an appendix to the justly acclaimed *Mysteries of Christianity*, he offers tentatively:

> In deriving Eve from the side of Adam, God wished to bring about the procession of human nature in the representatives of family unity (father, mother, child) from one principle, just as the divine nature is transmitted from the Father to the Son, and from the Father and the Son to the Holy Spirit. He wished to exhibit family unity in mankind as the truest possible imitation of the unity in nature of the divine persons. As in God, the Son alone proceeds from the Father, and the Holy Spirit is the fruit, the crown, and the seal of their unity, so in mankind the woman was first to proceed from the man alone, and the child was to be the fruit and crown of the union of man and woman. The differences which spring to mind in this comparison serve but to strengthen it.
>
> In the human family the son appears as the third person, and his origin as the second procession; but in God the Son is the Second Person, and His origin is the first procession. But why? Duality, the twofold principle of act and potency, rules throughout creation; human nature, too, is split into two principles, one predominantly active, the man, and one predominantly passive, the woman. Therefore, also generation, the supreme act of nature, results from the union of the members of the species. In God, on the contrary, in whom there is no partition into act and

potency, who is the purest and most perfect nature, generation as the principal and most natural act of the divine nature must proceed immediately and exclusively from the First Person. With men generation is the *ultimum in executione* (last step in order of execution), because it presupposes the difference between the sexes for its realization, while at the same time it is the *primum in intentione* (first objective in the order of intention), because the difference between the sexes exists only on account of it. But in God it must be absolutely the first production in every respect. For the very reason that generation in God is true generation, it must proceed from one person, not from two persons.

Nevertheless the Third Person in God functions as mediator between Father and Son, although in an incomparably higher sense than the mother does between father and child in human nature. As the mother is the bond of love between father and child, so in God the Holy Spirit is the bond of love between the Father and the Son; and as she brings forth the child in unity of nature with the father by transmitting the nature from the father to the child, so the Holy Spirit manifests the unity of nature between the Father and the Son, not of course by transmitting the divine nature to the Son, but because He himself is the fruit of their mutual unity and love. In God, the Son proceeds from the Father as perfect Son without requiring the intermediacy of another person for His origin and constitution. The fecundity of generation in God requires as a consequence the bond of union which is a necessary condition for generation among human beings: although the Son has His origin from the Father alone, His supreme unity with the Father requires the production of a personal bond him whom the Father and the Son express their love for each other. The functions of the individual persons concerned in both cases are assigned in different sequence; but this change of order lies in the very nature of things, in the difference between divine and human nature (Herder ed., pp. 182-3).

Theology doesn't lend itself to epigrammatic style, so quotations tend to be long and unwieldy. I'd like to reproduce here all Fr. Scheeben's reasoning as he develops his thought step by step from this point, but anyway, he concludes:

The woman would represent the Holy Spirit not partially, but wholly, not merely in her origin but also in her nature, if without being wife and mother she could be the center of love between father and son in the family as a virgin. Hence, if we prescind from those relationships, *we may to some extent regard the Third Person as the representative of feminine attributes*, (italics mine) that is, of love and tenderness, among the divine persons" (*op. cit.*, p. 188).

At this point Fr. Scheeben's conclusions become fraught with the most shattering implications for even the lowliest housewife, be she virginal or married to a human spouse. If Father's construction is correct—and we must remember that his position remains undefined and disputed among theologians—woman's role in the world is one analogous to that of the Holy Spirit. Furthermore, the more spiritual her role, the closer the analogy. The thought is rather terrifying, if you intend to act on it!

Let her who dares aspire to be perfect as God is perfect, try to understand these things! Here at ground level, it seems to me imperative to ascertain as soon as possible just what it is the Holy Spirit does, so we can adjust our schedules accordingly. Searching the Scriptures for myself thus far, I'm overcome by the impression that whatever it is He does, it's never anything *trifling*. Wherever we detect His presence, there's something mighty afoot. He stirred over the waters at the birththroes of the world; He was the "finger of God" who wrote the Law for Moses on Sinai; and with the birth of the Church at Pentecost, He casts Himself over the whole earth, renewing it in wind and flame.

Veni, Creator!

Is this being feminine? Who can bring this awesome hidden Spirit down to us so we can imitate Him in our kitchens?

Only Mary. She brought the Holy Spirit down once to a house in Nazareth, and she will continue to do so until the end of time. Surely she will help us. St. Ephraem of Syria says of her, "After the Trinity, she is the *Domina* of all; after the Paraclete, she is another paraclete." She is the Mother of Good Counsel, the Help of Christians, the Virgin most prudent.

"Coming upon" her at the Annunciation, the Holy Spirit made her His perfect instrument and representative in the world of men. "The Spirit of God which originally descended over the chaos as principle of light and life and which formed the first creation, now forms the second and higher creation out of the Virgin," says Fr. Scheeben (*Mariology*, Vol. I, p. 75).

"Woman, behold thy son!" the Christ told her from the cross, "sending" her to St. John and all mankind, as after His Ascension He sends them the Holy Spirit from the bosom of the Blessed Trinity. In theological language:

> ... toward the Logos the Holy Ghost represents the divine nature in the same manner as the woman represents the human nature next to the man. In like manner both these types unite in Mary as the woman animated by the Holy Ghost to a supernatural figure of the heavenly and spiritual Eve, in a manner analogous, in Christ, to the "type" of the Logos

and that of the man uniting to form the type of the heavenly and spiritual Adam (*op. cit.*, p. 213).

If this is true, it would seem the so-called "feminine" attributes of God so hidden from our gaze in the inaccessible Godhead can be known to us after all in human terms, simply by gazing on Mary, the "moon" who reflects the light of the Sun of Justice. Through the pure creature, Mary, the divine Model comes closer to us, tempered to our weak vision. Her, perhaps, we can find the presumption to imitate.

Only the Mother 'Of God rises to the heights possible to woman under the new dispensation. Fr. Scheeben speaks of her as:

> ... made a mother in a supernatural manner by the power of the Holy Spirit and who, through the same Holy Spirit and with Him, is the bond of love between the Father and His Son become man, just as He is between the Father and the Son in the Godhead. ... But this idea of supernatural, glorified womanhood is not so much a visible, independent image that leads us to a knowledge of the Third Person in God, as rather a reflection, invisible in itself, of His personal character, a reflection which can be conceived and understood only in and from the personal character of the Holy Spirit." (*Mysteries of Christianity*, p. 188-9).

Isn't it wonderful that the Father, the Son, and the Holy Spirit are all *Persons*? Elsewhere Fr. Scheeben says:

> It is not accidental that for the highest elevation of nature the male sex was chosen (Christ), and for the elevation of the person, the female (Mary). This nature, hypostatically united to God, must represent God Himself in His position of royalty and as bridegroom of the creature; the male sex alone could do this. On the other hand, the highest elevation of a created person to the union with God finds its expression in the relationship of the bride to the bridegroom, and for that reason it is naturally represented in the female sex (*Mariology*, I, p. 68).

So *there*, Herr Schopenhauerl Here's real ammunition for the suffragettes!

It's through woman that God's relations with mankind are cemented. *I believe in Jesus Christ ... who was conceived by the Holy Ghost, born of the Virgin Mary.* This must be, for,

> ... in the redemption, since it is the work of the triune God, both the Persons who proceed from the Father, not only the Son, but also the Holy Ghost, must be represented by a special created agent. The community of power and activity between Christ and Mary is so close and all-embracing

that nowhere on earth can a perfect likeness of it be found in the cooperation of any two persons. It can be understood and valued aright only by the supernatural prototype which it had in the community of action between the Holy Ghost and the Logos, between the humanity and the divinity of Christ, as well as by the wonderful community of life between Christ and Mary before His birth. In the natural order, the cooperation and mutual influence on each other of head and heart provide the only fitting analogue (*Op. cit.*, p. 190).

In the light of these truths, devotion to Mary isn't just sentimental attachment to a woman who is outstandingly good, powerful and sympathetic, with whom a poor housewife can speak "woman to woman" about troubles no man would understand. She is all this, it's true, but most of all she is our indispensable means to eternal life, the one Pope Pius IX called the "Neck" of the Mystical Body. By her close cooperation with the Blessed Trinity, the Holy Spirit is pleased to pour the divine life abroad, both in Nazareth and Jerusalem. As St. Grignon de Montfort clearly saw, going to God through Mary is no roundabout way, but the inside track!

Is it possible I once tried even for a moment to stop thinking about the Blessed Trinity by shifting my thoughts to *Mary*! Fr. Scheeben calls her the bride of the Son by virginity and His mother by fecundity. Her union with God was so perfect, she was able as instrument of the Holy Spirit to bear as Child the same God she knew as Bridegroom. What unutterable mystery! What unheard of fruitfulness is this Woman's! Only in the Godhead can more perfect generation be found.

Bringing the processions of the Trinity down to earth, she makes the divine Triad visible to us in human guise as the Holy Family of Nazareth, where the Son acts in His own Person, St. Joseph plays the part of God the Father, and Mary herself acts in, through, and for the creative Spirit.

When St. Paul quoted Genesis, saying, "For this cause a man shall leave his father and mother, and cleave to his wife; and the two shall become one flesh. This is a great mystery—I mean in reference to Christ and to the Church," he may have been uttering a strong parable of the Incarnation, whereby the Son "leaves" Father and Holy Spirit in heaven to become one flesh with human nature, his own "wife." If Fr. Scheeben's theory is correct, women caught up in like activity, where they must play the part of the Holy Spirit of God, can't afford to dilly-dally through life. Like Mary, they are engaged in a supernatural, Trinitarian work through which Christ is produced spiritually, prolonging in time, space, and human souls the missions within the Blessed Trinity.

When you come right down to it, the Holy Spirit and a housewife have more in comman than at first appears. The Liturgy calls the Spirit:

> *Consolator optime,*
> *Dulcis hospes animae,*
> *Dulce refrigerium.*
> *In lab ore requies,*
> *In aestu iemperies,*
> *In fletu solatium.* (Sequence for Pentecost)

Like any good mother, He is the spirit of refreshment and consolation, to whom we run whenever anything hurts. Adam of St. Victor called Him *Consolator alme*, "nourishing consoler," which is even more motherly a term. He is the Paraclete, the Advocate, the one who, like a mother, pleads the child's case through love, tempering the father's just punishments.

He is the very spirit of compassion, best shown forth in the world of men by the female sex, who are always feeling sorry for somebody for no logical reason. Women have little trouble placing mercy above justice, for their pity operates quite independently of moral judgments. A mother loves her children no matter how bad they are, or how homely. It's even possible that she loves the bad ones most.

Man primarily reflects God's generative power; woman primarily reflects His nourishing mercy. Man has chin-whiskers—his glory is in his head. He is meant to reflect a God whose generation within the Blessed Trinity is a perfect Act of divine intellect. Man's proper virtue is therefore justice. Woman's proper virtue is mercy, and her very physiology proves her glory is in her heart, her bosom. Like the Holy Spirit, she is the *fons vivus, ignis, caritas* of the home, the living fountain who offers her breast, her warmth, and her love.

It was "daughters," not "sons" of Jerusalem who extended sorrowing sympathy to our Lord on the way to Golgotha, and scholars tell us it was a society of pious women who regularly supplied to dying criminals the drugged wine He was offered on the cross. The Holy Spirit not only pities and consoles, He is the very spirit of forgiveness. "Receive the Holy Spirit," said our Lord, breathing Him out on His Apostles. "Whose sins you shall forgive, they are forgiven them; and whose sins you shall retain, they are retained" (*John 20:22,23*) .

"You shall be carried at the breasts. As one whom the mother caresseth, so will I comfort you," He promises through His prophet

(*Isa. 66:12-13*). As Pope Pius XI pointed out, it is the woman who is the heart of the home, the representative of these specifically divine attributes of love and boundless mercy. Like the Spirit of love, she is designed to transform, sanctify, and beautify everything and everyone with whom she comes in intimate contact.

Like Him, she should be a *dulcis hospes animae*—pleasant company. "When I go into my house, I shall repose myself with her," says the author of Wisdom, "for her conversation hath no bitterness, nor her company any tediousness, but joy and gladness" (*Wis. 8:16*). Joy is the infallible mark of the presence of God, says Leon Bloy, and we might add, of the good wife in whom God dwells. "House and riches are given by parents, but a prudent wife is properly from the Lord," whose Spirit is sweet (*Prov. 19:14*).

Da perenne gaudium! we ask the Holy Spirit, looking to Him for eternal happiness. More than Mary, He is the First Cause of our Joy.

Dulce refrigerium, aestu temperies we call Him, whose sweet coolness tempers heat. Modern woman seems to have forgotten that her function in man's world is primarily to allay concupiscence, not to arouse it. She feeds the hungry, pays the marriage debt, soothes ruffled tempers, all in a spirit of love. The woman who starts fights, can't cook, and spends her time willfully inflaming men's passions to acquire status as an irresistible siren is simply no woman at all. She's pure devil, and spends her life doing what devils do: tempting others.

A good woman has good work to do, and plenty of it. From the Holy Spirit is her genius for detail. "For the Spirit searches all things, even the deep things of God" (*I Cor. 2:16*), says St. Paul. He is the *Digitus Paternae dexterae*, the Finger of the Father's right Hand, who puts the finishing touches on all the Father's work. Holy Wisdom, the Spirit of God, who is the divine Housekeeper of creation, "praising her own self!" says, "I alone have compassed the circuit of heaven, and have penetrated into the bottom of the deep, and have walked in the waves of the sea. And I have stood in all the earth; and in every people" (*Ecclus. 24:1-9, passim*).

"For wisdom is more active than all active things: and reacheth everywhere by reason of her purity" (*Wis. 7:24*). Ever the good housewife, "she reacheth therefore from end to end mightily and ordereth all things sweetly" (*Wis. 8:1*). "She shall fill all her house with her increase, and the storehouses with her treasures," says Ecclesiasticus (*1:21*).

> Blessed is the man ... who looketh in at her windows, and hearkeneth at her door: He that lodgeth near her house, and fastening a pin in her

walls shall set up his tent nigh unto her, where good things shall rest in his lodging for ever. He shall set his children under her shelter, and shall lodge under her branches: He shall be protected under her covering from the heat, and shall rest in her glory" (*Ecclus. 14:24-27*).

Father Scheeben says:

> Wisdom thus occupies a central place between God and Creation, in which it appears as existing and working outside God, not haphazardly ... but in a most particular way, similar to the essential characteristics and working of a mother. It is like a mother, who in the fulfillment of her task, the arrangement of her household, the care and government of the inmates, and above all the care of the children, acts as the main figure of the family and becomes a child with and among her children. In such a position Wisdom, too, with regard to its origin, ought to be thought of not as "son" but as "child," more correctly, as "daughter of God." In this quality it is represented here in a beautiful way, and rightly so, for affectionate habitation and association with men comes forward as the continuation and crowning of that action by which with God it constructed the cosmos in the beginning and continually rules and governs it, "playing with Him" (Ecclus. 24:5), i.e., lightly and lovingly (*Mariology*, I, p. 32).

These perfections are proper to Wisdom, who is called "the unspotted mirror of God's majesty" (*Wis. 7:26*). Our Lady, herself the Mirror of Justice, is the human model of the efficient spiritual housewife, for whom no detail is beneath notice. A good wife and mother must keep track of everything and increase and perfect whatever is confided to her, be it a good steak, a small child, or some muslin to do up into curtains.

We beg the Holy Spirit,

> *Lava quod est sordidum,*
> *Riga quod est aridum,*
> *Sana quod est saucium,*
> *Flecte quod est rigidum,*
> *Fove quod est frigidum,*
> *Rege quod est deviuml*

Please, we ask, wash what's dirty, water what's dry, heal what's sick, soften what's hard, and straighten out whatever's out of line. This sounds like the ordinary housewife's day, laundering and scrubbing, sprinkling the ironing or watering the flowers on the windowsill, giving medicine to the baby, and tidying up every minute. "Make ready the way of the Lord, make straight His paths" (*Matt. 3:3*), she might mutter if she knows what housekeeping is really all about.

Woman has a deep instinct to beautify, to rectify, to reform. If she sees a man whose tie is crooked, she wants to straighten it for him, even if that man happens to be the President of the United States.

Gone wrong, it's this instict that can make a woman so infernally bossy; used rightly, it's her normal way of expressing love of neighbor. Veronica, seeing our Lord's face covered with filth, blood, and sweat, ran to wipe it with her veil without ever thinking twice about what might be the reaction of the mob.

Woman is a terrific organizer and regulator of both home and society, preparing mankind for the last day. Hers is the *actio unitiva* ascribed to the Holy Spirit in the Blessed Trinity, for good housekeeping is nothing but a drive towards simplification, order, and unity, the natural fruits of wisdom.

It follows that the good housewife is never obtrusive. As a matter of fact, the better she is at her job, the less she's noticed. A badly kept house with dirty windows, rugs askew, children unwashed, and with buttons missing from their clothes immediately proclaims the woman responsible. A hostess whose dinner preoccupies her to the point of neglecting her guests is conspicuous by her absence from the parlor, as well as by the long waits between courses when dinner finally does appear.

Like the Holy Spirit in the Church, the perfect wife and hostess is hardly noticed at all. Who sees buttons that are sewed on? Is there anything less visible than a really clean windowpane? Anything less remarkable than a rug that is perfectly straight? Like our Lady behind the scenes at Cana, the good housewife makes no fanfare, but sees to everything quietly and efficiently.

"They have no wine," Mary says simply and quietly to Christ.

To the servants she says merely, "Do whatever He tells you."

That's all. She is the go-between of God and men, a bond of love like the Third Person of the Blessed Trinity. As far as we know, not one of the guests at Cana ever suspected there was a domestic crisis. If our Lady hadn't attended to it, however, what a hullaballoo would have arisen!

Evidently Mary's mission did not include a participation in Christ's public activity *ad extra*, either at His side, or as His representative. Therefore, since she had no position in the visible and social organism of the Church, she had no particular right to hold a public teaching office or to exercise His priesthood. Her cooperation with Christ, like that of the heart with the head, remains a silent and hidden cooperation in its interior activity and in the interior communication of life to the members. But for that reason she cooperates precisely in that activity by which Christ preeminently discharges His mission as Redeemer (*Mariology*, II, 192).

Didn't I say women were contemplatives? Later on, Fr. Scheeben explains that Mary's part in Christ's sacrifice was prefigured in Mosaic ritual by the unbloody and incidental cereal offerings prescribe to accompany the bloody sacrifices. Hers is primarily a spiritual, supporting role, and this applies to all women who would be real women, and not men in skirts. When St. Paul told Timothy "I do not allow a woman to teach or to exercise authority over men; but she is to keep quiet" (*I Tim. 2:12*) he wasn't being mean. He had been caught up to the Third Heaven and was just trying to set us women straight in our relations with the Blessed Trinity.

Our Lord was exposed naked on the raised Cross to the gaze of all during His Passion, but not so the veiled Mary, whose com-Passion took place standing on the earth at its foot. Though she conformed to Christ more closely than any other human creature, she remained hidden, like the Holy Spirit.

A woman who can't be hidden can't be truly a woman, let alone pattern her life on the Holy Spirit, whose action is so powerful, yet never seen, and whose trademark is a dove, the most gentle and guileless of creatures. The Holy Spirit put order into the primordial chaos as a housewife puts order in a topsy-turvy house, and filled the earth with life when "there was not yet any field shrub on the earth, nor had the plants of the field sprung up, for the Lord God had sent no rain on the earth and there was no man to till the soil; but the mist rose from the earth and watered all the surface of the ground" (*Gen. 2:5-6*). This gentle "mist" was taken by the Fathers as a figure of our Lady, who like the Spirit unobtrusively "waters what is dry," and produces living beings in the order of grace. If it applies to our Lady, it also applies, I'm afraid, to us.

But that's not all. The Holy Spirit is not only the transforming Spirit of Love, characterized by the fire of Pentecost; He is also the Spirit of Prayer, characterized by the mighty invisible wind which shook the whole house. By theological definition He is the mutual Spiration of the Father and the Son, their very Breath, or Sigh of Love, breathed out by them together as the Third Person of the Blessed Trinity. This means that in the final analysis, to receive divine inspiration is nothing less than to receive the Holy Spirit, an Inspiration not to be taken in lightly.

The little breeze the prophet Elias detected on Mount Horeb, which caused him to cover his face with his mantle, was the self-same one which later became the whirlwind which took him in the fiery chariot to heaven. This is supposed to happen to all of us, for, *"Emitte spiritum tuum et creabuntur/Et renooabis faciem terrae!"* is a pentecostal, eschatological cry. It began in the first sentence in Genesis, blowing over the surface of the waters and soon to breathe the living soul into Adam, and eventually it will animate all the elect.

Teaching God's ways in action parables, the prophets Elias and Eliseus restored life to the dead by breathing into them. When Christ before His Ascension appeared to His Apostles to give them the power of the Holy Spirit, He "breathed upon them," anticipating the rushing wind He would send at Pentecost, when the divine Breath would enter the Mystical Body, so that, like Adam's, it might become "a living soul." So "wisdom inspireth life into her children" (*Ecclus. 4:12*) and animates the Church.

This is real Inspiration, of which every other kind of breathing, huffing, puffing, sputtering and wheezing is the merest parody. And a woman, of course, is supposed to be an inspiration. She may not be able to darn socks or boil water, but she must inspire some man, somehow, to something. There's evidently nothing a man won't do if he's properly inspired by some woman. Even the world knows this. For good or ill, every Petrarch is expected to have his Laura, every Dante his Beatrice, and every Macbeth his lady. Not trusting this important function entirely to earthly females, the pagan Greeks employed nine Muses to do the job on a higher plane. With proper female inspiration, a man can be made to kill, build bridges, write poetry, rob banks, commute a hundred miles a day, dry the dishes, or walk the dog. He may buy a new hat.

He may even become very holy.

The Holy Spirit being both Fire and Wind, woman is inescapably bound up with both aspects if she takes her divine model seriously. She must love, and she must pray. Only through loving prayer can she hope to animate, regulate, and sanctify her home, bringing all within it into God. This isn't accomplished by rushing out for extra courses in home economics—though these might help in difficult cases!

Breathing is the perfect analogy of prayer, as necessary to physical life as prayer is to supernatural life. It may be hard to pray, but it's much, much harder not to pray. Prayer purifies and sustains. The more perfect it is, the more it resembles easy breathing, which is unceasing and largely unconscious. When our attention is unduly directed to the mechanics of breathing, we can be sure something is wrong with the breathing apparatus or the oxygen supply. Asthma? Paralysis? A bad cold? Or did somebody seal up the windows and turn off the air conditioning?

So too, the greater the lung capacity, the deeper the breathing. Shallow breathers must breathe fast under effort, and when they try to breathe deeply they gulp. The soul far advanced in prayer has his second wind. He breathes calmly even under heavy effort. Artificial respiration, breathing exercises, or even an iron lung may be necessary at times for the best of us in this fallen world, but these aren't considered normal. To take such artificialities for granted reveals the chronic invalid.

By the same token, elaborate methods of discursive meditation may be a godsend to those who can't breathe God naturally, but they're in the nature of a last resort, not *sine qua non*. The Little Flower said flatly that most books on prayer gave her a headache, they were so complicated. I agree with her all the way, and so I think would most women, who as a sex are more affective than cerebral in their relations with God, once they let themselves go. Mme. Claude Martin (later Venerable Marie de l'Incarnation), after trying various "methods," said, "I did myself so much violence that it was for me like a head bandage which wounded me notably, from which I suffered very much pain!" She had the good fortune to be told by her director to stop the foolishness immediately and let the Holy Spirit continue to pray in her as before. A healthy breather like her in an iron lung is pretty silly.

Perhaps, like me, you've wondered why it is Mother Church is so partial to the blessing of throats on the feast of St. Blaise. every February third. Why the throat? Can't we hurt all over? The blessing reads: "Through the intercession of St. Blaise, Bishop and Martyr, may God deliver you from ailments of the throat, and from every other evil; in the name of the Father, and of the Son, and of the Holy Spirit. *Amen*,"

Amen. This year the point of it all dawned on me at last: the throat is the indispensable entry for food and breath into the body. You'd think anybody would know that. A clogged throat means certain death, and surely the child with a fishbone caught in his, whom St. Blaise as Bishop of Sebaste cured, almost died. Taken in a spiritual sense, the words of the blessing become crystal clear, for if the spiritual throat ails, the soul becomes incapable of prayer or receiving the Bread of Life. The full import of our Lady's function as "Neck" of the Mystical Body comes to light through St. Blaise, who blesses our throats, incidentally, with candles from our Lady's feast of the Purification, celebrated the day before.

"May God deliver us from ailments of the throat and from every other evil!" Without the breath of healthy prayer, the spiritual life becomes a drama of slow suffocation, parallel to the death of Christ on the cross. If queried, only too many Christians will tell you our Lord bled to death on Calvary, but that was only part of His agony. Modern research has unearthed evidence to show that He in fact suffocated by drowning in body fluids, deprived of the breath of life by the cramping of the chest muscles which was the specific torture of crucifixion.[5] Scripture says as much to those who read the Passion carefully, for the texts use exclusively such terms as "gave up His spirit (breath) ," and "ex-spired." Recording the death of God, St. Luke says in fact, "He cried out at the last with a loud voice, 'Father, into thy hands I commend my spirit:'"

The Christ can die in no other way. Breath, spirit, soul,all can be the same word in each of the trinity of sacred languages, Hebrew, Greek, and Latin. Is it surprising? Christ suffocated to death through the hatred of Satan, and this horror continues to take place in the world today wherever the life of God is crushed out of a human soul by the suffocation of its prayer—the one indispensable means to Him. This is the extinction of the Spirit.

"Pray without ceasing. ... Do not extinguish the Spirit!" pleads St. Paul (*1 Thes. 5:17,19*).

The forces of evil bend every effort to this end, for it is Christ they suffocate. He breathed out the divine Breath and poured out His Blood for the redemption of the world as He himself is sent out as Second Person within the Blessed Trinity. This divine action, now taking place on earth, Satan seeks to interrupt at all costs. Who dies as long as he breathes? Where there's breath, there's hope.

I once taught catechism to a little girl who by no stretch of the imagination could have been called a good student. She wasn't as backward as she appeared, however, for she soon discovered one answer that could be made to apply somehow to all questions. When stumped—and that was often—she would look up at me wide-eyed and serious and reply, "Prayer!"

After the first six weeks of this invariable answer, I became convinced she was on to something, for I was amazed at how often her answer made sense. And surely without prayer, even catechism is a waste of time. So are the liturgy, the sacraments and Redemption itself. Can God save a soul who doesn't pray any more than a doctor can save

---

[5] *Vide* Barbet, *A Doctor at Calvary* (Kenedy)

a patient who won't breathe? Could it be that holding your breath is the unforgivable "sin against the Holy Spirit"?

Women, I'm afraid, may be largely responsible for the shallow breathing that goes on in this workaday world, forgetting they're supposed to be an in-spiration, breathing God in, and then breathing Him out on others, producing Christ by the power of the Holy Spiration. He helps our weakness, says St. Paul, "for we do not know what we should pray for as we ought, but the Spirit himself pleads for us with unutterable groanings" (*Rom. 8:26*). No woman can be the instrument of the Holy Spirit who doesn't allow Him to pray in her.

Dominus vobiscum.

Et cum Spiritu tuo.

No doubt one reason our breathing is so erratic is that we can't sit still. We're always out of breath, if you know what I mean. (And I'll bet you do!) *In labore requies* is a divine "feminine" attribute, providing rest in the very midst of action, which woman is designed to reflect. Sirach says a good wife isn't only a man's helper, but "a pillar of rest" (*Ecclus. 36:26*). In perfect accord, the Psalmist prayed, "May our daughters (be) like wrought columns such as stand at the corners of the temple!" (*Ps. 143:12*). Apparently a good woman must above all provide peace, stability, and refuge to the human family to whom she, like the Holy Spirit, is "sent."

Pillars and columns can't bang around like open doors, shifting the whole center of gravity in the building. They stay put and support the edifice. If they go down, the roof caves in, no matter how sound the other structural parts may be. This may upset our ideas a little, considering the woman, and not the man, as the "support" of the home; but I think the problem is merely semantic. It's true men support the home, but mainly in the sense of protecting and providing for it, and exercising stabilizing authority over it. Interior stability-emotional, moral, spiritual, or whatever—depends particularly on the wife. This is another natural truth well known to classical antiquity, for not only the Hebrews, but the Greeks and the Romans supported their temples with caryatids—columns carved in the semblance of beautiful *female* figures, not men with bulging muscles.

"As golden pillars upon bases of silver, so are the firm feet upon the soles of a steady woman. As everlasting foundations upon a solid rock, so the commandments of God in the heart of a holy woman!" continues Sirach (*Ecclus. 26:23-4*).

"A wrangling wife is like a roof continually dropping through," adds Proverbs bitterly (*Prov. 19:13*).

Juvenile delinquency is just one of the more obvious evils that follow on women who can't stay home spiritually and hold the family together. Women who can't stay put can't pray, can't run their homes properly, can't give good counsel, can't comfort and console—can't *love*. Those committed to their care are denied their rightful vision in the flesh of God, the Good Mother, for it takes two parents to play the role of God for a child in full dimension. Without a mother, he may have no visible figure of "the Father of mercies and the God of all comfort, who comforts us in our afflictions, that we also may be able to comfort those who are in any distress by the comfort wherewith we ourselves are comforted by God" (*II Cor. 1:3-4*). In a child's mind, it's a short step from "there's no mother in the house," to "there's no God in the Church."

In modern society, the extent to which a mother can devote herself to interests other than her family is the subject of much debate. Advocates of "A Career outside the Home for Every Housewife" grow more vociferous daily, abetted by a woman-power-hungry economy, current false values, and a large proportion of the housewives themselves, spiritually too immature to recognize the issues at stake. Besides, the problem is enormously complicated. Not every woman is called to live a prayer life in her own home approaching that of the desert fathers. Also, we must agree that many women who have no outside careers are still not home in the true sense of the word, though they may be so physically.

Putting aside for the moment the woman who can't stay home because she's too proud, selfish, and disintegrated to face the death of self which marriage confers, still we can't overlook matrons like St. Lydia in the Gospels, who sold "purple" in Thyatira without detriment to her sanctity. The Valiant Woman herself in Proverbs wasn't above manufacturing a "girdle for the Canaanite" in her spare time to sell on the outside, and in modern times Zélie Martin ran a lace-making business (at God's suggestion) from her home and still managed to produce the Little Flower and her sisters.

When St. Teresa, driven to traveling all over Spain to make new foundations for the Carmelite reform, was reminded by her persecutors of St. Paul's injunction to women to "stay home," our Lord Himself came to allay her scruples. He said, "Tell them they are not to follow one part of the Scripture by itself, without looking to the other parts also; perhaps, if they could, they would like to tie My hands!" (*Relations*, III).

No one can presume to pass judgment on married women's activities outside the home as such, but that doesn't mean judgments can't be formed about their "staying home." There are certain points that stick in my mind in this regard. First of all, the so-called outside activities of St. Lydia, the Valiant Woman, Mme. Martin and others like them were rooted in and managed from the home. In a spiritual sense, this was also true of St. Teresa, whose foundations were after all only an extension of her spiritual family, whom she was bound to "increase and multiply" like any good mother. These women were undoubtedly very busy, but remained "pillars of rest." They were there for those who depended on them.

What St. Paul said to Titus on the subject of staying home was precisely that younger women should be trained by the older women "to be wise, to love their husbands and their children, to be discreet, chaste, *domestic*, gentle, obedient to their husbands, so that the word of God be not reviled" (*Tit. 2:4-5*). The word *domestic* is the English translation for two Greek variants, one meaning "home-worker" and the other "stayer at home" or "housewife." The gist is clear. A married woman with children must, whatever she does, remain centrally located at her own hearth! That St. Paul should forbid her to radiate from that center, however, is quite unthinkable. Isn't he called *the* Apostle? Would he want God's word dammed up in four walls?

Our blessed Mother Mary is Queen of Apostles, and I can't help being struck by the fact that the only occasions on which the Gospels reveal her even taking an interest in anything outside her immediate family occur either before the birth of our Lord, or after He was grown. Between her charitable visit to her cousin Elizabeth and her concern for the failing wine at Cana there stretches a period of some thirty years of luminous, mysterious, and fruitful silence, broken only by the one incident of the boy Jesus lost in Jerusalem, and that incident reveals only her motherly devotion to Him.

It seems to me that in the contemplation of this pregnant thirty-year silence must lie the answers to all the problems that can bedevil the Christian woman with minor children. Here each searcher travels alone. Even outside Nazareth, however, our Lady's contact with the world was always what you might call family-motivated. Elizabeth was, after all, her cousin. It's quite likely, too, that she was related to the couple married at Cana, for her concern there was hardly that of an outsider. As for her activity as nurse of the infant Church from Pentecost until her death and ever after, well, if the Church isn't our Lady's family, what is it?

Any woman who finds life as a wife and mother *confining* must have somehow got herself trapped in the broom closet. That's no place for the woman "come upon" by the Holy Spirit in everything she does, caught up on earth into the operation of the Blessed Trinity in eternity. Woman's work takes breadth of vision. Being "the unspotted mirror of God's majesty" (*Wis. 7:26*) is no little chore to be accomplished on the run.

It means staying home in a big way.

Would you believe it, the Holy Spirit and our Blessed Mother never leave the Church for a minute?

The Worship of Groop

CHAPTER 12

> Blessed be the name of the Lord from eternity and for evermore: for wisdom and fortitude are his. And he ... giveth wisdom to the wise, and knowledge to them that have understanding. He revealeth deep and hidden things, and knoweth what is in darkness: and light is with him. To thee, O God of our fathers, I give thanks, and I praise thee, because thou hast given me wisdom and strength: and now thou hast shown me what we desired of thee!

SO PRAYED Daniel the prophet after the mystery of Nabuchodonosor's dream "was revealed to him by a vision in the night" (*Dan. 2:20-23*).

When Daniel wanted to know something, he had a very simple and direct method of finding out: he asked God to tell him. Knowing that God gives wisdom to those already wise enough to know this means, and accords "knowledge to them that have understanding" of how it's done, Daniel earned himself the title "man of desires" from the angels sent to satisfy his unquenchable thirst for truth. Only very holy people think of acquiring knowledge this way, because only very holy people have the fortitude to face truth wholly, or to persevere in the self-denial that makes really learning the lessons of God possible.

"Daniel, thou man of desires," an angel tells him, "understand the words that I speak to thee, and stand upright: for I am sent now to thee."

"And when he had said this word to me, I stood trembling," recalls Daniel.

"Fear not," returns the angel, "for from the first day that thou didst set thy heart to understand, to afflict thyself in the sight of thy God, thy words have been heard: and I am come for thy words. ... I will tell thee what is set down in the scripture of truth" (*10:11,12,21*).

Daniel, who asked for, and got, explanations from heaven is the prophet most like our Lady, Queen of Prophets. He too was visited by the angel Gabriel; and like her he was frightened and told not to fear.

"For thou," Gabriel later told Mary, "hast found grace with God. Behold, thou shalt conceive in thy womb and shalt bring forth a son; and thou shalt call his name Jesus. He shall be great and shall be called the Son of the Most High; and the Lord God will give him the throne of David his father, and he shall be king over the house of Jacob forever; and of his kingdom there shall be no end" (*Luke 1:30-33*).

When she asked, "How shall this happen?" Gabriel told her, and consenting to this knowledge, the young Mary conceived in flesh the fulfillment of a prophecy which had first been accorded to Daniel only in a "vision of the night" of the Old Testament.

Says the prophet to us today:

> I beheld, and lo, one like the son of man came with the clouds of heaven, and he came even to the Ancient of days: and they presented him before him. And he gave him power, and glory, and a kingdom: and all peoples, tribes and tongues shall serve him: his power is an everlasting power that shall not be taken away: and his kingdom that shall not be destroyed (*7:13-14*).

And Daniel, like our Lady, "was affrighted at these things."

Like her he "went to one of them that stood by and asked the truth of him, and he told me the interpretation" (*7:16*).

On receiving the interpretation, Daniel's similarity to her rises to new heights, for like her, when filled with overwhelming mystery, he "kept the word in his heart" (*7:28*). Daniel, it seems, was a "ponderer in the heart" too, for Scripture notes elsewhere that he was particularly given to "silently thinking within himself" (*4:16*). Revealing to him the tremendous prophecy of the Seventy Weeks, Gabriel tells Daniel, "From the beginning of thy prayers the word came forth," for Christ always springs from the prayer of the holy, the Word generated in the bosom of the Blessed Trinity dwelling in the soul of man.

It seems to me the gentle Daniel, defender of Susanna, was a prophet like no other. A man of prayer, he is described as going "into his house: and opening the windows in his upper chambers towards Jerusalem" (surely a figure of contemplation!), he knelt down three times a day. Rather than discontinue these quiet but persevering triune habits, he allowed himself on at least one occasion to be thrown to hungry lions.

Daniel never berates, roars, or thunders maledictions like the other major prophets. Even when reproving the king of Babylon for using the vessels of the Temple at his profane banquets, Daniel is restrained by comparison. Always he seems more acted upon than acting, though his power with both God and men was certainly considerable. His apocalyptic visions still remain in large part utterly beyond us, so grand and cosmic are they in their implications.

Deported in his youth to exile in Babylon, he soon distinguished himself there by his extraordinary talents as an interpreter of dreams, in fact rising thereby to "the third place in the kingdom." Apparently he never returned to Jerusalem, even in his old age when the Temple was finally restored under Cyrus. He lived his entire adult life in the heathen capital far from home, performing valuable services for its pagan monarchs while never deviating one iota from his devotion to the God of Israel.

Though apparently not dying a martyr's death, he is, I do believe, something of an Old Testament St. Thomas More who has much to teach us in our time on how to live a spiritual life in a secular world filled with evil. Like St. Thomas and Elias of old, Daniel was quite a wit. Never employing the extraordinary measures of the astounding Elias, Daniel prefers to outsmart the conniving priests of Bel much as St. Thomas might have done, by a simple human ruse all the more devastating.

Scripture says that on this occasion "Daniel laughed," and it was funny. To prove to the king that Bel, the idol, was no living god and wasn't really eating the food offerings left for him every night (which were nevertheless always gone the next morning), Daniel spreads the floor of Bel's temple with fine ash before retiring and has the doors sealed in the king's presence. The unsuspecting priests and their families, coming up through a trapdoor under the table as was their custom, feast off the victuals during the night. Unfortunately not noticing the ashy floor, they leave an awful lot of footprints when they leave at daybreak.

It was the next morning that Daniel laughed. He tells the king, "Behold the pavement, mark whose footsteps these are," and that's the end of the seventy priests of Bel, destroyed by Daniel without his ever laying a finger on them. If there's one thing a king can't stand, it's having been made a fool of in public.

Very few, if any, male characters in the Old Testament can be taken wholly as figures of contemplation, but stories like this one about Daniel show how close this prophet can come to meeting the requirements. Like the Blessed Mary and all contemplatives, he has little use for wrath or violence of any kind. He never resorts to the miraculous, though he often produces miraculous results from ordinary means. His outstanding characteristic seems to be just plain intelligence, especially that superior brand of intelligence which goes by the name of "common" sense. With this he outwits the most cunning evil, defending Susanna much as he protects himself from pagan kings, hungry lions, or the priests of Bel. In reading Daniel it's well to keep in mind that St. Thomas Aquinas specifically recognized contemplation as a supra-sensible operation of the intelligence.

Like the Books of Judith, Wisdom, Tobias, and others which come to grips with the quiet mysterious power of higher prayer over evil, these particular stories about Daniel occur in chapters of his book not included in the present Hebrew Bible, and forming part of the so-called Protestant Apocrypha. Among the missing is a story I specially dote on, the one about Daniel and the Dragon, found in chapter fourteen of the Catholic Book of Daniel.

Therein the king of Babylon, pretty discouraged after the Bel episode, nevertheless kept trying to find a god that Daniel could somehow bring himself to worship, but which the king could *see*. After all, it didn't look good to have a high councilor who wouldn't have anything to do with the official deities, and the situation which developed must have been something like that of Henry VIII trying to get his old favorite Sir Thomas to kowtow to Anne Boleyn, if only for the sake of appearances.

Daniel steadfastly refused to worship anything but some "living God." In fact he had rejected Bel "because I do not worship idols made with hands, but the living God, that created heaven and earth, and hath power over all flesh" (*14:4*). The king, we must remember, had been trying to prove to Daniel that Bel was a living god because he presumably ate the food which disappeared before him every night, and, well, that's where we came in.

Our next episode about the Dragon then begins:

> And there was a great dragon in that place, and the Babylonians worshipped him.
> And the king said to Daniel, "Behold thou canst not say now, that this is not a living god. Adore him therefore."
> And Daniel said, "I adore the Lord my God: for he is the living God: but that is no living god." (I suppose Daniel said this pointing to the poor dragon in disgust.) "But give me leave, O king, and I will kill this dragon without sword or club."
> And the king said, "I give thee leave."

Then Daniel took pitch, fat, and hair, and boiled them together, and he made lumps, and put them into the dragon's mouth, and the dragon burst asunder. And he said, "Behold him whom you worshipped."

And when the Babylonians had heard this, they took great indignation, and being gathered together against the king, they said, "The king has become a Jew. He hath destroyed Bel, he hath killed the dragon, and he hath put the priests to death."

Needless to say, Daniel soon finds himself in the lions' den again. But that's another story. That dragon fascinates me. What was it?

The word itself is plain enough; the Greek δρακών (*drakon*) was coined to represent some mythological beast or other. According to the information I can gather on dragons in Scripture, this word was actually used only as the best available approximation in Greek of two Hebrew words which might designate either a jackal, a snake, or some water monster. It could have meant, I discovered, a crocodile.

In all my imaginary representations of this dragon, henceforth, I must admit I always have thought of him as a cold, scaly crocodile, with jaws that bite, hung beneath a bird-brain completely overbalanced at the other end by an excessively disproportionate tail. That's just the way I see him. Whether De Quincey had anything to do with this view of mine I couldn't say without prohibitively expensive psychoanalytic probing into my surcharged subconscious. But there he is.

I have a pet name, even, for this creature. I call him the *Groop*. The idea came to me some weeks ago when I happened to see a Sunday supplement survey of America's recreational activities. As I remember, the pollsters discovered in their investigations that we like to bowl, play cards, go to parties, watch ball games, and do lots of other things; but there's one activity that overshadows all others. For both men and women, first on the list of national pastimes was *attending meetings*. According to statistics, America would rather attend a meeting than anything else in the world, any kind of meeting.

There must be deep sociological reasons for this. Being an American presupposes a background of any number of foreign extractions, and even the most superficial analyst can see that being able to get together, smooth out differences, and act as one was for us from the beginning bound up with elementary survival. By this time we've become so awfully good at getting together that we find ourselves in the position of teaching our developed organizational techniques to the whole world, and we're doing it.

Among ourselves we take for granted cooperative procedures which are anything but obvious to less-developed observers. Naive foreign careerists, who think democracy is natural to man and will, therefore, be accepted whenever many at the tea table. Democracy, I have learned, is in fact a highly intricate skill in which Americans are trained from the cradle by almost everyone with whom they come in contact, much as Japanese are taught the difficult feat of squatting gracefully for hours on a bare floor.

Any tendency to unity is of itself good, and group activity is no exception; but like every good in a fallen world, it has its own built-in propensity to nothingness. As it is, it's easy to believe an American will do most anything, provided he doesn't have to do it alone. Our pow-wow mania assumes such proportions among certain elements of the population that we might be led to conclude anything worth doing is worth doing in a group. There are those who might go so far as to maintain that what the group can't do isn't worth doing at all! That America produces few great vocations to the artistic or intellectual life is a simple corollary. When the meeting-mania takes over the spiritual life, however, the effects are far worse.

My own view of the matter is something less than national, but not long ago I did hear a young woman say, "Let's get a club together so we can study Scripture. I've always wanted to study Scripture *seriously!*" as if no serious study of Scripture would be possible without visible support from others.

She was soon drowned out by a gentleman who was thinking bigger. He was planning a large metropolitan center where "people could get together and exchange ideas."

"What ideas?" I inquired naively. Honest, I just wanted to know.

"*Any* ideas!" he informed me, stooping to my level. "There's got to be a place where everybody can *communicate.*"

I was outnumbered, so I didn't have the nerve then to ask where the ideas were coming from, if there weren't also some place a few people could go to be alone long enough to think up some, but I'll ask now. (I'm alone with the typewriter.) Groups are very intimidating, and *their* idea, namely that something good is sure to evolve wherever enough commotion can be made, is certainly one that has been abundantly communicated.

Then there's the lady who telephones to announce a friendly meeting at her house to discuss taking Mrs. X's needy family some extra groceries. No, says she, she hadn't planned to call on Mrs. X personally. She thought the *Groop* would handle it.

Now, the *Groop* isn't one to give alms in secret. He makes it his business to keep both left and right hand in view of all, and he trumpets. For a sack of potatoes and a can of beans around the corner, he exacts honor before men and due reward. The *Groop* in America often subjects the poor, already humiliated in a land where poverty itself is almost a sin, to the added humiliation of *Groop* interest. Where a delicate and guarded personal charity might effect everything necessary in a given case, the *Groop* must lay bare to the whole community the embarrassing small needs and deficiencies of the poor person under consideration. Because we seem to have lost the courage for individual initiative, our beneficiaries often pay for a few cast-off garments by being stripped naked before their fellows, who make the most intimate affairs of the poor neighbor a matter for *Groop* discussion.

Meetings are certainly time-consuming, the boon of the bored, and the bane of the busy; yet they are looked to as the universal panacea for all ills. Housewives who suddenly start worrying about the poverty of their interior lives cry, "Let's have a meeting!" "Let's form a little *Groop!*" they decide, clapping their dainty dishpan hands.

This is idolatry.

"For the beginning of fornication is the devising of idols: and the invention of them is the corruption of life" (*Wis. 14:12*).

Before you can say Dark-Night-of-the-Soul, however, the ladies have engaged themselves a speaker—as often as not some other housewife who can't stay home either, but who has learned to talk about it amusingly. And there you are. The agonizing civil war requiring personal initiative, and which can be resolved only on the inside, has been shifted painlessly outward, much as a smart dictator diverts attention from inner political tensions he can't control by nurturing foreign complications.

That wild Frenchman Pascal would have found the American meeting mania an interesting proof of his classic contention that "all the misfortunes of mankind spring from not knowing how to remain peacefully in one room for any length of time." To this human weakness he ascribed all fruitless endeavor pursued as an end in itself, whether taking the form of rabbit hunting, wars, dances, card playing, or just idle conversation. "The only thing that consoles us in our miseries is distraction," says he. "Nevertheless, this is the greatest of our miseries, for this is what primarily prevents us from thinking about ourselves."

How about a little group thinking along these lines, so we can exchange ideas? Pascal for President? We'll appoint the committees Tuesday. Apparently America has no interior life, and we'd better get organized and do something about it. At least we can talk about it, get it out in the open! No man is an island ...

This sort of thing scares the wits out of me, this worship of the *Groop* as if he were a living god.

The living God, it must not be forgotten for a moment, is a Group. Although God is a Person, it is theologically false to say the Blessed Trinity is a Person. God is an exchange of Persons who are One, and as such He is the exemplar of all human groups, whether the family, the state, the College of Cardinals, mining corporations, the beer party down the street, or the PTA. To be like God, we must engage in cooperative activity. The group life of God is reflected even in the organization of matter, in the disposition of stars as well as molecules, let alone wolf packs, quail coveys, and schools of fish, so we can safely conclude group life is God-ordained and here to stay. Even the human body is an organization.

What an organization really is, however, can be rather puzzling, when it comes to people. I think it's a mystery, but my husband, who teaches a course on the subject in a graduate school one night a week, puts this relatively short definition under my nose:

> A social organization is a continuing system of differentiated and coordinated human activities, utilizing, transforming, and welding together a specific set of human, material, capital, ideational, and natural resources into a unique problem-solving whole engaged in satisfying particular human needs in interaction with other systems of human activities and resources in its environment.

This is quoted from *Concept of the Social Organization*, by E. Wight Bakke, who appends thirty-five pages of explanation. I don't mind admitting I don't quite follow him, even breathing hard. For my limited purposes here at home, I'm forced to be original, i.e., return to origins, and remind myself that the Greeks who coined the word organize meant by it to "make music," as did Richard Rolle. That means that for me, people who don't make music aren't really organized.

Good music, entailing as it does order and harmony, requires God. Our natural desire for the company and cooperation of others in our works and aspirations is so firmly derived from the circumincessions of divine Persons in the Blessed Trinity, that we must deny both our God and our own humanity even to attempt to divorce ourselves from society. The desire to do so is satanic pride and essentially it's impossible to accomplish. Even M. Sartre will allow that, although he bases all social intercourse on hate, ordered to abstracting integrity from others!

The Incarnation produced a Corporation of Saints, bound to worship and imitate the Group who is God. Given the Incarnation, who can even pray privately? There's now no such thing as private prayer, for a Christian who kneels to pray alone in his room inevitably draws all humanity with him. The closer our union with the Divine Group, the closer do we draw others, and the closer are we drawn to others.

"It is better therefore that two should be together, than one: for they have the advantage of their society," says Ecclesiastes. "If one fall he shall be supported by the other. Woe to him that is alone, for when he falleth, he hath none to lift him up. And if two lie together, they shall warm one another. How shall one alone be warmed? And if a man prevail against one, two shall withstand him. A threefold cord is not easily broken" (*4:9-12*).

Ultimately this "threefold cord" can be nothing other than the Three Divine Persons united with the individual human soul and uniting her to all others. The relationship is transcendentally and wholly supernatural and personal. To maintain it, we can't worship false gods like the *Groop*. Daniel chose lions in preference to that, and we must be prepared to follow suit if necessary.

Any group existing as an end in itself, not bound together by the Threefold Cord, is a *Groop*. Evil mocks good by aping it, as we have seen, and nowhere does it betray its methods more clearly than in *groop* activity, an activity that looks like the real thing, but isn't. Surely the king of Babylon's crocodile exhibited exteriorly all the proper signs of life. He moved, he glared, and he ate, and the king didn't see why Daniel should be so darn particular. Only Daniel knew better. The *Groop* was good enough for the Babylonians, but not good enough for Daniel, a figure of the predestined.

To get a more detailed picture of the animal Daniel scorned, perhaps we might borrow a little from the Book of Job, for there the evil crocodile emerges in better light than he does at the zoo or in De Quincey's dreams. As interpreted by the Fathers, the description of the crocodile in Job is a word study of Satan himself, splendid in perverted majesty and grandeur. Apart from its divine message, it's still just about the most gorgeous poetry that ever filtered through human consciousness:

"Canst thou draw out the leviathan (crocodile) with a hook, or canst thou tie his tongue with a cord?" the God of the whirlwind asks Job. Rebelling against the "threefold cord" is precisely Satan's sin!

> Will he make supplication to thee, or speak soft words to thee? Will
> he make a covenant with thee, and wilt thou take him to be a servant

forever? ... Shalt thou play with him as with a bird, or tie him up for thy handmaids? ... Lay thy hand upon him: remember the battle, and speak no morel Behold his hope shall fail him, and in the sight of all he shall be cast down. ... Who can open the doors of his face? His teeth are terrible round about. His body is like molten shields, shut close up with scales pressing upon one another, and not so much as any air can come between them:

They stick to one another and they hold one another fast, and shall not be separated. His sneezing is like the shining of fire and his eyes like the eyelids of the morning.

... Out of his nostrils goeth smoke, like that of a pot heated and boiling. ... His heart shall be as hard as a stone, and as firm as a smith's anvil. ... The archer shall not put him to flight, the stones of the sling are to him like stubble. ... The beams of the sun shall be under him, and he shall strew gold under him like mire. He shall make the deep sea to boil like a pot, and shall make it as when ointments boil. ... There is no power on earth that can be compared with him who was made to fear no one. He beholdeth every high thing, he is king over all the children of pride (Ch. 40-41, *passim*).

You may think this a hyper-sensitive portrait of Daniel's *Groop* as applied to the local chowder society, but if we bear in mind the satanic nature of the "dragon," the description becomes very revealing. Anyone who has taken on a *Groop* alone knows they have hard hearts, and pour smoke and fire through their nostrils, for they thrive, not on justice, but on intimidation. They are tightly organized, their members in fact "stick one to another and they hold one another fast, and shall not be separated."

The *Groop* makes a lot of commotion, moves fast, and hard. He sneezes and stares and fears no one. He accomplishes nothing lasting, but just try to "lay thy hand upon him," says Scripture, and you'll "remember the battle and speak no more." If you don't believe this, just try getting up at the next *Groop* meeting you attend and ask, "What are we really doing here?" I dare you. This will get you nowhere anyway, for "the stones of the sling are to him like stubble." Any organization man who "plays with him as a bird" or "takes him to be a servant," ends by being devoured by him. Books are being written nowadays about this, so I won't elaborate.

The only way to dispatch a *Groop* is the way Daniel dispatched the dragon, "without sword or club." He must be gorged to death. Give him plenty of pitch, fat, and hair, and let him "burst asunder in the midst" as Judas did. In this incontrovertible fashion does the *Groop* reveal himself for what he is, when "his hope shall fail him and in the sight of all he shall be cast down," like Satan.

For a long time now I've wondered what Scripture means by this pitch, fat, and hair so fatal to dragons, and taking my cue from Daniel, I haven't neglected to ask divine enlightenment. What occurs to me is rather obvious, and therefore just might be the answer. As expected, it's anti-trinitarian. Pitch, fat, and hair must be symbols of the world, the flesh, and the devil, or stated otherwise, the well-known concupiscence of the eyes, the concupiscence of the flesh, and the pride of life so familiar to ascetical theology. Opposed to the three theological virtues uniting us to God, they are the contraries of poverty, chastity, and obedience.

"He that toucheth pitch shall be defiled with it," warns Sirach (*13.1*); and the *Groop*, a creature of this world possessing no supernatural life, literally gluts himself on this pitch of worldly riches, boiled together with fat and hair in one savory lump. God told Job, "he shall strew gold under him like mire," and sure enough, a *Groop* can raise more money than anybody would believe possible. Sometimes he has to plan whole conventions to take care of the surplus.

Fat, the second ingredient, occurs throughout Scripture as a figure of sensual gratification. The well-known expression "fat of the land" explains its significance, though of course it's not always used in a bad sense. When the Judge Aod dispatched the Moabite usurper Eglon by sinking a dagger into his belly, however, Scripture sees fit to tell us that "the hilt also went in after the blade, and the fat closed over the blade because he did not withdraw the dagger from his body" (*Judges 3:22*) Obesity has always been a number one health problem, complicating all other ills, even assassination. This is true in the spiritual life too, if I get the message right.

Hair, a universal symbol of glory and virility, reminds us easily of the luckless Samson, as well as the holy prophet Habbacuc who was "carried by the hair of the head" to take some dinner to the hungry Daniel in the lions' den. In the reprobate, hair becomes a figure of false human glory or status-seeking, in other words, pride. Even a scrap drive can raise this hair on some people; and it's the downfall of the *Groop*, who feeds on publicity, being "king over all the children of pride." In order to decapitate the drunken Holofernes, holy Judith first "took him by the hair of the head," for always "pride goeth before destruction," as Proverbs warns (*16:18*).

As we said, the *Groop* looks like a living god, but he isn't. By the same token, there are thousands of human organizations which look like the real thing, but aren't. I suppose the highest manifestation of

Groop activity is organized heresy. It apes the structure and purposes of the true Church, but like all *Groops*, it's doomed to burst asunder in good time. History is patently strewn with the rotting carcasses of heretical *Groops* which have gorged and died on concupiscence and pride.

On lower levels, *Groops* elect officers like mad, are terribly busy, wear badges and uniforms, collect heaps of money or its equivalent, hold meetings with exemplary regularity, distribute goods of all kinds, confer awards, and get nothing eternal done. Above all, they talk!

"Canst thou tie his tongue with a cord?" Oh, no!

With due apologies to Lewis Carroll, anyone trying to lead a spiritual life in the world should especially "Beware the Jabber-*Groop*, My son!/The jaws that bite, the claws that catch!" for he's one of the worst of the *groops*, and the chances are he feels you're pretty uncooperative if you don't join the fracas. The Discussion-*Groop* is probably the commonest garden variety of Jabber-*Groop* among spiritual dilettantes, though he is found in all ranks of secular life.

"Adore him, therefore!"

Any old *Groop* will have you believe that man exists purely for top-level organization. The end of marriage, says he, is dues-paying membership in a Family Movement. He'll try to push wife or husband, preferably both, into spearheading a little cell *groop* that meets three evenings a week away from home, tackling problems they have become too civic-minded to face on their own hearths. With cub scouts, bowling, choir practice, and a Charity-*Groop* or two thrown in, there shouldn't be one day when the entire family is together in a physical body, let alone spiritually.

A really dedicated *Groop* will drive us to receive Holy Communion with our respective *groops* rather than as the God-formed social nucleus a human family truly is. Really spiritual persons are catching on to the modern *Groop*, in spiritual guise, which seeks to impose on the family unnatural forms of spiritual organization designed primarily for religious or single persons in the world. Archbishop Heenan of Liverpool said at a conference on family life:

> We do a great deal innocently to destroy family life. Even in our spiritual life in the Church we do a great deal to harm family relations. We have men's Communion Sunday and women's Communion Sunday. We have children's Masses. ... As a parish priest I abolished (First) Communion breakfast and wrote to the parents, saying, "This is your great day. Take the children home with you."

The family needs a spirituality where grace can truly build on the natural structure, and not one which rides roughshod over the mystical body's most basic social cell.

The Archbishop said that the Church regards the family as the "most important society on earth—every other society is subordinate. In every Christian civilization there is this recognition of the primacy of the family." Going on to scold materialistic fathers and mothers of small children who prefer to work outside the home, His Excellency concluded with a jibe at the Bingo-*Groop*: "Better for a diocese to go bankrupt financially than spiritually."

Satan knows the weaknesses of gregarious nature. He knows, too, that acting for the *Groop*, human beings will descend to perversities they would never stoop to as individuals, because *groops* are out to shift individual responsibility and initiative onto themselves, and they feed on cowardice and human respect. Nazism and atheistic communism are *groop* examples so trite that I hate to mention them, but there they are.

The same *groop* mentality, however, can infect ladies' prayer clubs, as easily as large political systems. I'm ashamed to say I was once associated with a Church group, which as a group, saw nothing wrong with holding a Communion Breakfast in a public restaurant which refused to serve its one negro member. Individually the situation was deplored; but this didn't make it possible for the negro member to attend.

"It's only *one*," some of the ladies said. "It's better than not having a Breakfast at all."

Caiphas put it very much the same way. Speaking for the Sanhedrin Groop, he said, "It is expedient for us that one man die for the people, instead of the whole nation perishing" (*John 11:50*).

This is *Groop* morality, and in it lie the seeds of its own destruction. Come to think of it, the aforementioned ladies' group no longer meets today, and neither does the Sanhedrin. Coincidence? Such gathering can be groups, and again, they can be *Groops*. This depends—and here we return to the painful crux of the problem—on the supernatural life of the individual members, their real motives, the depth of their interior lives, and the lengths to which they are prepared to go to withstand the irate tail-thrashing of the *Groop*.

The *Groop* aim is never complicated. He means only to usurp the rights and duties of the person, diverting them from God to himself. He'll call you self-centered, opinionated, unpatriotic, stupid, godless, childish, in fact, anything to get you to come around. If driven to

extreme measures, he'll pronounce you in a state of mortal sin if you
don't goose-step through the liturgy. "Adore him, therefore!"

Speaking of this gambit, Dietrich von Hildebrand remarks:

> Certain religious theorists today seem to assume that we can only get
> rid of narrow egotism and become imbued with a truly theocentric attitude
> if one ceases to attach any weight to one's relationship with Christ insofar
> as this relation is experienced by one's own consciousness. They would
> express their theories something like this: "What am I; what are my
> longing and my love for Christ—is not all this much too small and
> unimportant to be something in the eyes of God? The only thing that
> matters is for us to keep step with the great objective rhythm of the holy
> Church, and, without thinking of our personal problems and situations at
> all, dedicate ourselves exclusively to the great community of the Mystical
> Body of Christ; for the latter alone, and surely not our petty little ego,
> means something to God." The more I succeed in effacing my personality,
> the more, they would say, my attitude must become an "objective" and
> "theocentric" one. It is these speculations also that have brought forth an
> attempt at dividing the saints into those having a predominantly
> "objective" outlook and those having a predominantly "subjective"
> outlook—as though the idea of a saint of a 'subjective' outlook were
> anything but a contradiction in terms.
>
> *The error that underlies this conception is the more dangerous as it
> corresponds with the anti-personal spirit of the age*, which tends toward a
> glorification of the 'collective' as such. (Italics mine.) The propagators of
> this error give proof of their shallowness of mind by equating personality
> and subjectivity and measuring objectivity by the standard of
> impersonality. They forget that God, the Origin of all objective reality and
> validity, is a Person. They attach the derogatory label of "subjectivity" to
> ethos and even to the personal conscious mode of being. ... They are blind
> to the fact that God is Love—in Which we participate according to the
> measure of our own supernatural love. They disregard the basic truth that
> it is only by confronting myself with God, by my loving adoration of
> Christ—and not by any consciousness of being a mere part of a big
> Whole—that I can transcend the narrow limits of my ego. ... They forget
> the moving grandeur and eternal importance of every immortal soul. St.
> Teresa of Avila says, "Christ would also have died to save one single
> soul."
>
> ... The error of anti-personalism ... is present, for example, in certain
> enthusiasts of the so-called "liturgical movement." These liturgists are
> prone to regard distrustfully the mystic and ascetical elements in religion.
> Any intense emotional attitude towards Christ—any "I and Thou"
> relationship with Him—appears to them suspect, "subjective." In all
> depersonalization, on the other hand, they are inclined to see religious
> progress. Yet, in truth, every religious progress in our life means a higher

stage in our becoming, *qua* persons, transformed in Christ and participants in His holy life. This life, again, means love—charity unconfined and unending towards God and one's fellow persons (*Transformation in Christ*, pp. 392 ff.).

God is greater even than His sacraments or His liturgy. To worship anything less than Him is idolatry, no matter how excellent it may be in itself.

"Worship God!" commanded the glorious angel in the Apocalypse. When St. John, overcome at the sight of him, fell down at his feet, "Thou must not do that!" he warned (*Apoc. 22:9*).

Paradoxically enough, personal conformity to Christ produces the highest group activity. It produces the Church, a visible organization whose holiness is only the sum of the holiness of the individual souls composing her hierarchical ranks. It also produces the holy Christian family, the Christian state, and conceivably, the holy bridge club and marching society. It brings to earth the Group life of the Most Holy Trinity, whose Unity is not diminished, but intensified, by distinction of Persons. God is three Persons, and He won't have us forget it.

Not only sharing the life of God, but actually transmitting it to one another, individual souls are the stuff of true group life, rooted in the Blessed Trinity and acting and dwelling in the individual. As Father de Langeac said, "In the manner by which the Father is related to the Son by communication, and the Son to the Holy Ghost, so are interior souls to one another and to mankind." This is the real group activity of which all associations and assemblies are merely figures. Human organizations, not informed by this life, are *groops* and nothing more, even though much natural, temporal good might result from them. After all, even the King of Babylon's *Groop* must have served to cement national solidarity by a common worship, and to effect a stability better than none!

The *Groop* would have us believe anything you can do he can do better. He gets things done, he says, and on a large scale! Still, *Groops* don't read Scripture. *Groops* don't give to the poor. *Groops* don't think, or love, or pray. Only persons can do these things. Only persons can be born, suffer, and die. Only they can sin and repent and be saved. Only they can be agents of supernatural life for others, and those others—persons. Nobody has ever converted a *Groop* and never will, for only persons can be converted.

Nobody knows all this like the housewife, whose whole life is at the service of a group of persons. The day she gets thoroughly "organized" and leaves her family for *Groop* activity will be the day society falls to bits. While the *Groop* plugs for day nurseries to release her pent-up energies in his direction, let her get to her prayer like Mary and Daniel and "kill this dragon without sword or club." Let's make no mistake. It wasn't pitch, fat, hair, or plain human intelligence that destroyed Bel and the dragon. These were only means. What really killed them was Daniel's "pondering in the heart" that went before.

This brand of pondering is *wisdom*, the fruit of knowledge and love, as produced by the Group Life of the Blessed Trinity in the human breast. The housewife who wishes to safeguard this Life within herself must be prepared to forgo much needless group activity on a merely human level. Souls who withdraw from their fellows for this high reason, as do, for instance, monks into their cloisters or housewives into their homes, are not being anti-social, but suprasocial. They mean to save the world by bringing God down into it more intensely. Certainly they should be excused from the bridge club, as well as from a lot of spiritual puttering and distraction!

With considerable dismay I read recently in a publication directed to married women that, "In marriage one so quickly and easily becomes caught up and absorbed in all the many details of homemaking and family life—to remain God-centered, group support is absolutely essential." Dear me, doesn't the gift of knowledge bestowed in baptism invest the details of homemaking with the revelation of God? If the married woman must have a group besides her family, the Communion of Saints, and the Blessed Trinity to work out her salvation, we're doomed.

Holiness for the housewife can't depend on banding together with other housewives and forming federations outside the home. It depends on getting together with God, who gives himself abundantly to the silent and hidden who need Him. The woman with the hemorrhage saw that! She came alone, secretly, and touched Him "from behind," getting everything she needed. This is true cloister spirituality, not the kind that always looks to others for what only God can give.

In the world, spiritual activity with others degenerates so easily into merely keeping up with current spiritual fads and fashions, learning current spiritual terminology, or spiritual celebrity-hunting. This season, we must quote Dom So-and-so, or say "Christocentric," to show we know what's what. Next season it may be someone else, and the catchword will be "theandric." Simple souls, who can't keep abreast of the jargon, must be content with trying to be like God, year after year. God bless them!

There's something especially perverted about a woman who sells herself to the *Groop*, for she rather than man is meant to exemplify the exaltation of the human person, as Fr. Scheeben saw so penetratingly. This is a vital role she must play in any organization of which she is a part. As representative of the Holy Spirit, woman is humanity's surest guarantee against depersonalization and heartless objectivity.

Cardinal Suhard said:

> The reign of God being presupposed, the human person is first in the creative intention in relation to society. To forget it is to sacrifice the unique drama of the life of each one for the eschatological success of the whole, and to transfer unduly to the group prerogatives and an autonomy which belongs only to man himself. "In every physical living body." the Encyclical *Mystici Corporis* states, "all the different members are ultimately destined to the good of the whole alone: while every moral association of men, if we look to its ultimate usefulness, is in the end directed to the advancement of all and of every single member. For they are persons. To ignore this truth, by reversing the order of values, is to prepare and legitimize every bondage and all sorrows. This is a precious reminder against the invading collectivism.

And again,

> Especially today, when the social form is acquiring such importance and is increasing so much in its pressures, not only the individual but the group itself must become a missionary. These groups are the natural communities: the family, those of a building, or a neighborhood, those who work or take their recreation together, etc., which ought to bear witness and communicate the message.
>
> This is conditioned, however, on not yielding to what might be called the "temptation of Thabor": "Lord it is good for us to be here," that is, the community must not become a closed group forgetful of its essential mission. These communities do not have their end in themselves. They are both the result and the starting point of a missionary movement. They should nourish the spiritual life but not stop their members on the way; these refresh themselves and pass on (*The Church Today, Growth or Decline?*).

Women are specially equipped to discern and safeguard the rights of the individual person wherever they may find themselves, but in the home especially. This doesn't mean housewives should be hermits. They couldn't if they tried! (I've tried.) There is, however, such a thing as over-organization, and the housewife occupies the most advantageous position in the whole secular world in that she can dispense with all artificial organization outside her home and her

Church if she so chooses, and can devote her extra time to prayer and study, vitalizing the Mystical Body from the heart.

In her house, the Holy Spirit can blow as hard and as free as She (!) pleases. If the holy housewife Mary claimed membership in a housewives' union outside the Holy Family, Scripture sees fit not to tell us. When she begged wine at Cana from our Lord, she was speaking for no party or "movement" but humanity. One doesn't, after all, have to be attached to an Apostolic *Groop* before daring to slip a copy of *The Question Box* to a neighbor inquiring about the Church. Nor does one have to kowtow to a Discussion-*Groop* in order to improve one's mind. It doesn't take a Charity-*Groop* to give a couple of hungry children a square meal now and then. How many people affiliated with Literary-*Groops* ever write books? The sad truth is, not many of us have time both to do and attend meetings. A choice must be made.

(Just the other day I learned of a nursing-*groop*, at whose meetings members are invited to breast-feed their babies in common. Evidently even this intimate activity is best not indulged in alone! What next?)

Though the wife and mother may be denied wide exterior activity, she's never denied deep activity that may become very wide indeed, and even deeper in due course of time. If one of the few souls she brings closer to God in her own home turns out to be a St. Pius X, as Signora Sarto's son turned out to be, I think it's safe to say she can dispense with almost every other group activity on the human level! Did ever a human life seem more narrow than our Blessed Mother's?

Of all women, Mary was most conformed to Christ, who took such pains with the individual. Was it a *Groop* which accosted the Samaritan woman? Not even the group of Apostles did this. Scripture relates of our Lord that "all who had *persons* sick with various diseases brought them to Him. And He laid his hands upon *each of them* and cured them." One wonders sometimes that He didn't just wave His arms over all of them at once, as a group, and save time. Wasn't He God? Yes, and God is a Person who leaves a group of ninety-nine sheep to go searching for just one that got lost. *Groops* find this sentimental.

At Pentecost, the Holy Spirit descended upon a group of some one hundred and twenty people in an upper room, you'll say. "And suddenly there came a sound from heaven, as of a violent wind blowing," says Scripture, "and it filled the whole house where they were sitting. And there appeared to them parted tongues as of fire." But note. Scripture adds carefully that these fiery tongues "settled upon *each of them*," who forthwith "began to speak in foreign tongues, even as the Holy Spirit prompted them to speak," that is, prompted each of them to speak (*Acts 2:2-4*).

Since that day every Christian speaks a foreign tongue in this world, as the Holy Spirit prompts him. No *Groop* can ever understand him well enough to legislate for him, for as an individual he will always be incomprehensible. This is the mystery of the human soul, unique before God. This is the mystery the housewife grapples with every day, for no matter how many children she has, each one is always an only child.

Our Lord, the Second Person of the Divine Group, is the Only Child of the Father in heaven, and the Only Child of Mary on earth. He understands these things. He made himself personally responsible for the whole world, and daily He tells other persons to "Follow Me!"

One who followed Him was the aforementioned housewife Elizabeth Leseur. From her own experience she concluded, "I believe much more in individual effort and in the good that may be done by addressing oneself not to the mass but to particular souls. The effect is deeper and more durable" (Mar. 28, 1900).

This is the hidden, humble way of Nazareth. There's little public recognition for this kind of approach unless the individual you strike happens to be famous, so I daresay the *Groop* will give you no competition here. Mme. Leseur summed up her own group activity in a nutshell when she remarked, "Each soul that uplifts itself uplifts the world."

After her death, her atheist husband became a Dominican priest.

This is what can come of membership in the Communion of Saints. They're a *grand* Group! You'll love them! Maybe someday we can all get together and ...

Caesar's Household

CHAPTER 13

"GREET every saint in Christ Jesus!" says St. Paul, not standing on ceremony. He has been leaning over the bar of heaven some two thousand years now, trying to get us all together.

Every saint?

"All the saints greet *you*," he rejoins, making it plain those above aren't like us waiting for formal introductions, *"especially those of Caesar's household"* (*Phil. 4:21*).

My goodness, who are these holy people?

St. Paul was writing to the Philippians from prison in Rome, and when he said, "The brethren with me here greet you," he was simply transferring good wishes from one segment of Christianity to another, without more ado. That they probably had never met in the flesh mattered little, then as now. "Our citizenship," St. Paul reminds us, "is in heaven" (*Phil. 3:20*).

I believe in the Catholic Church, the Communion of Saints ... and life everlasting. Don't you?

Caesar's household, who greet us especially, must have been working for Nero at the time. They might have been domestics or slaves, political appointees, soldiers, or professional people of all sorts, including respective wives, husbands, children, or dependent relatives. It's not unlikely Nero's establishment regularly employed untold numbers of cooks, hairdressers, landscape gardeners, actors, tailors, armorers, artists, smiths, plumbers, secretaries, accountants or cleaning women, not to mention a wide variety of tradespeople wont to supply royalty with goods "By Special Appointment to His Majesty."

Some of them were undoubtedly bureaucrats. Let's not mince words; bureaucrats can be saints. And besides, my husband works for the government, which means I know something firsthand about Caesar's household, or I think I do. Trying to imagine some worldly calling Caesar wouldn't find useful at one time or another is wasted effort. Caesar's household could be anybody, that is, anybody who's *secular*. The Age of the Laity began with Adam and Eve. Gaining real momentum with our Lady and St. Joseph, the number of lay saints has been growing all the time, and must be just about bursting heaven by now.

In Christ Jesus, *hello*! Hello, Perpetua! Hello, Felicity!

It's easy to forget that our Lord's injunction to "render unto Caesar" is a command as binding in its own way as "render unto God." Caesar, poor fellow, does have his rights. Whoever doesn't give him his due can never be perfect as God is perfect, for it's positively scandalous the way God has always been interested in secular affairs.

Scripture is quite uncompromising about this.

When King Cyrus of Persia conquered Babylon and liberated the Jews after their long exile there, he may have thought he was merely being a mighty monarch, but it was God, says Scripture, who told Cyrus, "Thou art my shepherd, and thou shalt perform all my pleasure" (*Is. 44:28*).

"Thou wouldst have no power at all over me were it not given thee from above" (*John 19:11*), said Christ Jesus to Pilate, also of Caesar's household.

Through Isaias God spoke to the one He called,

> my anointed Cyrus, whose right hand I have taken hold of, to subdue nations before his face, and to turn the backs of kings, and to open the doors before him, and the gates shall not be shut. ... I am the Lord, that make all things, that alone stretch out the heavens, that establish the earth, and there is none with me. ... Who say to Jerusalem: Thou shalt be built: and to the temple: Thy foundations shall be laid (*Is. 45:1,44:24,28*).

Xenophon actually refers to Cyrus the Great as "God's shepherd," and the Jewish historian Josephus quotes the following edict of Cyrus:

> Since God Almighty hath appointed me to be king of the habitable earth, I believe that he is that God which the nation of the Israelites worship; for indeed he foretold my name by the prophets; and that I should build him a house at Jerusalem, in the country of Judea.

Though far from an objective chronicler, Josephus nevertheless adds, "This was known to Cyrus by his reading the book which Isaias left behind him of his prophecies. ... Accordingly, when Cyrus read this and admired the divine power, an earnest desire and ambition seized upon him to fulfill what was so written" (*Antiq.* XI, I, i-2).

If this is true, Cyrus was hardly a bad sort. As a matter of fact, God takes so much interest in secular affairs, He has been known time and time again in these latter days to put saints on earthly thrones or give them political appointments. St. Clothilde and St. Louis of France, St. Henry of Germany, St. Elizabeth of Hungary, St. Charlemagne, St. Wenceslas, St. Helen, St. Edward the Confessor, St. Margaret of Scotland, St. Thomas More and others are just a sampling of those we happen to know about. There must be thousands more we don't know about. To call our flagging attention to His ordinarily unnoticed concern for our world, God sent a young laywoman named Joan to accomplish for her nation what Cyrus did for the Jews. She told us her helpers from above were an angel, St. Michael, and two other laywomen like herself, the bluestocking St. Catherine of Alexandria and the primitive St. Margaret of Antioch. So many people found this so unduly secular, it took five hundred years to canonize Joan, who rendered unto God precisely by rendering unto Caesar. God, perhaps, should stay in church?

Yet, "these things I speak in the world, in order that they may have my joy made full in themselves ... I do not pray that thou take them out of the world, but that thou keep them from evil" (*John 17:13,15*). Our Lord, it seems, was like His Father also exceedingly secular. He took the world so seriously that as far as that world could see, His life on earth was nothing more than the life of a God-fearing *layman*.

This is quite astounding when you stop to think of it, and small wonder the Protestant reformers were able to make so much of it in their quarrel with the See of Peter. Nevertheless, it's true that our Lord sanctified the life of the laity here on earth quite simply by living it for the greater part of His life. In one sense He lived it all His life, and this was a source of much of His trouble with the Pharisees, culminating in His condemnation by the high priest Caiphas.

Unlike His cousin John the Baptist, our Lord was no scion of a levitical family of hereditary priests, but merely a descendant of the layman King David. The Pharisees never dared direct against John the accusations they leveled at our Lord, for John's spiritual position in their society was quite impregnable from a legal standpoint. When our Lord asked them, "Was the baptism of John from heaven or from men? (*Mark 11:30*)" He caught them fairly, for by acknowledging its divine origin, they would have to confirm John's witness of Christ, and by denying it, would impugn the hereditary priesthood before the people. They had to say they didn't know.

Before John's denial of his own claim, it had been clearly hoped that he was the Messias, who it was assumed would spring from the priestly class. Scripture says "the Jews sent to him from Jerusalem priests and Levites to ask him, 'Who art thou? ... Art thou the

Prophet?'" (*Jn. 1:19,21*). John's "No" must have disappointed them sadly.

It remains that in His life on earth, our Lord never performed one specifically priestly act sanctioned by Mosaic Law—as far as the Jews could see. Even the sort of preaching He did was often engaged in by laymen in His day both in and out of the synagogue. Rabbi Sandmel, in *A Jewish Understanding of the New Testament*, explains that,

> The Temple was administered by a hereditary priesthood. The synagogue, however, could be served by any Jew, whatever his birth; and the historical distinctiveness of the synagogue was its lay character. The man who expounded Scripture had no ecclesiastical office, but only an acknowledged great measure of learning; the expounder and the one to whom matters were expounded were equal in religious rank (p. 22).

Even officiating at the Last Supper was—viewed from the outside—no more than any lay rabbi or father of a family did in those days or now at the yearly Passover.

When the Pharisees rebuked our Lord for allowing His disciples to pick grain on the sabbath, not even then does He arrogate to himself the rights of the levitical priesthood, but appeals to the precedent set by His ancestor David who once when hungry ate the loaves of proposition "which neither he nor those with him could lawfully eat, but only the priests ..." who according to the Law can "in the temple break the Sabbath and are guiltless" (*Matt. 12:4-5*). At this time Christ tells them simply He is Lord of the Sabbath and greater than the Temple, quite above and beyond the levitical clergy.

The Pharisees and Scribes had no objection to an earthly Messias springing from the line of David; in fact they would welcome His releasing them from Roman rule. Indeed they acknowledge he is to spring from David's line, but when our Lord begins to take unto Himself the other-worldly role of priestly Messias, they become enraged. "By what authority dost thou do these things? And who gave you this authority?" (*Matt. 21:23*) is the line they take with Him when they find Him teaching in the Temple or casting out money-changers. The treatment they mete out to Him is what they feel should be accorded to any such presumptuous layman.

"Who do you think you are?" is always the gist of their reaction. When He tells them point blank who He is before the Council, He is officially condemned for blasphemy and dies excommunicate outside the walls, according to the prophecy. Had He been a member of a levitical family, perhaps the treatment might have been very different.

Certainly His priestly cousin, St. John the Baptist, had suffered no indignity from the Sanhedrin, but had been executed by Herod. They didn't mark, of course, that before the birth of John, the priest Zachary, as figure of the Old Law, was struck dumb for unbelief.

That this obstacle to faith continued to plague the primitive Church is well attested to by the famous Epistle to the Hebrews, a masterly apologia for the high-priestly claims of Christ who is Son of God, Son of David, Son of Man, but not Son of Aaron or Levi. He is presented therefore as High Priest forever according to the order of Melchisedec "without genealogy" who enters once and for all the Holy of Holies as eternal Mediator and perfect Sacrifice.

This line of argument is still hard for those who never see anyone but the inspired layman in our Lord. There are others, however, who may be equally hampered by never seeing anyone but the divine High Priest in Him. To them the converted Pharisee St. Paul says, "Remember that Jesus Christ rose from the dead and was descended from David. This is my gospel!"

Fr. Charles de Foucauld would agree. He writes to himself in his diary in July, 1905,

> Jesus has established you for good in the life of Nazareth; the missionary life and life in solitude are only exceptions for you as they were for him. Practice these whenever such is clearly His will. Immediately this is no longer the case, return to the life of Nazareth.

What golden advice for the housewife in Caesar's household!

> ... Whether you are alone or with a group of other brothers, take the life of Nazareth in its simplicity and broadness [how well put!] as your objective in every way and for every purpose ... no costume or habit—like Jesus at Nazareth ... no enclosure—like Jesus at Nazareth ... no isolated place of abode, but close by some village—like Jesus at Nazareth ... not less than eight hours of work (manual or otherwise, but the former as far as possible) per day—like Jesus at Nazareth ... neither large properties, nor large buildings, nor large expenditures, nor even large sums in alms, but real poverty in every respect—like Jesus at Nazareth. In short Jesus at Nazareth in everything.
>
> Do not seek to organize; simply prepare the establishment of the Little Brothers ... if alone, live as if you were always to remain alone; if you are two, or three, or more, live as if there were never to be more of you. Pray as Jesus prayed, pray as much as Jesus prayed; always make plenty of room for prayer ... and, again, like Him, do plenty of manual work, for manual work does not mean time taken from prayer but time

given to prayer. ... The life of Nazareth can be led anywhere at all: lead it where it will be the most helpful to your neighbor.

Greet every saint in Christ Jesus—especially those of Caesar's household!

By human standards, the Christ like His mother led a very narrow life. In the light of His divine-human perfections, we may well wonder at the staggering list of what He *didn't* do, rather than of what He did: the masterpieces He never painted, the books He never wrote, the cities He never planned, the devices He never invented, the mathematics He never developed, or even the trips He never took, soon assume astronomical proportions. We could hardly find these deficiencies compatible with incarnate Godhood if we didn't reflect that the mystical Christ accomplishes these things by us, His Body.

Caesar's household is the mystical Christ-Layman. They have work to do.

Sirach says of such people, "They shall strengthen the state of the world, and their prayer shall be in the work of their craft, applying their soul, and *searching in the law of the Most High*" (*38:39*). Here, I gather, is another way of searching Majesty. And here, I also gather, is mystery.

Well, don't you think it's awfully mysterious?

Why does one man have a vocation to carpentry and another to horticulture, or to opera singing, or tent-making? Or why does he join the navy? What I mean is, why can't we all do the same thing, considering we all are destined for the same end? I realize this is like asking why grass is green, but then, as I keep reminding, housewives are about the only ones left who ask these questions. Specialists don't worry about the grand and obvious.

Why did Lydia sell dye-stuffs, and Zélie Martin make lace? Why did Joan, on the other hand, put on man's armor, get on a horse and ride to battle? (Ah, there was a girl the world would easily set down as a spiritual lesbian! That shows how much the world knows. Joan herself said, "When it comes to sewing and spinning, I fear no woman!" She had a firm grasp of fundamentals.)

But what I'm getting at is, what's in a vocation? We often hear the dire consequences of denying a call to religious life, and we ponder with due sadness the rich young man in the Gospel who turned sorrowfully away from our Lord's invitation, but do we ponder sufficiently the probable consequences of turning one's back on, say, a vocation to plumbing? It's worth thinking about. After all, everyone has a religious vocation in the sense that everyone is called to union with God, but only plumbers have vocations to plumbing. For them, this is a mysterious and special means to the Godhead.

As Benedict XV laid down, "Sanctity properly consists in Simple conformity to the Divine Will expressed in an exact and constant fulfillment of the duties of one's proper state." If the duties of one's proper state are a plumber's, plumbing can be mighty important. This is all so obvious, I find it properly terrifying.

There must be more here than meets the eye. Why was St. Joseph a carpenter? Couldn't he have been a silversmith? And why was our Lady a housewife? Why did St. Paul make tents and St. Peter fish? Couldn't they have done something else just as well? Who cares?

Apparently God does, who persists in taking so much interest in secular affairs. Anyway, I'm not taking any chances around here. My youngest at this precise moment, believe it or not, has just asked me, "Mother, why do you keep on writing books?" That's easy. If I'm supposed to, I'm scared not to, that's why.

Even Cardinals are troubled this way. John Henry Newman finally concluded:

> God created me to do Him some definite service; He has committed some work to me which He has not committed to another. I have my mission—I may never know it in this life, but I shall be told it in the next. I am a link in a chain, a bond of connection between persons. He has not created me for naught. I shall do good, I shall be an angel of peace, a preacher of truth in my own place while not intending it—if I do but keep His Commandments. Therefore, I will trust Him. Whatever, wherever I am, I can never be thrown away.

"Each one has his own gift from God, one in this way, and another in that" (*I Cor. 7:7*).

It's all too true that seeing as darkly as we do, we may never know our real mission in this life, but I'm sure the good Cardinal would have been the first to agree that we can easily get a few glimmers. "God's gifts," says St. Paul, "are without repentance." What He gives once He never takes away, unless we willfully spurn it. On the contrary, we must "increase and multiply" our talents. It follows that any temporal vocation fully lived in a supernatural manner must trigger an eternal deployment in the spiritual sphere. Caught up into the activity of the Blessed Trinity, finite tasks take on infinity. This earth, given to us "to till and to keep" is very important.

The prophet Jeremias was once imprisoned by the reigning monarch for prophesying that the kingdom was doomed to be conquered by the Chaldeans. Paradoxically enough, God—always interested in secular things—chooses this particularly inauspicious moment to order the imprisoned Jeremias to invest in family real estate.

"Behold," He says, "Hanameel, the son of Sellum, thy cousin, shall come to thee saying, 'Buy thee my field.'"

"I understood that this was the word of the Lord," says Jeremias, who duly purchases the field, weighing out the money somehow and recording the deed before witnesses, but he doesn't neglect to ask God for an explanation. "Sayest thou to me, O Lord God: Buy a field for money, and take witnesses, whereas the city is given into the hands of the Chaldeans?" (*32:25*). Today this question takes the form of, "Why bother about this world, when it's going to disappear anyway?"

God deigns to answer through His prophets, saying that the land will be indeed laid waste, but the day will come again, He promises, when "they shall be my people and I will be their God," and "fields shall be purchased in this land, whereof you say that it is desolate" (*32:38,43*).

If we are to credit the prophet, this earth is matter for transfiguration and we're fools not to invest in its promising future! Like the little acorn which produces the giant oak, our earthly life supplies the "form" our eternal destiny must take. At least, this is what I get out of Jeremias' story. Though nobody could imagine an oak tree from looking at an acorn, there's no getting around the fact that there's a relationship, and that every leaf of the oak is present in the acorn. If only we had the means of discerning, we could see everything there.

Chides St. Paul:

> Senseless man, ... when thou sowest, thou dost not sow the body that shall be, but a bare grain ... If there is a natural body, there is also a spiritual body ... but it is not the spiritual that comes first, but the physical, and then the spiritual! ... Therefore, my beloved brethren, be steadfast and immovable, always abounding in the work of the Lord, knowing that your labor is not in vain in the Lord" (*1 Cor. 15, passim*).

Cardinal Newman wrote to a friend once:

> I understood ... that the exterior world, physical and historical, was but the manifestation to our senses of realities greater than itself. Nature was a parable, Scripture was an allegory, pagan literature, philosophy and mythology, properly understood, were but a preparation for the Gospel.

We have already noted how eminently congruous was St. Paul's tent-making to one' whose mission was setting up tabernacles over all the Gentile nations. Not to be overlooked are a couple of other tent-makers who went into business with him in Corinth—the married couple Priscilla and Aquila. Revealed to us in the Acts of the Apostles, these were genuine lay apostles and tent-makers, who not only aided in spreading the kingdom of God, but actually "expounded the Way of God more precisely" to the eloquent Apollos, so "mighty in the Scriptures" (*Acts 18:24-26*).

St. Peter, quite properly, fished. And thereby hangs a tale, for God had once told Joshua on the threshold of the promised land, "As I promised Moses, I will deliver. to you every place where you set foot" (*Jos. 1:3*). With characteristic impetuosity, St. Peter once asked our Lord whether he might set foot with Him on the sea, and walk on it. He did, and of course ran straight into that ancient promise without repentance. The whole sea was delivered to Peter to fish in, for as we know, our Lord eventually made him pope.

So does temporal action bring forth the eternal, for good or ill. Our works follow us into heaven. St. Peter still "walks on the water," as does every pope since and, indeed, every true follower of Christ who dares take the plunge. St. Paul, with St. Priscilla and St. Aquila, is still making tents; and his convert Lydia, bless her heart, is, I'm sure, "selling purple" spiritually as fast as customers will buy. Don't the Proverbs tell us every good housewife must be clothed in "fine line and purple," the garb of predestined royalty? *Cherchez la femme* behind St. Paul—and Lydia may well turn up. Come to think of it, we might find St. Paul's tents dyed with her purple, which in those days came from shellfish pulled in turn from St. Peter's preserve. Call the analogy labored if you like, but there's no getting around the fact that in God's economy, everything is dangerously interrelated.

Certainly St. Louis and St. Joan are still looking out for Frenchmen. According to the testimony of Count Dunois at her re-trial, Joan had told him:

> I am bringing you better help than ever you got from any soldier or city. It is the help of the King of Heaven. It does not come through love for me, but from God Himself who, on the petition of Saint Louis and Saint Charlemagne, has had pity on the town of Orleans and refused to suffer the enemy to have both the body of the lord of Orleans and of his City.

Isn't that something?

As for St. Joseph's carpentering, I hesitate to dwell on that too much, for fear I'll start another book before I've finished this one. Even thinking of the cosmic implications of being an ordinary plumber, perhaps ultimately responsible for conveying the waters of grace throughout creation, is too much. As for a spiritual electrician, providing others with power and light, or a musician "organizing" like Richard Rolle throughout eternity, well ... doing God's Will is no trifling occupation, however trifling it might look from here.

In a plan where the last are so often first, care must be taken. Especially by housewives. A woman who has been handed the same vocation as the Mother of God may well tremble. She can be responsible for almost anything, being a walking figure of the wisdom which orders and contains all things. I'd rather be a housewife than anything. Perhaps I shouldn't say so, but then, it's an acknowledged characteristic of wisdom that she "praises her own self," so I might as well carry out the figure. A woman who has even one child, either physically or spiritually, becomes in a sense the mother of all children. She can have who knows how many descendants, for whom she must "cook" spiritually, and make "double garments," and who must be taught their manners.

The prayer of Christ for "those whom Thou hast given me" must be the prayer of every Christian who seeks to imitate Him fully. We may be responsible for untold thousands still unborn and like Christ, be meant to be "glorified in them" (*John 17:9-10*). Thérèse of Lisieux understood Christ's prayer in this sense, and prophesied that she would spend her heaven doing good on earth. Who wants to acquire a lifetime of hard-earned know-how just to bury it under six feet of earth? I don't know about you, but I'm just beginning to catch on to how to run a house and bring up children. When I die, I expect to be useful in the life to come! Surely no one is idle in heaven, where we can begin at last to do perfectly what we're really supposed to.

The blessed now in glory yearn for the end of time when soul and body can be reunited, and they work unceasingly toward that end. We're not without help in our share of the work, any more than St. Joan was. The Church Triumphant forms with the Church Suffering and the Church Militant a very important representation of the Blessed Trinity, whose personal exchanges are the sublime activity called the Communion of Saints. This doctrine underlies all the Church's attitude toward saints, who are designated "patrons" of the most varied occupations, predicaments, and endeavors. Unbelievers, lacking knowledge in solid theology, consider our petitions to saints pious nonsense, but we know better. It's not just happenstance that St. Blaise should be in charge of throats, or St. Monica an adviser on outstanding wayward children like St. Augustine.

Whoever has bookkeeping problems can certainly apply to St. Matthew. Paratroopers, I understand, look to St. Michael, and postal employees favor St. Gabriel, who brought the greatest message ever. As for me, when I need help really badly on some secular problem that's humdrum but critically important, I'm inclined to apply to Caesar's household—the vast array of uncanonized saints. If they don't know how to live a spiritual life in the world, who does? I have a feeling they're bursting to help with their specialties, but hardly anybody ever asks them, just because we don't know who they are.

Isn't that silly? Why wouldn't heaven be full of glorious people nobody ever heard of? Alas for the status-seekers, "Charity is not pretentious, is not puffed up, is not ambitious" (*I Cor. 13:4*). It's one thing not to notice these people on earth, but not to notice them in heaven is really too much. Who are we to rob God of His glory in them?

"Greet every saint in Christ Jesus ... All the saints greet you!"

The Communion of saints, it would seem, is like the Blessed Trinity, no one-way exchange. There must be something we can do for the saints. What? How can we help them fulfill their heavenly missions as they help us fulfill our earthly ones? They have no earthly help but us. Can't we ever do *them* a favor? I hate to think of all those thousands upon thousands of saints, filled with God's grace they're yearning to dispense, not being able to find friends down here to carryon for them. No wonder the Last Day is so long coming!

Well, in Christ Jesus, we can offer Holy Mass.

> *Suscipe, Sancta Trinitas*, this offering we are making to Thee in remembrance of the Passion, Resurrection and Ascension of Jesus Christ, our Lord ... and of all the saints; that it may add to their honor and aid our salvation; and may they deign to intercede in heaven for us who honor their memory here on earth.

This is pretty heady, you know, when a housewife like me is told she can *add to the honor* of saints. There's no telling what might come of it, because of course saints are notoriously grateful. St. Teresa admitted she could be bribed with a sardine. I can hardly bear to think what she does when Mass is offered in her honor, even *nobis quoque peccatoribus*, yet members of God's household, who ask "some part and fellowship with ... all thy saints, through Christ our Lord."

Anybody could feed a hungry child for Don Bosco or teach catechism for St. Peter Canisius. Couldn't we combat race prejudice in some small way at our doorsteps for the negro girl, St. Emerentiana, who was herself stoned to death for praying at the tomb of her white foster-sister St. Agnes? And how about all Caesar's household? Can they get through to us? How about St. Paul himself, who still has so many Gentiles to convert, not to mention the Jews?

He may be reading over my shoulder. He says, "I have rejoiced in the Lord greatly that now at last your concern for me has revived! Not that I am eager for the gift," he explains, "but I am eager for the profit accumulating to your account. I have all and more than enough" (*Phil. 4:10,17*).

What in the world are we waiting for?

Workers of the world, unite! You have nothing to lose but your chains, your boredom, and maybe your double chins! "*Communicantes et memoriam venerantes* of all Thy saints ... Graciously accept, O Lord, this service of our worship and that of all thy household!"

The warrior Josue provides, I think, a most wonderful figure of the honest layman. A sort of Figaro-factotum to the man of God, Moses, he implements faithfully God's commands at the operational level. He is one of the faithful spies who reconnoiter the promised land when its borders are reached. At Raphidim, on the way, Josue had defeated the Amalecites in battle on the plain while Moses, supported by the priests Aaron and Hur, kept his hands raised in prayer on top of the hill.

"As long as Moses kept his hands raised up," says Scripture, "Israel had the better of the fight" (*Ex. 17:11*). There's no reason to suppose this order has been reversed at any time. Supported by His priests, our Lord, the new Moses, intercedes eternally, while the laity battles till sunset and "mows down Amalec" (*Exod. 17:13*). This is the lay-clergy dialogue as it has always taken place.

The Lord said to Moses at Raphidim, "Write this down in a document as something to be remembered, and recite it in the ears of Josue: I will completely blot out the memory of Amalec from the heavens" (*Exod. 17:14*). This fight is fixed, I think, as long as Josue can be depended on to do his part.

As Moses' successor, Josue eventually reaches the promised land and lays siege to Jericho, where an interesting strategy is followed. The Lord commands Josue,

> Have all the soldiers circle the city, marching once around it. Do this for six days, with seven priests carrying rams' horns ahead of the Ark. On the seventh day march around the city seven times, and have the priests blow the horns. When they give a long blast on the ram's horn and you hear that Signal, all the people shall shout aloud. The wall of the city will collapse, and they will be able to make a frontal attack (*Jos. 6:3-5*).

This order was followed. "In front of the priests with the horns marched the picked troops; the rear guard followed the Ark, and the blowing of horns was kept up continually as they marched. But the people had been commanded by Josue not to shout or make any noise or outcry until he gave the word: only then were they to shout" (*6:9-10*).

"On the seventh day," Scripture tells us, "beginning at daybreak, they marched around the city seven times in the same manner; on that day only did they march around the city seven times. The seventh time around, the priests blew the horns and Josue said to the people, 'Now shout, for the Lord has given you the city and everything in it! It is under the Lord's ban" (*15-17*).

As we know, that did it.

> As the horns blew, the people began to shout. When they heard the signal horn, they raised a tremendous shout. The wall collapsed, and the people stormed the city in a frontal attack and took it. They observed the ban by putting to the sword all living creatures in the city: men and women, young and old, as well as oxen, sheep and asses (*20-21*).

"Here is wisdom," says St. John again. "He who has understanding, let him calculate the number of the beast, for it is the number of a man; and its number is 666" (*Apo. 13:18*). The notes to our Bible here at home tell us the Hebrew characters making up 666 also spell Nero, and that this number "symbolizes extreme imperfection, for each digit is one short of seven, the number that signifies perfection."

Here we are again at sixes and sevens.

That explains a lot about Jericho, where apparently only the standard cubit is used. An anti-trinity of three sixes, 666, must have been Jericho's number too. Certainly man left to himself there works hard for six long days, only to find that for him there's no Sunday at the end of the week. Even 666 times around the clock on the sixth day will never get a beast to the Seventh. Hell is simple arithmetic. Or should we say, simple arithmetic is Hell? Against Jericho, only Josue's sevenfold logistics can prevail. The people of God, perfect as their God is perfect, can "calculate the number of the beast" in no time, using the royal cubit, the higher calculus of supernaturalized existence.

I'm not one to expect the End of the World next Tuesday, but I think it's safe to predict it is coming. When the lowliest housewife in Caesar's household can stock cheap glassware that Nero would have coveted, I think something pretty big is going on. We may well wonder, along with Fr. de Chardin and many others, at the acceleration of change and the material abundance that has come upon us, not to mention population explosions and the quickening of communication. Scientific discoveries have inevitably deepened the natural mysteries, and science itself, like the prodigal son, finds itself returning to its parent philosophy for support in its perplexities. It looks like a whirlwind.

"You know then how to read the face of the sky, but cannot read the signs of the times?" (*Matt. 16:4*).

Even the times seem faster. Is it Saturday night already? If, as Cardinal Newman says, the exterior world is physical and historical parable, we are today witnessing through our senses a lively, progressive parody of the invisible grace of Pentecost, whose unspeakable fullness is overwhelming the whole world with power from on high!

"Behold, I come quickly!"

Wait for me! Overcome by the fact that only on the seventh day, the seventh time around, were "the people" allowed to shout, I notice, nevertheless, that only then was Jericho taken. Priests and "picked troops" apparently couldn't do the job alone, even bearing the Ark of the Covenant, symbol of the Mother of God. Every dog has his day, and the seventh lap on the Seventh Day must be D-Day for the laity, when God commands "*all* the people" to "shout"—a figure for intense prayer, say the Apostolic Fathers.

Caesar's household are people. Even women are people, when you come right down to it. So, if that's the signal horn I hear, "Now shout! For the Lord has given you the city and everything in it!"

That Josue should lead us needn't surprise anyone. It happens "Josue" is simply an older form of the name Jesus, the Savior. We might have known that all along. Without Him, we can do nothing. He is both High Priest and Victim for all the people, who like Him "suffered under Pontius Pilate" on their way to the Father, and who share in His work. (This suffering under Pilate may take no more dreadful shape than filling out income tax forms, but no secular escapes entirely.)

This Christ, who supplanted the hereditary priesthood of flesh, wrought a very great thing in that now the priests ordained to blow the horns before the Ark no longer perpetuate themselves, but spring from "all the people." This was the end of division between priesthood and laity, the end of the Pharisees, whose very name means "separated ones," who condemned the carpenter's Son to death.

When the priesthood springs from the laity, who is to blame the priest? When the laity follows the priesthood, who is to blame the layman?

We are one at last.

"Like people, like priest!" (*Osee 3:9*)

Either presuming to criticize or condemn the other must do so in the light of his own examination of conscience, for the priest can only reflect the culture and spirituality of the people who produce him, and the people can only respond to the kind of leadership he provides them.

Dominus vobiscum, says the one. "The Lord be with you!"

Et cum spiritu tuo, says the other. "And with your spirit!"

Spiritually "conversing and arguing together" like the two disciples at Emmaus, they confer Christ on each other in much the same way married people do, one subject to the other, yet one flesh in the Mystical Body.

Isaias prophesied, "It shall be with the people, so with the priest" at the Last Judgment, for as the Lord promised Moses after Raphidim, "You shall be to me a kingdom of priests, a holy nation. That is what you must tell the Israelites!" (*Exod. 19:6*)

Listen, Israelites. We seculars may become very holy indeed, for it happens that our High Priest, sprung from us people, is also the Word, the Second Person of the Most Holy Trinity.

> He was in the world,
> and the world was made through him,
> and the world knew him not.
> But to as many as received him
> he gave the power of becoming sons of God;
> to those who believe in his name.
> And of his fullness
> we have all received,
> grace for grace.
> For the Law was given through Moses;
> grace and truth came through Jesus Christ.
> No one has at any time seen God.
> The only-begotten Son,
> who is in the bosom of the Father,
> he has revealed him.

"All things were made through him, and without him was made nothing that has been made," says St. John, and we housewife-theologians might add respectfully, "or that ever will or can be made." Whether it frightens us or not, those incorporated with the Son through the Holy Spirit into the Unity of the Godhead will be bound to take part in any and all subsequent worlds God the Father may deign to create, in *saecula saeculorum*. Isn't that what Mother Church ends her prayers with—"through worlds of worlds"?

That's being really *saecular*!

Per Dominum Jesum Christum, I do believe we should be as worldly as possible. Think of the eternal employment awaiting spiritual plumbers, electricians, carpenters, farmers, city planners, scientists, artists, garbage collectors, office workers and everybody now, with an infinity of incalculable construction ahead of us. Oh dear, just think of the work this will make for the housewife!

> Eye has not seen nor ear heard,
> Nor has it entered into the heart of man,
> What things God has prepared for those who love him (*1 Cor. 2:9*).

St. Joseph the workman, father of the whole Christ, friend of the dying, pray for us!

GLORIA PATRI

et FILIO

et SPIRITUI SANCTO

Sicut erat in principia, et nunc, et semper,

et

IN SAECULA SAECULORUM!

Amen.

ABOUT THE AUTHOR

An established writer before the Second Vatican Council, Solange Strong Hertz wrote for most major Catholic periodicals and had five books to her credit, one a selection of the Catholic Literary Foundation. When she refused to adjust her theology to the new "Spirit of Vatican II," her manuscripts almost overnight became unacceptable to her former editors. After a series on feminine spirituality for the old *Triumph* magazine, she continued speaking for tradition by successfully producing on her own *The Thought of His Heart* (1974) and *Sin Revisited (1975)*. The former was republished in 1994 by Veritas Press under the title *The Thought of Their Heart* and the latter was republished in 1996.

In 1973 Mrs. Hertz began writing the Big Rock Papers, published privately throughout the next decade and the source of the highly acclaimed *Star Spangled Heresy:* Americanism (Veritas Press, 1992). In 1993 Veritas was privileged to publish her monumental collection on the confrontation between the universal republic and the reign of Christ the King, *Utopia:* Nowhere Now Here, and in 1995 *Beyond Politics:* A Layman's Guide to What Keeps on Happening.

The present volume contains her most recent work on the Church in our time. Mrs. Hertz is a regular contributor to *The Remnant* and her articles can be found abroad in *Apropos, Christian Order* and *Action Familiale et Scholaire.* She is universally regarded as one of traditional Catholicism's foremost contemporary writers.

Other books by Solange Hertz

∞

Published by Tumblar House

On The Contrary

Beyond Politics

Utopia Nowhere

The Star-Spangled Heresy: Americanism

Apostasy in America

Sin Revisited

The Thought of their Heart

∞

Published by Remnant Press

The Battle for Amerindia

The Sixth Trumpet

59941199R00151

Made in the USA
Charleston, SC
17 August 2016